L. TOM PERRY

An Uncommon Life

Years of Preparation

L. TOM PERRY

AN UNCOMMON LIFE
Years of Preparation

LEE TOM PERRY

SALT LAKE CITY, UTAH

All photographs courtesy L. Tom Perry family

Visit us at DeseretBook.com

Library of Congress Cataloging-in-Publication Data

Perry, Lee Tom, author.
L. Tom Perry, an uncommon life : years of preparation / Lee Tom Perry.
pages cm
Includes bibliographical references and index.
ISBN 978-1-60907-462-3 (hardbound : alk. paper) 1. Perry, L. Tom, 1922–
2. Perry family. 3. The Church of Jesus Christ of Latter-day Saints—Apostles—Biography. I. Title.
BX8695.P47P47 2013
289.3092—dc23
[B] 2012050172

Printed in the United States of America
Publishers Printing, Salt Lake City, UT

10 9 8 7 6 5 4 3 2

Contents

Foreword

Anyone who's spent much time with Elder L. Tom Perry has likely heard him say that he is "as common as dirt"[1]—and he says it with such conviction that one senses he actually believes it. But, truth be told, there is nothing common or ordinary about this distinctive and distinguished man who has now served for forty years in the presiding councils of The Church of Jesus Christ of Latter-day Saints, thirty-eight of those as a member of the Quorum of the Twelve Apostles.

Elder Perry is, in a phrase, larger than life. His six-foot-four frame and booming voice brimming with energy help create that initial impression, but the explanation for his engaging persona goes much deeper. He is the embodiment of *joie de vivre,* exhibit A of the title of his book *Living with Enthusiasm.*

In volume one of *L. Tom Perry: An Uncommon Life,* Elder Perry's son, Lee, presents us with an open, candid, heart-warming look inside the first fifty-three years of his father's life. These were, in many respects, formative years, the years of Elder Perry's preparation leading to his call in 1972 as a General Authority and two years later as a member of the Quorum of the Twelve Apostles.

In Lee Perry's recounting of his father's life, we see Tom Perry as a boy under the watchful influence of a priesthood-leader father and a mother who enlisted his help rendering compassionate service throughout the neighborhood and then stood outside his bedroom door at night long enough to be sure he said his prayers. We walk alongside the youthful but maturing Tom Perry as he enters the Northern States Mission, where he discovers the power of the Book of Mormon, and then returns home to join the United States Marine Corps during World War II. We see him protected during this tumultuous time against danger as well as unsavory influences, and we observe elements of his emerging personality and character.

"I just hate to be second," he has said, describing his time in the marines but much more as well, "so when we'd be on forced marches, I'd drag myself to the front of the line and stay there."[2] The young marine was among the first of the occupation troops to enter Japan after Hiroshima and Nagasaki, where he saw firsthand the devastation of war. His heart immediately went out to a people who just months earlier had been the enemy, and in Nagasaki he rallied a group of servicemen to help rebuild Christian churches. Later, when his unit shipped out, two hundred members of that Japanese congregation lined the railroad tracks to touch hands with the marines as the train rolled by.

With Tom Perry home from the war, we see him smitten by the inner and outer beauty of Virginia Lee, and we follow the two of them as they fall in love, marry in 1947, begin their family, and then proceed to build a life together. As his work takes their family from Idaho to California, then to New York, and finally to Massachusetts, we see him deal with the pressures of establishing a career while calls to serve in the Church come one after another.

And, at the end of this volume, we share in Elder Perry's pain when the love of his life is diagnosed with cancer and passes away just months after his call as an Apostle. Following Virginia's death, Elder Perry determines to throw himself into his work and to be more productive than ever. But he instead finds it nearly impossible to concentrate or be effective. He learns quickly, as he often says, that "the combination of husband and wife working together is more than one and one make two."

Through it all—the ups and downs, the achievements and growth interspersed with struggle, the setbacks embedded in progress—there is much to learn from the life of Elder L. Tom Perry. There is power and purpose in biography—power to enlighten and inspire, to warn and teach. This is particularly the case when a biography chronicles the life of a person worthy of emulation.

In this regard, Lee Perry likens his father to the man in the Savior's parable who was given two talents rather than five: "My father has often said about himself and others: 'I don't care as much about where someone currently stands relative to someone else as about whether they're improving.' My father's approach to eternal progression has been sure and steady."[3]

It has also been practical and achievable. And those elements form the basis for this important biography. Elder Perry may be an uncommon man, but he understands real life. He understands both joy and pain. He has experienced failure and success. He knows both the heartache of losing his eternal companion and the thrill of meeting men and women the world over whose lives have been transformed because they have chosen to love and follow Jesus Christ.

In Elder Perry's first general conference address after being called to the Quorum of the Twelve Apostles, he told about a time when he was a child in Primary and his father helped him memorize the names of the members of the Quorum of the Twelve. "As I was thinking about this assignment [to speak today], I thought, what if there is some father in the Church who would like to spend some time in family home evening telling [his children] about the current members of the Twelve. The thought startled me. What could he ever tell about me? As I thought and searched, I realized there is a theme to my life which is worthy of being repeated and I think would be of value to those young children in your homes. It is this: He was raised in a home in which his parents loved and appreciated the gospel of Jesus Christ. They understood the admonition of Paul to the Ephesian saints when he wrote: 'Finally, my brethren, be strong in the Lord, and in the power of his might.'"[4]

Everything in the life of Elder L. Tom Perry points to and bears witness of the power of Jesus Christ to transform all who willingly turn their lives over to Him. In short, this compelling biography of a truly uncommon man—a man who understands what each of us is experiencing in this adventure called mortality—will help each of us want to do better and to be better.

SHERI DEW

Preface

Throughout my adult life I have been asked what it was like growing up in the home of an Apostle. My quick answer is that I didn't actually grow up in the home of an Apostle—I was a returned missionary and college senior when my father was called as a member of the Quorum of the Twelve Apostles of The Church of Jesus Christ of Latter-day Saints. If pressed further, however, I will often explain that I was blessed to be raised by wonderful parents who loved my sisters and me and that our home life was typical of that of many other strong LDS families. Like many of my peers, I grew up with a deep respect, even awe, of the General Authorities of the Church. Even as an adult I retain a similar sense of awe for these remarkable men who serve as the General Authorities of the Church and the families who support them in their special callings. I believe they truly are set apart. It continues to be difficult for me to grasp the concept that many people see me as part of this amazing cast of characters. I often admit to feeling incredibly blessed to have had a front-row seat from which to observe my father's uncommon life, but I see myself as part of the audience, not of the cast.

Perhaps the most difficult challenge associated with writing any book, especially a biography, is finding the right voice. It is challenging because it cannot be planned, at least not as precisely as the book's content. Usually it involves learning by trial and error what works—that is, what resonates and sounds genuine—and what doesn't. I have not written any book, including this one, in which I settled on a voice before I began to write. Thus writing even a fully outlined book has for me always involved the exercise of faith, especially around selecting the voice. In my experience, then, writing a book is a spiritual process—as Nephi observed about himself when he was asked by his father to return to Jerusalem to secure the brass plates, it involves being led by the Spirit without entirely knowing beforehand the things we should do.[1]

As I experimented with and pondered the right voice for this book, I wanted it to be very personal and also allow me to represent my father as thoughtfully and accurately as possible. It felt very right and natural to shift between first and third person as I told stories about my father, his ancestors, parents, siblings, and my mother—stories I had heard since I was a small boy. This choice set the stage for intermittently using first person to comment about my father's life history, much as Mormon did in commenting about the history of his people as he abridged the record with which he had been entrusted. Accordingly, in the first fourteen chapters of this volume I granted myself license to insert commentary about my father's uncommon life.

Chapter 15 relates the time my father, mother, and older sister, Barbara, moved from Logan, Utah, to Boise, Idaho, and also coincides with when I was born. While it had worked to shift occasionally into first-person commentary in an account of my father's life before I was born, I realized such a shift was likely to confuse the account after I was born. Moreover, if I used first person to tell about an experience in which I had participated, I would seem to be telling it from my point of view and I would be at the center of the account. To avoid these and other potentially adverse consequences, I adjusted how I told my father's life story in the remaining chapters. As John the Baptist taught regarding the Savior and himself: "He [in this case, my father] must increase, but I must decrease" in the telling of his story.[2]

At the outset, you should know this is the first volume of a two-volume biography. This was a decision I made and my father endorsed around the same time I was pondering and experimenting with the right voice to use to tell his story. Something I struggled with during this period was how to treat my mother, Virginia, and my stepmother, Barbara, in a fair and balanced way in a single-volume work. Both women have played significant and extraordinary roles in my father's life, but their roles were and have been very different. Virginia helped shape my father into a man who was prepared to be called as an Apostle of the Lord, but she died soon after his call to the holy apostleship very near the beginning of his forty-year ministry. Barbara has been my father's constant companion for most of his long ministry, and she is the Sister Perry most Church members know and love. She has traveled to the ends of the earth with my father, and together they have testified of the truthfulness of the gospel of Jesus Christ. It felt like inspiration when it occurred to me that I could divide my father's life story into two volumes to highlight the influences of each of his two exceedingly influential eternal companions.

In the end, this is my father's story, and I humbly and sincerely hope the choices I have made help more than they hinder the telling of it. When I think of my father's life, a scene of a movie comes to mind—it is the closing scene of the 1946 film *The Razor's Edge,* based on W. Somerset Maugham's 1944 novel. The film and the novel are partially autobiographical—Mr. Maugham is not the central character in the story, but he is a participant in it. He shares the closing scene with Isabel Bradley. The two of them are talking about Larry Darrell, who is the central character in the story. Mr. Maugham explains to Isabel: "My dear, Larry has found what we all want, and very few of us ever get. I don't think anyone can fail to be better and nobler, kinder from knowing him. You see, my dear, goodness is, after all, the greatest force in the world. And he's got it."

I concur that goodness, especially the goodness stemming from God, is the greatest force in the world. I also believe my father has it. I know this because I am better and nobler and kinder sitting in my front-row seat and knowing him. If this book represents him accurately, and it's my hope that it does, I believe anyone can become better and nobler and kinder by reading it.

Acknowledgments

In the eighteenth chapter of Mosiah in the Book of Mormon, we learn about a group of people who gathered with Alma and were taught, converted to the gospel of Jesus Christ, and baptized in the waters of Mormon. They became the church of Christ, and about them it was said, "their hearts [were] knit together in unity and in love one towards another" (Mosiah 18:21).

In writing my father's biography, I have felt my heart knit together with the hearts of many people who love and respect him. My heart has been knit to my sister Linda Gay as we have reminisced about our noble father and mother. I have felt my heart knit together with two of my cousins—one from my father's side, Laraine Ferguson, and the other from my mother's side, Kay Erickson. They gathered, organized, and shared family memories, and, most important, letters their respective mothers—Gay Kowallis (my father's older sister) and Jessie

Seamons (my mother's older sister)—received from my parents. Without these memories and letters, much of my father and mother's history would have been lost. In a similar way, I am grateful to my stepmother, Barbara Perry, for transcribing the correspondence between my father and his father. More than anything else, all of these letters brought this biography to life, and I am deeply grateful to their preservers and caretakers. My uncle Ted Perry (my father's younger brother) also made a substantial contribution to my understanding of my father's boyhood when he republished and added commentary to the life history of my grandfather Leslie Thomas Perry.

I am reminded of another scriptural metaphor—the "welding link" between ancestral fathers and children (Doctrine and Covenants 128:18). I have felt a particularly strong welding link with three individuals who left behind wonderful histories: my grandfather, the first L. Tom Perry, who took time in 1964 to write his life history; his brother Albert, who wrote about their parents (my great-grandparents) Henry Morgan and Fannie Young Perry; and Conway Sonne, a second cousin, who wrote about the history of the Sonne family in his biography of his father, Elder Alma Sonne, older brother of my father's mother, Nora Sonne Perry. On many occasions, I have also felt a welding link to many other family members who have passed away, from Gustavus Adolphus Perry, the first known member of the Perry line to join the restored Church of Jesus Christ, to my dear mother and to my older sister, Barbara. I have a deep and personal witness that persons on the other side of the veil were concerned enough about the accurate telling of my father's life story to intervene when I needed their special help.

I could not have written my father's biography without other supporters with whom I have felt knit and welded together. As a professor at the Marriott School at Brigham Young University, I received encouragement from my group leader, Paul Godfrey, my department chair, Jeff Dyer, and my dean, Gary Cornia, to put aside other projects to focus on this one. I believe they rightly deemed this project more important than the others. I am grateful to my father's secretary, Kari Smith, and to my secretary, LuAnn Hart, who have always been ready, willing, and able to lend a helping hand. I am enormously blessed by strong family support from my wife, Carolyn, and our children, Audrey, Tom, Justin, Diana, Christina, and Rachel. I am especially grateful to Justin, who is a far more gifted writer than I am, for his help and insights whenever I needed the listening ear of another writer. I have also appreciated my association with my friends at Deseret Book who have helped move the biography along—Sheri Dew, Cory Maxwell, Richard Erickson, and especially my editor, Suzanne Brady. They have been wonderfully supportive collaborators.

Finally, I would like to acknowledge my father, Elder L. Tom Perry. We have a very special relationship, and I am both humbled and honored to be his son. I have appreciated this extraordinary opportunity to write about his uncommon life.

١

CHAPTER 1

INTRODUCTION

My grandfather Leslie Thomas Perry was hired by the family of President Joseph F. Smith to milk their two cows. This afforded him the opportunity to live in the Beehive House for three and a half years. In his personal history, he wrote the following about the Prophet Joseph F. Smith: "Most great men that I have known have been deflated by intimate contact. Not so with the Prophet Joseph F. Smith. Each common every day act added inches to his greatness. To me he was a Prophet even while washing his hands or untying his shoes."[1]

My grandfather was a skilled debater and a trained attorney and judge who knew how to build and argue a case. If he were asked to defend his statement about President Joseph F. Smith, he would quickly concede the point that his subjectivity might have clouded his objectivity. He would then build and argue the case from its major strength—his unrestricted daily access to the prophet. He saw President Smith in so many situations that he possessed a unique vantage point for taking a true measure of the man.

I begin my father's biography with my grandfather's experience in the home of a prophet because I recently realized how closely it resembles my own experiences growing up in the home of a future Apostle—a prophet, seer, and revelator. What my grandfather's personal history has helped me appreciate is the unique value of a firsthand account. I have loved the stories about his years in the Beehive House since they were told to me as a boy. They powerfully affect me because he was personally experiencing the prophet's daily routines. I firmly believe that my grandfather's stories about President Smith are not simply family treasures but also hidden gems of Church history.

I have come to view my lifetime of experiences with my father in much the same way—as hidden gems of Church history. Not only do they describe what he has accomplished in his uncommon life but they also give a true measure of the man, a man whom the Lord has prepared and refined for what is now nine-tenths of a century. In addition, the substantial part of my father's life I have personally observed leads me to much the same conclusion about him as my grandfather made about President Joseph F. Smith: "Each common everyday act [has] added inches to his greatness."

An Uncommon Life

My father has a talent for deflecting compliments and rarely allows praise to inflate his perception of himself. He is also someone who lives in the present, and he seldom dwells on previous accomplishments. This presented a formidable challenge for me as his biographer. On the rare occasions when he reflects on his uncommon life, he does not cast himself as the central character in the story he tells. It is usually someone else who receives the credit or plays the hero. And when pushed about his role, he dismisses its significance. He'll shake his head, smile, and even laugh at the thought that perhaps he's not attaching sufficient significance to his role. Then he'll often say, "I'm as common as dirt."

How can someone remain so unaffected by his uncommon, even extraordinary life? It is an adult life that encompasses a twenty-year professional career that took him from his first job as an internal auditor for C. C. Anderson's department store in Boise, Idaho, to executive positions on the West Coast and the East Coast. It is a life that saw him called at fifty years of age by a prophet of God to be a General Authority of the Church and later, with the death of that prophet, President Harold B. Lee, to fill the position left vacant in the Quorum of the Twelve Apostles. Perhaps his humility is simply what happens to men who serve as Apostles of the Lord Jesus Christ for forty years. I'm sure it is, but there are additional reasons my father has retained uncommon humility throughout his life.

First, my father was a late bloomer. His father, my grandfather, was a man of rare intelligence, and he valued education and academic honors above all else except the gospel and his family. Even when my grandfather wrote his personal history when he was nearly eighty years old, he recalled what his favorite teacher from elementary school, Fred J. Holton, told his parents when he was only nine years old: "Your other boys may be successful farmers, and you should train them for that occupation, but Leslie is different. He will never be a farmer. Training him in that line will be wasted effort. You cannot put a square peg in a round hole. His heart is set on being a teacher or a lawyer. You must provide for him a higher education."

My grandfather was immensely proud of his accomplished children, but my father is quick to note that his birth order was unfortunate. He was preceded by an older sister and followed by a younger brother who were near-geniuses, and he never measured up to their many impressive academic achievements. My grandfather's personal history contains long paragraphs about all of his children and their accomplishments—except my father. All he said about him was, "Tom has surprised us."

My father had just received and read his father's personal history when he told his father about a promotion in a letter written January 5, 1965: "The President and Sr. Vice President of our firm called me and wanted to take me to lunch. At lunch I was told that at the board meeting on the following Wednesday, I was to be elected a vice president. I am now V.P. and Secretary-Treasurer of a $200,000,000 business. It just shows what good home and church experience can do for the family's poorest student."

My father prefers to think of himself as an overachiever rather than gifted. In a letter he wrote to his father dated March 6, 1955, my father said:

"As I think over the many inventories I have taken of myself, I have yet to find a situation in which the assets I received through inheritance [the inheritance he received from nature and nurturing, not a financial one] have not been ample to give me the desired result if I was willing to work for it. I am also very thankful that the assets I have received through inheritance were not those which produced a desired result, but rather those which grant the opportunity for self-expression and initiative to produce the desired result."

Essentially, my father was saying he was grateful he was not as naturally gifted as others. He felt fortunate that things didn't come easily for him and that he was given only enough natural ability to be successful when he was conscientious and applied himself.

Perhaps my father is more like the servant given two talents than the servant given five.[2] Given his competitive nature, my father might relish competing as the underdog against the servant with five talents. His goal would not be to win but to improve himself as much as possible and to gain the greatest possible increase with the talents he has been given. Regarding self-improvement, my father has often said about himself and others, "I don't care as much about where someone currently stands relative to someone else as about whether they're improving." A person's slope of improvement does not even need to be particularly steep when he or she is continuously improving. My father's approach to eternal progression has always been sure and steady—more like continuous climbing than on-again, off-again siege climbing.

Second, my father always seems to be able to see the big picture as context for the roles he plays. Perhaps this ability partially explains his steadiness and resilience. He has experienced his share of life's hardships, but he remains Teflon-coated against discouragement. He drives my sister Linda and me crazy when he says, "I've never had a bad day in my life," though both our mother and our older sister have died of cancer. And though our rose-colored glasses are not as deeply tinted as his, we know he genuinely believes it. He has the kind of unshakable optimism that is possible only to someone with his faith in God and His eternal plan.

I have seen the process many times as my father has accepted new callings or assignments. Initially, he is humbled and overwhelmed by the challenge that has been handed to him. He wonders how he is going to accomplish the task—for example, serving as the president of the Europe Central Area and moving to Frankfurt, Germany, at age eighty-two, or, more recently, chairing the Church's Public Affairs Committee. He accepts these assignments solely on faith. He firmly believes that anybody else would be more qualified to do them. It may take him a few days to embrace such assignments, but step by step a vision is revealed to him, and he knows exactly what to do. And it is usually in the doing that my father excels, for as anyone who works with him learns quickly, he practices the principle of accountability so consistently that it is second nature to him.

My father thinks about the progress of the Church in much the same way that a grandfather in John Steinbeck's short story "The Leader of the People" speaks about westering, the nineteenth-century push westward by the pioneers. In that story, the grandfather says: "It was westering and westering. . . . I was the leader, but if I hadn't been there, someone else would have been the head. . . . The westering was as big as God, and the slow steps that made the movement piled up and piled up until the continent was crossed."[3]

Clearly my father sees himself as one member of the cast in an unimaginably expansive drama, and whether he is acting in the role of a senior apostle in the latter-day Church of Jesus Christ or a home teacher, he always strives to make a positive difference.

Finally, my father stays grounded because he knows who directs his life and leads the Church. His life's story has never been about him—it has been about doing what he has been called and chosen to do to fulfill God's eternal plan. Like any other faithful member of the Church, my father is simply following the Lord's lead. All that really matters to him is doing the will of Jesus Christ and receiving His divine accolade: "Well done, thou good and faithful servant: . . . enter thou into the joy of the lord" (Matthew 25:21).

A Purposeful Biography

A few years ago, one of my father's grade-school friends told me that my father had made a presentation to the other fourth-grade boys about how they should get dressed in the morning. As a ten-year-old, he was emphatic that boys put on their shirts first. Why? Because if they put on their trousers first, they need to unbutton or unzip them to tuck in their shirts.

Aspects of my father's life appear as if they were the result of a time-and-motion study. He has always been someone who prefers not to waste time or movement. He can relax, but he's very clear about when he's relaxing and when he's working. In his mind, work is meant to be efficient and purposeful. For example, Richard Bushman, the noted LDS Church historian and biographer of the Prophet Joseph Smith, served for a time as my father's counselor in the Boston stake presidency, and he recalls their first stake presidency meeting together. My father pulled out an egg timer along with the meeting's agenda, and he announced that he was going to hold all reports to their allocated minutes on the agenda. This was quite a shock to a university professor like President Bushman, who was used to a very different set of norms for meetings.

My father has given me little direction about his biography, but he has made one request—it should have a purpose. In other words, it ought to teach something to everyone who reads it. He does not want a biography that makes him appear larger than life or chronicles all his accomplishments and travels. For him, the value of life's experiences is mostly determined by the value of the lessons they teach. His life's lessons are consistently positive lessons because he is such a positive person. He also has lived a life of faithfulness to God, family, and country, and his life is filled with faith-promoting experiences. That is why I believe my father wants his biography to be both uplifting and inspirational. He would view it as being of little worth unless it encourages others to live better lives by drawing closer to God, leading their families along the paths of righteousness, and selflessly serving their country in war and peace.

This biography has been written to commemorate my father's ninetieth birthday, but he shared a model of what he believes a biography should be when he celebrated his eightieth birthday with his family. On the Saturday before that birthday, he and Sister Perry gathered children and grandchildren for lunch in Perry, Utah, where members of the Perry family had settled after making the pioneer trek west to the Great Basin. Those early Utah settlers are the bedrock of my father's deep respect and enormous gratitude for his noble pioneer heritage.

After lunch we caravanned to Logan, where we made ten stops. At each one my father taught us an important lesson from his early life. That was the purposeful way he wanted to celebrate his eightieth birthday.

A Logan Boy, a Missionary, and a Marine

My father took us to Logan to teach us about his heritage and life so we could better appreciate the value of our heritage. The first stop in Logan was his birthplace, the home in which his mother's parents eventually lived. His lesson was about the sacrifices his ancestors had made and the sufferings they had endured to bless our lives today. It was a stop that was enriched by stories of family history, focusing mostly on his maternal grandparents, Christian and Eliza Sonne.

Then we went next door to the home in which my father grew up. He explained that much of the credit for his success in life should go to his parents, who gave him a wonderful start. He told stories about his parents and recalled their traits that impressed him most. He focused on how he had been given the name of his father, the first L. Tom Perry, and how he has always strived to honor that name.

At that point we drove to Logan's Comfort Inn. Before we checked in, however, my father told his family about the land on which the motel stood. He said, "Tonight we will sleep where my family's old cow pasture used to be." He also explained that a large part of the land had been used for a family garden, which he was grateful for because he grew up plowing, planting, tending, irrigating, and harvesting it. His principal lesson at this stop, however, was about the way things change. He wanted his grandchildren to understand that change is inevitable, and they should prepare for it and embrace it.

Our next stop was the old Logan Ninth Ward meetinghouse, where the Perry family attended church. My grandfather served as the bishop of the Logan Ninth Ward for eighteen years, and the Logan Ninth Ward chapel was constructed during the early years of his service. The completion of the chapel seventy-two years earlier was a miracle. Somehow during the early years of the Great Depression (1929–30), the members of the Logan Ninth Ward raised all of the money necessary to build the chapel. Bishop Perry recognized the challenges his ward would face when he proposed the building project to the General Authorities in Salt Lake City, but he acted on faith as the leader of the ward. He proposed the project partly because his ward needed a chapel but also to keep several of the craftsmen in his ward employed and hopeful during this difficult period.

Our fifth stop was the old Logan High School. My father's lesson there was about living up to one's potential. He explained to his grandchildren that during high school he was shy and seldom took full advantage of the opportunities available to him. He wished he had been more willing to try new things, for as he learned later in life, successive attempts at challenging tasks bring both confidence and the development of new talents.

Next we walked to his father's old law office, which had earlier been the location of the First National Bank of Logan. He explained that his father had been the bank's attorney, and he had wanted his eldest son to become a banker. Accordingly, that was the profession for which my father prepared. But after graduating from college, he received a lucrative offer in retailing, and he never became a banker. Still, preparing from an early age to become a banker focused him and eventually served him well in business. For example, he learned the lessons of integrity, character, ethics, faith, confidence, and industry. He also adopted the conservative financial philosophy of Depression-era bankers, which has benefited the Church many times during his decades of service as a General Authority.

The Logan Tabernacle was the seventh stop. There my father further highlighted the joy of service in the gospel. His father had served as a counselor or as president of the Logan Utah Cache Stake presidency for twenty years, and the Logan Tabernacle was where they held their stake conferences. My father explained: "You enter Church service with pure intent to build our Father in Heaven's kingdom. The Lord more than compensates you for your time and effort with blessings that increase your talents and abilities, which then are used in further service. It is impossible to stay even with the Lord."

Then we drove up the hill to the campus of Utah State University. My father's experience at what was then the Utah State Agricultural College was interrupted for five years between his freshman and sophomore years. He entered as a freshman in the fall of 1940 and completed the 1940–41 academic year, but he didn't return for his sophomore year until the fall of 1946. He served as a missionary in the Northern States Mission from January 1942 to January 1944. Upon returning home, he was drafted into military service and volunteered to be a marine. He was honorably discharged from the U.S. Marine Corps in late July 1946.

Because those experiences as a missionary and then as a marine occurred far from Logan, my father skipped them when telling the story of his early life at his eightieth birthday celebration. They are nonetheless critical episodes in his life, and it would be difficult to describe his college experience without accounting for the five-year gap between the 1940–41 and 1946–47 academic years. Accordingly, in telling the story of his early life, I will depart from my father's eightieth birthday script and interject his missionary and military experiences in their proper order. I do this primarily to preserve the chronology of his life's story. It is also important to recognize that once my father was discharged from the Marine Corps, he reenrolled at the Utah State Agricultural College under the GI Bill. This was a great financial blessing in his life and certainly expedited the completion of his college education.

As we walked around the quad at the USU campus on August 3, 2002, my father was flooded by memories. Especially prominent were his recollections of his courtship of Virginia Clare Lee, his first wife, our mother and grandmother. He said, "There was so much going on at this time of my life, but my courtship of Virginia became the most important thing. When this time comes to each of you [grandchildren], it affects everything that you do. Make it precious and special."

Our ninth stop was the Logan Utah Temple, where on July 18, 1947, he and Virginia were married for time and all eternity. On the temple grounds he taught us: "The center of our lives must be the temple. We must always be worthy to enter it. If we live worthy of the covenants we make with the Lord in His house, we bind the Lord to give us the blessings He has promised us. The Lord will fulfill His promises if we will be faithful to the covenants we make with him." The Logan Temple was the culmination of my parents' courtship and the beginning of their marriage of twenty-seven and a half years, during which they were blessed with three children.

By this time it was late in the afternoon, and we were ready for a treat. Our final stop was the Aggie Ice Cream store, which used to be on the main quad of the Utah State Campus.

Before we ordered ice cream, however, my father taught his family about family traditions. He noted that having an Aggie Ice Cream cone had become a tradition whenever he came to Logan. "There are far more important traditions," he explained, "like Church activity, Church service, and family celebrations." As he has taught on different occasions to members of the Church, each family should establish special traditions to help it endure, for families are eternal units in God's kingdom.

Life After Leaving Logan

Because my father, in celebrating his eightieth birthday, took his children and grandchildren to particular places in Perry and Logan, Utah, to teach them the lessons of his early life, I intend to follow the same order. What better way to tell the story of the first part of his life—the part for which Logan was the center—than the way he told it to his grandchildren?

The next part of my father's life took him to Idaho, California, New York, and Massachusetts before he returned to Utah in response to his call in October 1972 to be a General Authority of The Church of Jesus Christ of Latter-day Saints. During July 2012, in commemoration of his ninetieth birthday, he and Sister Perry traveled to all the places he had lived before he was called as a General Authority.

While I did not travel with my father and stepmother to the East Coast, I did join them on their trip to Sacramento, California, where our family had lived from late 1954 to 1962. My father was filled with a sense of adventure and personal history during this month-long celebration of his ninetieth birthday. He wanted to drive, not fly, to California to relive (in reverse and on a vastly improved highway) our family's annual trip to Utah. We arrived in Sacramento late Thursday evening, and early Friday morning he wanted to visit the meetinghouses he had helped build in the area. We also drove to and walked the sales floors of a department store in the Arden Fair Mall, one of the early suburban malls in California, that my father also helped plan and build while he worked as a retail executive there. In the evening we attended a gathering of old friends from the area.

Early Saturday morning, we drove up Highway 65 to Gridley, California, to attend the baptism and to enable my father and me to participate in the confirmation of his great-granddaughter Clare Wood. He and I also participated in the Aaronic Priesthood ordinations of two of his great-grandsons, Perry and Jensen Wood. Finally, on Sunday, my father spoke at a special sacrament meeting in the Mission Avenue chapel in Carmichael, California, one of the buildings that we had visited on Friday.

Places like Sacramento provide most of the structure for the second part of this volume of his biography, which includes the events of my father's and mother's family, church, and professional life before my father was called to serve as a General Authority and covers his service as a General Authority until the time he met Barbara Dayton, who became his second wife. His first wife, my mother, Virginia Lee Perry, passed away on December 14, 1974, seven months after he was called and sustained as a member of the Quorum of the Twelve Apostles. He met Barbara in January 1976, and the nearly forty years he has served as an Apostle with her standing nobly by his side will be the subject of a later volume.

L. Tom Perry Family

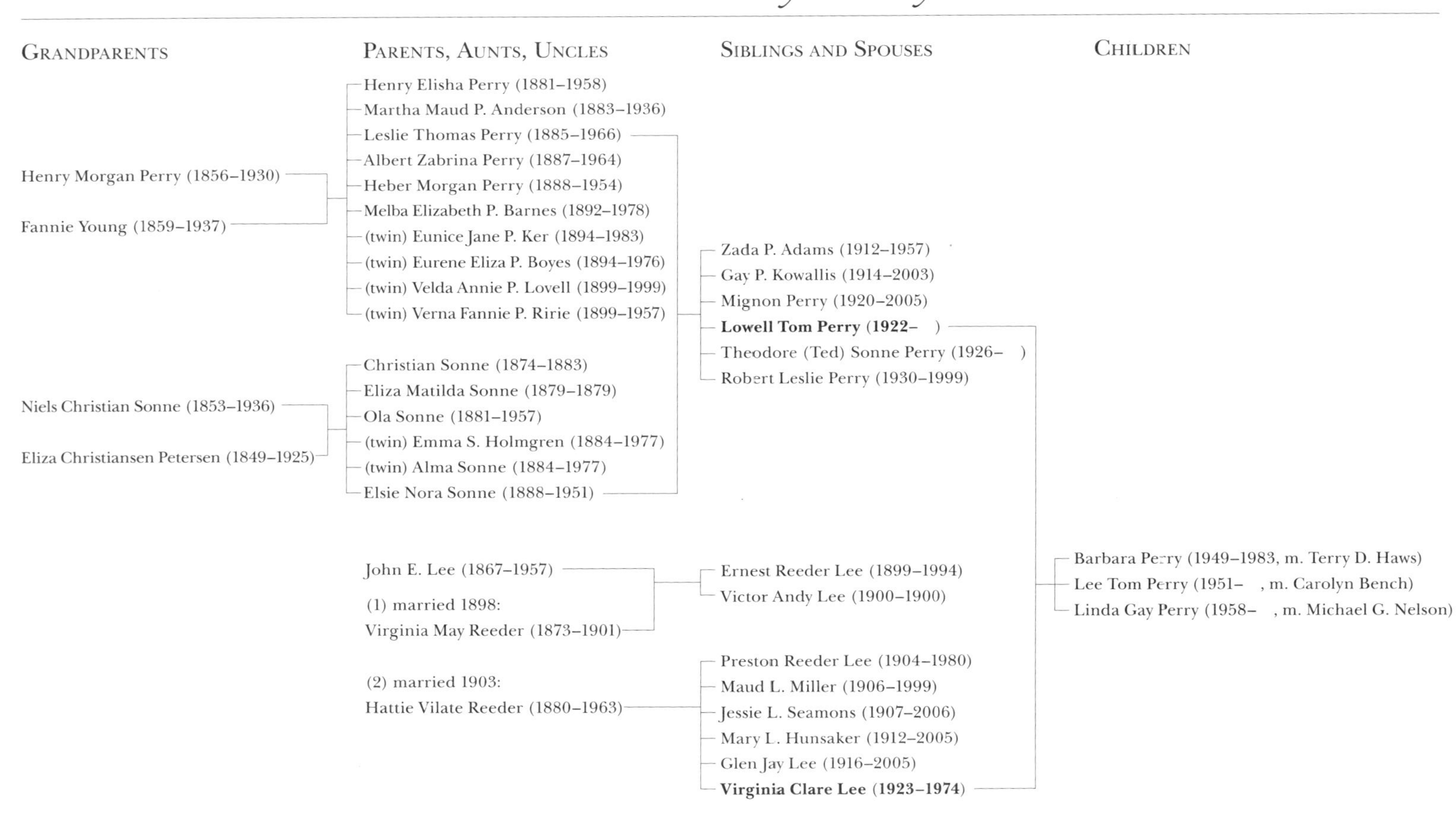

CHAPTER 2

PERRY, UTAH

The first members of the Perry family to join The Church of Jesus Christ of Latter-day Saints were the Gustavus Adolphus and Eunice Wing Perry family. They were living on their farm in Lewis, Essex County, New York, when they were visited by a mysterious stranger. This remarkable experience is recorded in the Perry family history:

"Close to the year 1830 on a dark, stormy evening, the Gustavus Adolphus Perry family was in the kitchen of their home, and the latch strings were drawn in for the night. The front door opened and they heard someone coming through the house toward the kitchen. When he entered the kitchen they saw that it was an old man with a white flowing beard. Although it was a stormy night there were no signs of raindrops on his clothes. He said 'God Bless You' and asked for food, and if he could spend the night with them. Although they were poor and had little bread they gave him food and shelter. When he came in he had a knapsack on his back with a little, black puppy which he gave to the children to play with. During the evening he took from his pocket, a book from which he read telling them it was soon to come forth and to get one at their first opportunity. As he was leaving the next morning he promised them that they would never want for bread, which promise was literally fulfilled. That very next day a man who owed them some money asked if they would take wheat for the debt. Although it was broad daylight when the stranger left none of neighbors saw him leave."[1]

In 1832 three LDS missionaries—Amasa M. Lyman, William E. McLellin, and Jared Carter—visited Lewis, New York. They met Gustavus Perry and prevailed upon him to buy a copy of the Book of Mormon. After supper, the family gathered to read from the Book of Mormon, and they immediately recognized it as the book from which the mysterious stranger had read. They found the missionaries to teach them the gospel, and they were soon baptized.

Gustavus Perry was ordained a high priest in Bolton, New York, in 1834 by John F. Boynton. With Brigham Young, Heber C. Kimball, and others, he signed a document that committed the funding for the purchase of land in Jackson County, Missouri, on behalf of the Church. The document, signed in Lewis, Essex County, New York, on October 20, 1834, reads:

"The members of a branch of the Church of Latter-Day-Saints agreeable to the requirements of heaven have striven to unite their hearts and views in order to be found spotless before the blazing throne of the Great Jehovah when He comes to make up His jewels, and for this end do send property by the hands of wise men appointed by the voice of the Church, agreeable to the revelation concerning the redemption of Zion for the purpose of purchasing land in Jackson County or counties round about for the inheritance of the Church. Agreeable to this we give our names with the affixed sums annexed."[2]

The sum for Gustavus was six dollars in property and no cash.

The Perry family migrated to Far West, Missouri, and they were among the Saints who were driven out of Missouri in the winter of 1838–39 after Governor Lilburn Boggs issued the extermination order. First, the main body of Saints stopped in Quincy, Adams County, Illinois, where they were treated hospitably and the last child of Gustavus and Eunice Perry was born—a daughter, Lucy Ann. They traveled up the Mississippi River approximately forty miles and stayed for a year in some empty cabins the owner allowed them to use. Finally, they joined the body of Saints who were settling Nauvoo, Illinois, where they remained until they were driven out in the bitter cold winter of 1846.

They trekked across Iowa and joined the Lake Branch at Winter Quarters. On March 22, 1847, while living at Winter Quarters, Gustavus was sealed to his first wife, Eunice, and also to his second wife, Sally Jenkins, by President Brigham Young. During their time in Winter Quarters, Gustavus served as a counselor in the branch presidency. The family remained in Winter Quarters until the summer of 1852, when they were instructed by President Young to close the branch, join a wagon train, and complete the long trek to the Salt Lake Valley.

Soon after the Perry family arrived in the Great Basin in early October 1852, they settled in North Cottonwood (now the Bountiful, Utah, area) and then Farmington, where they worked for the Harris Park family. While living in Farmington, Gustavus married a third wife, Elizabeth Wray Walker, whose previous husband had abandoned her and their children to go to California to find gold. Gustavus and Elizabeth were sealed in the Endowment House in Salt Lake City on April 10, 1853.

On May 1, 1853, Lorenzo Perry, second son of Gustavus and Eunice, married Elizabeth's daughter May. Lorenzo and May were the first in the Perry family to move north into Box Elder County, where they settled an area three miles from the center of Box Elder (now Brigham City). Initially, it was called the Welsh settlement, but soon it was renamed Three Mile Creek, after the small stream that furnished water for the settlers. By the spring of 1854, Gustavus moved his family to Three Mile Creek, and he was soon called to serve as the first presiding elder. Later, when the Three Mile Creek Branch was organized, Gustavus served as its first branch president.

Two sons of Gustavus and Eunice Perry did not make the trek to Utah with the rest of the family in 1852. Orrin Alonzo and Henry Elisha Perry had left Winter Quarters to find work in Missouri. Henry Elisha obtained work with a Roman Catholic man who owned 1,200 acres in the Missouri River bottoms. The man also ran a freight outfit that hauled provisions to Santa Fe, New Mexico, and Laramie, Wyoming. He soon placed Henry in charge of his freight operation, and Henry worked for him for four years. During this period Henry met and married Elizabeth Zabriske.

Elizabeth's father died and left her forty acres of land and some money. Henry and Elizabeth decided they could use her inheritance along with the wages he had earned to outfit themselves and Alonzo for the journey to Utah. When Henry approached his employer about leaving to go to Utah, the man offered to deed him all of his property if Henry would stay and continue to work for him. The man had so much confidence in Henry's honesty that he was willing to entrust him with everything he owned, knowing that Henry would take good care of him for the rest of his life. Henry, however, declined his employer's generous offer. His desire to join the Saints in Utah was greater than his desire for owning land and a lucrative freight business.

It turned out that Henry and Elizabeth had sufficient resources to help two other families make the trek west, which they happily did. They all joined the forty-six-wagon company of John Hindly and arrived in Three Mile Creek on September 3, 1855. Alonzo and Henry were each given a considerable tract of land by their father. Like his father, Henry served as the branch president of the Three Mile Creek Branch. When the branch became a ward, Alonzo was called as its first bishop. He served as the bishop of the Three Mile Creek Ward for nearly twenty years, and it was in his honor that the name was changed to the Perry Ward on March 5, 1901. The town was called Perry, Utah, thereafter.

Henry Morgan Perry

Henry Morgan Perry was the third child and first son born to Henry Elisha and Elizabeth Zabriske Perry. Henry was named after his father but given Morgan as a middle name to honor Jedediah Morgan Grant, a counselor to President Brigham Young who recently had died. Born Decembr 3, 1856, only a little over a year after his family's arrival in Three Mile Creek, Henry grew up under the harsh conditions of early pioneer life in the Great Basin. He was introduced to hard work at a very tender age.

Henry Elisha Perry died in 1875, when Henry Morgan was only eighteen years old. Suddenly, the responsibility to provide for the family fell to Henry Morgan. Over the next decade, he labored to sustain his mother and younger brothers and sisters in Three Mile Creek until they could sustain themselves.

Henry married Fannie Young in the Endowment House in Salt Lake City on February 24, 1881. She was the oldest daughter of Thomas and Martha Webb Campkin Young, two survivors of the Willie handcart company. Thomas and Martha were married approximately a year after their arrival in the Salt Lake Valley. Different accounts in the Perry family history suggest that Thomas was asked by President Brigham Young to marry Martha and take care of her five children. When they were married, Thomas was twenty-one and Martha was thirty-seven.

Martha was married to Isaac Campkin when they set sail with their five children from Liverpool, England, on the ship *Caravan* during the winter of 1856. Thomas Young also emigrated on the *Caravan*, and he and Isaac became close friends. Eventually they arrived in St. Louis, a gathering place for the Saints on their way to Utah. While in St. Louis, Isaac contracted a cold, which developed into pneumonia. Isaac died three days later, but before he died, Thomas Young promised to take care of Martha and the children on the trek west.

When Martha joined the Willie company, Captain James Willie tried to dissuade her. He said, "You can't pull a handcart alone, and it will be useless for you to think of going." Two sisters, Emily and Julia Hill, volunteered to help Martha pull the cart and tend her children. Thomas Young also helped once they reached the mountains. Remarkably, all of them arrived in Salt Lake City on November 9, 1856, after being rescued by the men sent by President Brigham Young.

Henry Morgan Perry decided soon after the birth of his and Fannie's third child, Leslie Thomas, to move their family north. He was frustrated by the lack of water and wood available in Three Mile Creek and how difficult it had become to support several growing families on the same tract of land. He reasoned that now that his brothers and sisters were grown, the family would be better off with one less family to support on the farm in Three Mile Creek.

Seeking a homestead offering better water and wood, Henry set out on his own after the spring planting in 1885. He traveled through Cache Valley, but he concluded that too many settlers were already there. He hiked through the rich lands of Blackfoot, Firth, Shelley, and Idaho Falls, Idaho. He found plenty of water in this area but insufficient wood. He continued to look until he came to the South Fork of the Snake River, near today's town of Ririe, Idaho. There he found a tract of land with plenty of water and an abundant supply of cedar and cottonwood. On the land he built a cabin of cottonwood logs plastered with mud, and he covered it with a roof of saplings and dirt before returning to Three Mile Creek for the winter.

In the spring of 1886 the Henry Morgan Perry family moved to Idaho. Baby Leslie was too young to remember the journey, but in his life history he recalled his mother telling the story of crossing the sand near Blackfoot. The teams were doubled, and their big Dunn wagon was pulled through the sand first. Fannie and the children waited all day with Indians nearby until Henry returned with the team. Then at night they walked over the sand.

At first, life was very difficult in southeastern Idaho. The nearest neighbor lived half a mile away, and the next two neighbors lived another mile farther on. Their small cabin was a single room with a dirt floor. Of course, there was plenty of work to do. Fannie planted a garden and milked cows so Henry could work late.

Fannie became extremely homesick for her mother. One day soon after they arrived, she took a walk with Leslie, and when he fell asleep, she laid him on a blanket under a cedar tree. She looked at her sleeping baby and then up at the tree. "Oh that my boy may grow up as strong, dark and handsome as this tree," she said. "So steadfast in purpose. So self-reliant, so protective to the weak, and they who are low in spirit." Then she wrote a short verse:

This tree that lifts its arms up high
And bends its back to the breeze
Twisting its toes firm in the soil
Nodding at other trees;
This tree that chills through winter's snow
And sweats 'neath a summer sky;
Were I a tree, ('tween you and me)
I'd go elsewhere to die.

Fannie's homesickness persisted. After giving birth to her seventh and eighth children, who were twins, she began to cry in the middle of the night. Her body shook with grief, and the shaking bed woke up Henry. Henry jumped out of the bed, looked at his sobbing wife, and said, "Mother, Mother, what in the world is the matter? Why are you crying?"

It took Fannie several minutes to compose herself and respond to her husband. "Take me back," she sobbed. "Take me back! I can stand it no longer. Take me back where there's singing and music and dancing; take me back to where there's books and learning. Take me back where there is culture and something to look forward to. There is nothing here nor ever will be. We left a nice home, and I came up here with you braving the hardships without a murmur. I have given you four sons and four daughters. What is there for them here? What is their outlook? No chance for higher education, and the coming generation is no better than the prairie they live in. Take me back, take me back!"

Henry promised her he would think about it, but in his heart he knew he would not be able to support his family if they returned to Utah. He started the fire, woke up the boys, and then went outside to begin the morning chores.

Fannie wiped her tears, dried her face, and looked in the mirror. "I'm sorry I let go like that, but maybe now I'll feel better." She dressed, went to the kitchen, put on her apron, and began to prepare breakfast. By the time Henry and the boys came back inside, she was radiant, smiling, and singing. She threw her arms around Henry's neck and kissed him. Then she served them breakfast.

Henry and Fannie Perry became pillars of the Rigby-Ririe-Rudy community. At a particularly busy time in his life, Henry was a bishop, president of the Great Feeder Canal Company, a stockholder and director of the Rigby Hardware & Manufacturing Company, chair of the school board of trustees, weekly correspondent for the local newspaper, farmer, husband, and father of ten children. He became the first bishop of a new ward, called in his honor the Perry Ward. As president of the Great Feeder Canal Company, he left a lasting legacy with the plentiful water it provided to this fertile farm community.

Henry's role as president of the Great Feeder Canal Company involved more hard labor than executive privilege. A story is told about a crew of men working on the canal threatening to go on strike. Henry listened to the crew's grievances from the man they'd appointed to take them to him. He politely listened to the man, and he promised to talk to the other directors about the crew's demand for better wages. Then he told the man, "But I'd like to plow the gravel bar first. It will be easy plowing this morning after the rain."

Henry walked out of his tent, harnessed two teams of horses, and began to plow the gravel bar. The work was difficult, and the horses needed to be prodded constantly. It took a little while, but eventually the men in the camp began to stir. One by one the men decided that if the boss could work, so could they. By 10 o'clock the strike was over, and the men were back at work.

When the Great Feeder Canal was finished with a final charge of dynamite, water rushed through it. As the assembled crowd cheered, the man who had been the spokesman for the striking crew ran up to Henry and said, "We've done it, Boss."

Henry replied, "Please don't call me boss anymore. I'm just one of you."

Henry and Leslie

Henry hired Leslie when he was eighteen years old to work on the Great Feeder Canal, hauling rocks from six miles away to build a dam. Leslie was paid by the load, and it was too far to make two loads each day. By starting at 3 a.m., however, he was able to make three loads in two days. The work was hard, but Leslie was working with a purpose. The job would help him earn money to attend Brigham Young University in the fall.

The summer ended, and Leslie received a check for $300.72, just enough to start at BYU. The check, however, had been made out to Henry, who chose to use it to pay taxes on the farm and buy winter clothing for the family. Even seventeen years after coming to southeastern Idaho, the family was still struggling to make ends meet. Leslie was disappointed, but he did not hold a grudge against his father. He understood there was a family of ten children to feed. His aspirations for higher education had to wait.

The circumstances under which Henry grew up never allowed him to receive much of a formal education. Still, both he and Fannie took their turns teaching at the one-room school in Rudy, Idaho, rather than send their children to the Ririe school six miles away. Moreover, he was a thoughtful man—endowed with a generous portion of common sense. Perhaps prodded by Fannie, he tried to make educational opportunities available to his son Leslie, who was able to attend Ricks

Academy in Rexburg.[3] He became the valedictorian of its first graduating class.

There is ample evidence to suggest that Leslie experienced occasional difficulty reconciling the teachings of the Church to the lessons he was learning about science and other subjects. Once, when he criticized his teachers at Ricks for being overly religious, his father counseled him: "My boy, be humble in your studies and remember your prayers. Yes, and in your prayers remember your studies."

Leslie, however, may not have immediately taken his father's wise and timeless counsel to heart. After graduating from Ricks Academy, he began to think he knew more than his father, and he challenged Henry to a debate to be held on a Sunday evening after Church services. The subject of the debate: "Resolved, that science has done more for the welfare of the human family than religion." Both Leslie and Henry were allowed fifteen minutes and a three-minute rebuttal. Leslie spoke first, and he was persuasive. It was reported that at the conclusion of his presentation, the attendees were ready to throw away their scriptures and take up arithmetic.

Henry spoke next, and he accepted the many merits of science, but he explained how religion had done many things to benefit mankind that science could never do. He sat down, not taking all of his allotted fifteen minutes.

Leslie stood up and began his rebuttal, but because his father had not been argumentative, he found he had very little to rebut. At first, and in typical debate fashion, he addressed what he had proven through argument. About midway through the rebuttal, however, he realized he had only proven what his father already accepted—that science had been a great benefit to mankind. He began to doubt the merits of his strong assertions. The spirit his father had brought to the debate melted his pride, and he suddenly recognized he might have created a false dichotomy between science and religion. Perhaps the reconciliation of science and religion advocated by his father was a better course than his attempt to prove the superiority of science. He became preoccupied with this possibility, lost focus, and was much less forceful at the end than at the beginning of his rebuttal.

Henry then stood up and said, "I give credit to science for what science has done. It has changed our way of life, and, in a way, our thinking. It has built, encircled, and constructed. None of us want to go back to yesterday when today holds so much, and tomorrow more." He paused, and then he spoke more deliberately. "But with all credit to its progress and all glory to its accomplishments, our scientists have not yet come up with anything that compares with the tenderness of the human heart."

With his brief, final words, Henry clearly won the debate. Leslie was the first to rush to his father, shake his hand, and congratulate him. The experience proved to be a turning point for Leslie. Inspiration had come so suddenly, it startled him and created newfound awe and respect for religious truth.

In his personal history, Leslie Thomas Perry wrote about the persons who had most influenced his life. He mentioned his father first. He said: "First there was my father—a public spirited man who was the first Bishop of the Perry Ward, a High Councilman in the Rigby Stake, and the President of the Great Feeder Canal Company. Father was not one to give advice. His influence came through example. He had a devotion to public duty, and he put the work of the public above his own private affairs. He greatly influenced my life."

CHAPTER 3

BIRTHPLACE

Lowell Tom Perry was born on August 5, 1922, at 472 North 100 West in Logan, Utah. The modest home, which is still standing, was built next door to the home of Niels Christian (Chris) and Eliza (Lise) Christiansen Petersen Sonne by their sons, Ola and Alma.[1] The new, smaller home was intended as a temporary home for Chris and Eliza while they remodeled the family home, a pioneer log home at 466 North 100 West. At the time the new home was being built, Chris and Eliza had no way of knowing that their youngest child, Nora, would move back to Logan with her husband, Leslie Thomas Perry, and their three daughters—Zada, Gay, and Mignon. When the Perrys were considering moving to Logan in the spring of 1922, they were invited to live in the 472 North home rent-free. Soon after their first son, Lowell Tom, was born, Chris and Eliza Sonne, placing the needs of Nora's growing family above their own, offered to trade homes, and the Perrys moved into the larger, remodeled

466 North home. Eliza died a few years later, in 1925, and Chris lived alone in the 472 North home until he died in 1936. In Chris's will, he left the home to his thirteen-year-old grandson, L. Tom Perry.

Niels Christian Sonne

The name *Sonne* is German in origin. It means "sun" in English. The history of the Sonne family traces back to the island of Bornholm, in the Baltic Sea, located closer to the coast of Denmark than of Germany. Today it is part of Denmark, but at various times the island has also been a possession of Sweden and Germany. The early inhabitants of Bornholm were Vikings, and they had a proud, free spirit. Its seamen were considered to be among the best in the world, but foreign sea captains would say they did not want more sailors from Bornholm than they had masts to tie them to.

Niels Christian Sonne was born on January 12, 1853, at Drastrup, Aalborg, Denmark, near the coastal towns that border the Baltic Sea on the Jutland Peninsula. Chris's father was a farmer, but farm labor was not the life Chris imagined as a boy. He was an excellent student, and, primarily through the efforts of a Lutheran minister, Chris was awarded a scholarship by the Danish government. He remained in school until he was nineteen, receiving an excellent education.

As Chris contemplated what to do next with his life, he received an offer he couldn't refuse. His uncle Ole C. Sonne had joined The Church of Jesus Christ of Latter-day Saints and migrated to America a few years earlier. Ole and his wife were childless, and he invited Chris to join them where they had settled—Mendon, Utah, a small community in Cache Valley.

Uncle Ole sent Chris enough money for his passage to Utah. Because Latter-day Saint missionaries had visited with Chris's parents in their home, Chris knew a little about the

Church, but he had not joined. He learned more about the Church crossing the Atlantic aboard the *SS Nevada* and traveling by rail to Utah with a company of Latter-day Saints, but he arrived in Mendon still unbaptized.

A rock church, the first chapel in Cache Valley, had been built across the street from Ole C. Sonne's home before Chris arrived in Mendon. Chris observed members going and returning from church each Sunday, and one day while he and his uncle were working together, he asked his uncle rather defensively why nobody had ever invited him to attend church with them. Ole, with characteristic bluntness, said, "The church is across the street, and its doors are open to anyone. Just go. You don't need an invitation." Then Uncle Ole went into the next room, brought back a worn copy of the Book of Mormon, and gave it to Chris. He then invited Chris to read it.

Chris did read the Book of Mormon. Every night he read a chapter or two before retiring to bed. After he'd completed it, he decided he wasn't particularly impressed. Then, a few days later as he was working alone in the fields, a question crossed his mind: How could Joseph Smith have written the Book of Mormon? The question bothered him, and because he had no satisfactory answer, he decided to read the Book of Mormon a second time. By the time he had finished it again, he knew the Book of Mormon was true, and he told his uncle he wanted to join the Church. On September 8, 1872, Chris was baptized and confirmed a member of The Church of Jesus Christ of Latter-day Saints.

Few men were as strong as Chris Sonne. I recall stories my father told me about his grandfather's strength. One wintry day he was driving down Logan Canyon on a horse-drawn sleigh with a load of logs. Farther down the road he saw four men struggling to load a big log on their sleigh. As he passed, one of the men yelled at him, "Chris, can you give us a hand?" Chris halted his horses, walked over to the log, waved the four men away, and single-handedly placed the log on the sleigh.

Another story my father told about his grandfather's strength was how he would pull timber fence posts out of the ground. This bear of a man would simply wrap his arms around a post, usually planted six feet deep, and lift it straight up out of the ground.

Chris's extra-large size sometimes presented unique challenges in pioneer Utah. For example, he had feet to match his large stature. He needed to travel to Salt Lake City even to hope to find a pair of shoes large enough to fit him. One day he went to ZCMI to buy shoes, and the clerk tried the largest pair of shoes in the store on Chris. They were too small. After going back to the storeroom to search a final time for a larger pair, the salesman returned holding two shoe boxes. Upon seeing a smile on the clerk's face, Chris momentarily assumed he had been successful. Then Chris noticed that the shoe boxes were empty. Seeing the disappointment on his customer's face, the clerk said, "I didn't find a pair of shoes that were big enough, but I can sell you a pair of shoe boxes that will fit." They both had a good laugh.

Eliza (Lise) Christiansen Petersen

Eliza Christiansen Petersen was born November 10, 1849, at Mosbjerg, Hjørring, Denmark, on the northern tip of the Jutland Peninsula. The name given her at birth was Lise Christiansen Petersen. She considered Lise to be her Danish name, but she was called by her American name, Eliza, most of her life.

Soon after she was born, the LDS missionaries visited her home, and her parents were converted to the gospel. Eliza's father, Søren Petersen, was a prosperous businessman, but in April 1863 he gave up his property to emigrate with his wife,

Elsie Marie, their children, and her parents to join the Saints in Utah. They sailed to England, where they boarded the *B.S. Kimball* with 657 other Saints for the voyage to New York City.

Eliza's family traveled from New York by rail to Florence, Nebraska, formerly known as Winter Quarters. They joined a company led by William B. Preston, an early settler who became the bishop of the Logan Ward. The Preston company departed on July 9, 1863, and arrived in the Salt Lake Valley on September 10. Later in life, Eliza would tell stories about her trip. She met Jim Bridger and other mountain men at Fort Laramie, Wyoming, but their rough, uncouth natures and lack of manners repelled her.

Eliza was equally unimpressed when her family arrived in the Salt Lake Valley. She cried in bitter disappointment after traveling so many miles and arriving in a land so desolate compared to her native Denmark. One of the teamsters in the Preston company convinced the family to settle in Cache Valley, which he described as fertile and beautiful. After traveling several days, they arrived in Cache Valley, where the teamster's mother prepared a meal for them and another family provided a wagon box that they used as shelter for the night. Only days after the Petersen family had arrived in Cache Valley, Eliza's baby sister, Cecilia, died of an illness she had contracted on the trek west.

By November the Petersen family had its own home—a cellar dug into the ground and covered with a dirt roof. Because winter was approaching and other families were still arriving in Cache Valley, they made room in their dugout for another family to live with them until spring.

Eliza and her mother knew how to card wool. They soon acquired small and large spinning wheels and did their spinning and weaving by the light of the wood fire that heated the dugout. Because the family's first crop was destroyed by crickets, it was Elsie and Eliza's spinning and weaving that provided the family with enough flour to sustain them through the next winter. Eliza also gleaned wheat and oats during the summer, like Ruth of the Bible. The staple of the Petersen family for many years was a cereal-like dish called lumpy dick made from flour and milk.

Logan was founded in 1859, only four years before the Petersen family arrived, so it was still a primitive, frontier settlement. Cache Valley was the traditional hunting ground for the Shoshones, and incidents with Indians were common for the Mormon settlers. One late-summer day, Elsie and Eliza were in their garden examining their crop of watermelons. Suddenly, a group of Indians rode up to them on their horses. They dismounted, picked up a few of the watermelons, and threw them at Elsie and Eliza. Although she knew nobody was nearby to hear her, Elsie began to scream. Her loud cries alarmed the Indians, and they hurriedly remounted their horses and rode away.

Eliza's reputation for weaving some of the finest pioneer cloth in Cache Valley helped her meet a recently baptized, six-foot, two-hundred-pound Danish immigrant named Niels Christian Sonne. Eliza had been employed by Ole Sonne, Chris's uncle, to do some weaving at his Mendon home. There was a mutual attraction between Chris and Eliza, and these two strong-willed Danes were married in the Salt Lake City Endowment House on November 24, 1874.

The newly married couple soon moved into a log house that Chris had built a block west of Main Street in Logan. This was Chris and Eliza's Logan home until they moved temporarily into the small, wood-framed house their two sons had built next door to accommodate them while the old log home was being remodeled.

Chris and Eliza: Parents of a General Authority, Grandparents of an Apostle

Chris acquired a farm in Petersboro, eight miles west of Logan, soon after he married Eliza. During the early years of their marriage, Chris and Eliza divided their time between two log homes—their home in Logan and another home on the Petersboro farm. Each spring Chris would move his family out to Petersboro, and in the fall he would reverse the process.

Eventually part of the family remained year-round in Logan. It was common for Chris to have only the companionship of a good book as he read by a kerosene lantern at the Petersboro farm. On days when the work was lighter than normal, Chris walked the eight miles to Logan to spend a night with Eliza and his children. Because he would arrive well past dark, Eliza would place a kerosene lantern in the window to help guide him home.

Chris and Eliza had six children. Their second child was a daughter, Eliza Matilda, who died shortly after birth. Their third child, son Ola, was born in 1881, almost two years before their eldest son, Christian, died of smallpox on January 31, 1883. As Christian was being examined by a local doctor before he died, the doctor thoughtlessly measured him for a coffin. Christian opened his eyes, realized what the doctor was doing, and pleaded with Eliza, "Mother, don't let them bury me alive."

The smallpox epidemic had caused a panic in Logan, and local authorities ordered that the dead be buried only at night. Chris and his father-in-law worked through the cold of the winter's night digging Christian's grave in the frozen ground, gently lowering the coffin, and filling the grave just as the first streaks of dawn peaked over the eastern mountains.

Eliza also became ill, and the Sonne home was quarantined for three months. During the quarantine, Chris was ordered to burn all clothing, bedding, and even the deeds to his property.

He was almost destitute, and when he asked a storekeeper to sell him supplies on credit, his request was denied.

Later, in 1884, the couple had twins—Alma and Emma. Alma was called to be one of the first Assistants to the Twelve in 1941, serving as a General Authority for thirty-six and a half years. Elsie Nora, the Sonnes' sixth child, was born in 1888. When Nora's son L. Tom Perry was called as an Assistant to the Twelve in October 1972, Alma Sonne was the longest-serving Assistant to the Twelve.

The Sonne home was a Danish home with Danish food and customs. The family socialized mostly with Danish neighbors. They even retained the Danish language, with Chris and Eliza conversing with each other and their closest friends in Danish. As parents, however, Chris and Eliza made certain that their children were proficient in both Danish and English.

Chris was a knowledgeable farmer who understood the importance of crop rotation, fertilizer, and proper irrigation. After many years of hard work and careful stewardship of his land, his Petersboro farm became more successful than most of the other farms in the valley. At first he had only a scythe and a rake to cut the grain and place it in windrows, but later he used a binder and threshing machine, and he acquired one of the first McCormick mowers. Chris increased his beef herd up to sixty Durham, or Shorthorn cattle, and he also had fifteen Holstein dairy cows, ten pigs, one hundred chickens, forty sheep, and a stable of ten horses. Until she became ill, Eliza also worked hard. She assisted in milking the cows, made butter and cheese, and continued to weave her fine cloth. Chris and Eliza were never affluent, but compared to their early years in Cache Valley, they became quite comfortable.

The Sonnes were deeply committed to their LDS faith. For many years Chris served as the high priests group leader of the Logan Fourth Ward. There were times in his life when Chris was unable to attend church as often as he liked because of the demands of a farm that was eight miles outside of town and because of Eliza's frequent illnesses. Both Chris and Eliza, however, believed in the power of prayer—both individual and family prayer. About Chris, his son Alma said: "My father seldom displayed any manifestation of religious zeal, but he prayed—for sufficient rainfall, the operations of the farm, and especially for my mother, who was ill much of the time. When he was particularly moved, he would pray in Danish, his native tongue."

Every morning and evening the Sonne family prayed together. Other times family members gathered together to pray for safety and protection. Once during the summer when Chris was at the Petersboro farm, a band of Indians set up camp only a few rods from the Sonnes' Logan home. Eliza took her children to a neighbor's home to stay for the night. In the middle of the night, she awakened her children and said, "We must pray." One of the sleepy-eyed children grumbled, "But we've already prayed." Eliza pointed outside to the Indians, who appeared restless and menacing, and replied, "We must pray again." Their prayer was soon answered when the Indians broke camp and left as quickly as they came.

When we consider the many hardships they endured and the central role that prayer played in Chris and Eliza's home, perhaps we see a bit more clearly why these two humble Danish immigrants were chosen by the Lord to be the parents of a General Authority and the grandparents of one of His Apostles.

CHAPTER 4

The Perry Family Home

The home at 466 North 100 West in Logan was remodeled a second time, starting when my father was seven years old. It was the beginning of the Great Depression, and young Tom's father was the bishop of the Logan Ninth Ward. Bishop Perry convinced the leaders of the Church to authorize his ward to build a chapel addition to the existing cultural hall that had been serving as the ward's meetinghouse. The chapel addition was certainly needed, but its construction was also Bishop Perry's attempt to keep some of the men in his ward employed during this difficult period. He, however, soon realized it was only a partial solution to the problem. The men needed other projects to earn enough to support their families. So when their work was not needed on the chapel project, the workmen were hired to remodel the Perry family home.

The remodeling project took nearly two years to complete because work on the Logan Ninth Ward chapel took priority.

The remodeling project afforded many opportunities for Bishop Perry to teach his son about the joys of honest labor. Elder Perry shared one of these lessons many years later in the October 1986 general conference. He said: "We were remodeling our house and tearing out some of the walls. In those days two-by-sixes were used as studding. To the studs was nailed the lath, and over the lath came the plaster. When tearing out walls, the slats and the plaster were easy to knock off, but, of course, that left the nails in the two-by-sixes.

"Each night after the workers had finished, I had the responsibility of gathering up the two-by-sixes and taking them out to the back lawn where there stood two sawhorses. There I was to make a pile of the two-by-sixes and then, one at a time, put them on the sawhorses, and with a crowbar remove the nails. After the nails had been pulled out of the studs, I was told to straighten them. Finally, I threw the straightened nails into a large green bucket and stacked the two-by-sixes in a neat pile.

"There was so much in this project that was of value to me in my young life. First, I was taught to be productive, to work, to be busily engaged, and not to waste my time in idleness. . . .

"Second, as a lad doing the job my father had assigned to me, I was taught not to waste, to conserve resources where possible. When the nails were pulled from them, the two-by-sixes could be used again—and we did use them. . . .

"Third, I will never forget my consternation as I watched the workmen using new nails as they built the walls back up and completed remodeling our home. The pile of nails that I had straightened and put in the green bucket grew and grew and was never used. I went to my father and said, 'Wouldn't it be better to save the new nails and use the ones I have straightened?' I was proud of the work I had accomplished.

"My father showed me something very important. He took a new nail and, using an odd angle, drove it into a board. He was able to drive it straight and true. Then he took one of the nails I had straightened so carefully, and, using the same odd angle, hit it again and again. It soon bent and was impossible to drive into the board. So I learned that a used, or bent nail, is never as strong as a new one. But then why had my father asked me to straighten those nails?

"As a boy, I never remembered receiving a satisfactory answer. It was not until I had a son of my own that I started to understand. . . . Work is something more than the final end result. It is a discipline. We must learn to do, and do well, before we can expect to receive tangible rewards for our labors. My father must have known that if he focused on the outcome of my labors, he would only become frustrated with how inadequately I did things then. So he found tasks that were difficult and would challenge me, to teach me the discipline of hard work. He was using the straightened nails not to rebuild our home but to build my character."[1]

There is a reason Elder L. Tom Perry often shares stories at general conference about lessons he learned from his parents—much of his character was shaped in the Perry family home at 466 North 100 West in Logan. Elder Perry also knows that embedded in the lives of his parents, Leslie Thomas and Nora Sonne Perry, are faith-promoting experiences and time-tested traditional values needed by every member of the worldwide Church.

Leslie Thomas Perry

Leslie Thomas Perry was endowed with an unusually keen intellect. Later in life he attended law school at both the University of Chicago and Stanford University, and he argued cases before the United States Supreme Court. While he was a man of humble means until his fortunes improved very late in life, he began life under extremely harsh circumstances. Perhaps his first year of life in Three Mile Creek, Utah, was not as difficult as the years that followed in Idaho, but it fills me with wonder when I consider where life took him from his first home in Rudy, a one-room log cabin covered by a roof made from sapling branches and dirt.

When Leslie was fifteen and a half years old, his parents arranged for him to attend a Church school, the Fremont Academy in Rexburg, which became the Ricks Academy before he graduated. Rexburg was twenty miles away from Rudy, Idaho, and Leslie claimed he remembered every turn of the road during that eventful trip.

Henry Morgan Perry could not afford to buy his son a new suit for school. All he could afford until the potato crop was harvested was a new hat. Leslie registered for school with some confidence because he believed that his schoolmates would fixate on his new hat, not the mended clothes he was wearing. He found the principal's office and politely laid his hat down on the principal's desk before he sat down. Leslie noticed that as the principal looked up, he seem startled by the hat sitting on his desk. As Leslie's eyes turned toward the hat, he realized that instead of his new hat, he had been wearing his old work hat. In his excitement to leave home in the early morning hours when it was still dark, he had mistakenly picked up the misshapen hat he had used the day before while working at the back of the straw carrier of the family's threshing machine. It was an inauspicious start, but a few years later, Leslie graduated as the valedictorian of the first graduating class of Ricks Academy.

Upon graduation, Leslie decided he didn't like his name—it was too feminine—so he assumed what he considered a more masculine form of his name, L. Tom Perry, by which he was known the rest of his life. After becoming certified to teach school in Idaho, Tom was hired to teach in the Rexburg Public School. This first job lasted two years.

Tom's desire for further education led him to Salt Lake City, which he reached by train from Idaho Falls. He had applied and been granted the opportunity to attend L.D.S. High School for two more years of secondary education. In his personal history, Tom wrote about arriving in Salt Lake in the evening: "It was my first trip to a city with more than five business buildings. What a thrill to view the Salt Lake Temple. I had dreamed of this since boyhood as I pondered over a picture of the temple on the cover page of the Juvenile Instructor."

Tom mixed well at L.D.S. High School. He was older than most of the students, and though they impressed him, he was not intimidated. He associated with the children of such Church leaders as Heber J. Grant, Orson F. Whitney, and a grandson of Brigham Young. He considered it a privilege to be taught economics by Bryant S. Hinckley, the father of future Church President Gordon B. Hinckley. He was elected by his fellow students to serve as the senior class president for the class of 1907.

Tom entered the University of Utah in the fall of 1907. During the years he attended the university, he milked the cows for the family of President Joseph F. Smith and lived at the Beehive House. Late one night as Tom entered the Beehive House, he accidentally bumped against a partially opened door and awakened the prophet. Many years later he considered the prophet's patience with him. He wrote:

"He [President Joseph F. Smith] turned on the light and, seeing who it was, came down the stairway and inquired concerning my difficulty.

"'The door is locked that leads to my room,' I explained. He went to the door and pulled instead of pushed, and the door opened. Had he been disturbed by my foolish blunder

I would not have been surprised, for I had robbed him of a precious night's sleep by a thoughtless act. He only smiled and stopped to inquire of a strange stable boy what I had stumbled into. I pointed to the half open door at the other end of the hall.

"'Let me show you something.' He took time at midnight to explain, 'When in the dark, never go groping with hands parted and outstretched; that permits doors to get by your guard and hit you. Keep your arms in front, but hands together; then you will feel with your hands and not your head.' I thanked him and moved to my quarters. He waited until I reached the rear stairway and then he retired.

"I had been alone at night with the nephew of the Prophet Joseph Smith who through his own worthiness was now [Joseph's] successor as the President, Prophet, Seer, and Revelator of the Church of Jesus Christ of Latter-day Saints. He had taken time to teach me a simple lesson, how to guard against danger as I walked through the darkness alone. He had lighted my path as I traveled to my resting place. Though clothed in night attire and not priestly robes, he was always a Prophet of God."

During Tom's time at the Beehive House, he witnessed firsthand some key moments in Church history. He was present one evening when President Smith returned home and announced to his wife Julina, "I have brought home the last of the bonds of the Church. I desire to destroy them." Tom was asked to make a fire in the fireplace, and once it was burning vigorously, President Smith opened his briefcase, took out the bonds, and threw them on the fire. This was 1907, and the history of the bonds dated back to December 1, 1898, when the Church was heavily in debt. Church leaders decided it was necessary to issue one million dollars in bonds, divided into two series, A and B, each in the sum of five hundred thousand dollars. It was a struggle, but the Church met every obligation when it came due.

Tom also participated in the Smith family prayer after the resolution against seating Reed Smoot in the U.S. Senate was defeated on February 20, 1907. Senator Smoot had been called as an Apostle in April 1900, and he received permission from President Smith to run for the United States Senate in 1902. Senator Smoot was elected, and he began serving on March 4, 1903. Questions arose, however, about whether Senator Smoot was eligible to serve as a U.S. Senator, given his high office in the LDS Church and evidence that the Church was not fully compliant with the 1890 Manifesto against plural marriage, although Smoot himself had never been a polygamist. The Smoot hearings began on January 16, 1904, and they lasted for more than three years.[2] In his prayer, President Smith offered a heartfelt expression of gratitude to the Lord and all the senators who had defended the Church. Later, at general conference, he said this about those who opposed Senator Smoot: "I forgive them and leave them in the hands of the Just Judge."

The young stable boy briefly served as a body guard for President Smith during the time when Thomas Kearns and the American Party were parading and rioting in Salt Lake City, and President Smith's safety was occasionally threatened. Kearns, who had served as a U.S. Senator from 1901 to 1905, included in his many business interests the publishing of the *Salt Lake Tribune.* With the newspaper's backing, the American Party opposed LDS Church influence in the politics and economics of Utah, and the party achieved significant backing in Salt Lake City and Ogden City government between 1904 and 1911. Tom admitted that his role as President Smith's body guard was uncomfortable. He said, "Even though I was rather large in size, I trembled for fear of attack."

Young Tom was at the Beehive House when distinguished guests visited, including Bathsheba Smith, general president of the Relief Society, and two future prophets, Heber J. Grant and George Albert Smith. Perhaps the most memorable visitor to the Beehive House was Joseph Smith III, the son of the Prophet Joseph Smith and President Smith's cousin. After observing their interactions together, Tom said: "The son of the Prophet Joseph Smith, a large ponderous man, seemed to be governed by the desires of the flesh; his face was full, his beard sandy, protruding forward. The son of the Patriarch Hyrum Smith, Joseph Fielding Smith, [was] calm, collected, full of the Spirit, whose passions had been subdued. I may have been prejudiced, but this was a testimony to me that I was following the man that God had chosen as the leader of His people."

During his senior year at the University of Utah, Tom was elected as the debating manager, and in that role he arranged debates with Colorado College and Denver University.[3] His debating skills proved invaluable when he was selected as the valedictorian for the class of 1910, but because he failed to submit his senior thesis by the deadline, the graduation committee refused to certify him for graduation. Tom pleaded his case before the president of the university, Joseph T. Kingsbury. He explained that his thesis had been in the hands of a typist in plenty of time to meet the deadline, and it was the typist's fault. Moreover, he argued, the university was ultimately at fault because it had allowed the typist to advertise in the school newspaper. He argued further that he was already on the program to give the valedictory address with Utah governor William Spry, who would be unimpressed if the student selected to represent the student body at graduation could not qualify for graduation. President Kingsbury overruled the graduation committee and allowed Tom to submit his thesis late and still graduate.

After graduating, Tom took a position teaching English and history at Rigby High School. Also teaching at Rigby High School during the 1910–11 academic year was a young woman from Logan who had recently graduated from the Agricultural College of Utah (now Utah State University) in home economics. She had been hired to teach domestic science, and her name was Elsie Nora Sonne.

Nora Sonne

The home in Logan in which Nora Sonne grew up was a Danish home. Her parents, brothers, and sister spoke Danish in the home, and the food and customs were Danish. Nora was the youngest in the family, and the task fell to her and her older sister, Emma, to care for their mother, Eliza, who was in poor health for many years.

Nora's three older siblings liked to play jokes on each other. For example, Alma and Emma once conspired to convince older brother Ola that Alma could solve in his head any arithmetic problem in their textbook. Unknown to Ola, Emma was signaling Alma the answers from the back of the book. Eventually, Ola caught on to their trick and stormed out of the room.

Another time, Emma pretended to sneak up on Alma with a pair of scissors and ruin his new haircut. When Alma complained to their mother, she could find nothing wrong with his haircut. Eventually, Emma confessed she had pulled a lock of his hair but had not cut it. What Alma didn't know was that she had cut a piece of paper to produce the sound that had alarmed him. Their mother laughed at the joke, but Alma found it less humorous.

Nora, being the youngest, received less teasing from her older siblings, who were protective of her. Moreover, Nora had a kind, sweet disposition that fostered adoration from her parents, brothers, and sister. Being the youngest in the family, however, did not excuse Nora from work. There was plenty of work to do, and like everyone else in the family, she was expected to do her fair share as soon as she was able. It could also be said of Nora that she had a streak of inner strength and independence common to many Danish women at that time.

Nora was an excellent student and a leader. She attended Brigham Young College in Logan and graduated in 1909 with a degree in domestic sciences. Nora served as student body vice president during her junior year, the only woman among the fourteen student body officers. She completed her education at the Agricultural College of Utah, where she was among the thirty-five graduates of the class of 1910.[4] At the Agricultural College, she served as the senior class vice president and participated on the college debate team. More relevant to her major, Nora took some commercial classes in drafting patterns for the complicated skirts and blouses of the era. This skill was greatly appreciated by her students the year she taught a Rigby High School. Three of her students, sisters of another teacher, Leslie Thomas Perry, soon became sisters-in-law.

Tom notes in his personal history that his initial encounter with Nora was not love at first sight. In the course of a brief hallway conversation, Tom mentioned an invitation he had received to a party for the school's faculty hosted by a Rigby matron. Nora, who had also been invited, said, "Good. I am glad I will not have to go alone." Nora always claimed all she meant by the comment was she would know at least one person at the party, but Tom assumed she mistakenly thought he had asked her to be his date. He arranged to pick her up at 7:30 that evening, and they were together nearly every evening after that, a use of time that Tom later admitted might have interfered with their daily lesson preparations.

Tom and Nora's courtship involved spending a lot of time together, but it was not particularly private time. Dating between teachers at the same school was mostly discouraged, and their principal imposed a rule that all their dates had to be chaperoned. They could be on the opposite side of a room so that there was an element of privacy to their conversations, but they always needed to be in view of their chaperone. Moreover, their contracts forbade them from marrying during the school year, so they waited until June 21, 1911, to be married in the Logan Temple. They spent their honeymoon riding in a wagon through Yellowstone National Park. By this time they were so accustomed to having someone else with them that they had invited Tom's youngest brother, Heber, and Nora's older sister, Emma, to join them on the trip.

L. Tom and Nora Perry: The Eleven Years Before Moving to Logan

Tom was hired to teach at Ricks Academy for the 1911–12 academic year. He was returning to the institution from which he had graduated as the valedictorian of the first graduating class. Tom taught at Ricks for three years, and he reminisced about those years as his most enjoyable and successful years of teaching.

The Perrys lived in the Rexburg Second Ward the first year, but then they purchased a home from Oliver Dalby, who was leaving to practice law in Box Elder County, Utah, and moved into the Rexburg First Ward. Oliver had been serving as the bishop of the Rexburg First Ward when he decided to move, and when the bishopric was reorganized, Tom was called by Bishop Robert G. Archibald to serve as his second counselor. Tom served in the bishopric for the next three years.

Tom left Ricks Academy to become superintendent of schools in Madison County, Idaho. The next year he was installed as principal of Rexburg Public Schools, a position that paid substantially better than his position as superintendent. In addition to being the principal, Tom taught eighth grade. He and Nora became pillars of the Rexburg community. In his usual self-effacing way, Tom wrote fondly of those years: "I loved to teach. After the faculty was selected during the summer months, there was little to do in the administrative line. I knew so little about the administrative work, I had few problems. There may have been problems, but I did not see them."

In addition to school administration and teaching, Tom operated a dry farm on a quarter section of land (160 acres) twenty miles east of Rigby near the Snake River. He homesteaded the land, and it needed to be cleared of sagebrush. By mid-August of his first summer on the farm, Tom had cleared a portion of the land, but it was tedious, difficult work. Then his plow broke. He decided to burn the sagebrush off his land, and after creating fire barriers, he waited until the wind was favorable and then struck a match.

All went according to plan until the second day of the burning, when a strong wind came from the opposite direction he had expected. The fire spread rapidly, and the wind was so strong that fire began to jump the barriers he'd established. Tom tried to put out the fire, but it was too big and moving too fast for one man to stop it. He narrowly escaped being surrounded by flames. As he ran, his one thought was that only God could save him, so he prayed. "I did not kneel," he wrote, "but poured out my soul to my Maker as I ran across the field."

Tom wanted to move a hay wagon out of the path of the fire, and he was prompted to get his horses to pull the wagon out of danger. He ran to where he kept his horses, harnessed his horse, Chub, rode him back, and hitched him to the wagon. He realized the fire was starting to burn the hay the horses had earlier dropped beneath the wagon, but still he was able to pull it, his only means of transportation, to safety.[4]

Tom's prayer was not answered immediately, but it was answered in time by an unusual change in the direction of the wind. He wrote: "A Southwester changing in the mid-afternoon was a thing unheard of in the Valley of the Upper Snake. More than sage was burned that afternoon, for there was scored in my soul a firm conviction of the power of prayer."

If this had been the end of the story, it would be remarkable, but apparently God had one more lesson to teach young Tom. Because of the sudden change in the direction of the wind, the fire threatened to jump another fire barrier on another border of his land. Two men joined Tom, but the wind made their efforts futile. At this point in the story, Tom recounted that the fire was out of control but that his faith remained undaunted: "God again took the helm. Once more the wind changed and this time its course held until the fire burned itself to naught."

A few years later, Tom had an experience that helped him decide he was not cut out to be a homesteader. One day he was resting in the fields reading a newspaper in the shade of his workhorse, Taft. He became engrossed in the paper's blow-by-blow account of a championship fight, and as the sun rose higher, Tom moved the paper so as to stay in the shade. Just as he was reading about the knockout punch, the paper tickled Taft's belly, and the horse delivered his own knockout blow. Taft's hoof caught Tom squarely above the eye, and when he came to his senses, his first thought was what Fred J. Holton, his favorite elementary school teacher, had told his parents—he would never be a farmer. Tom decided to sell the dry farm and pursue further education.

Tom had already been thinking seriously about going to law school. The previous summer he had attended summer school in San Francisco, where he took a course on contract law taught by Professor Samuel Williston of the Harvard Law SchooL. Tom was fascinated by law, and even without Taft's sudden intervention, it likely would have been his eventual career choice. Law suited his logical mind, his training in debate, and even his budding political aspirations. He enrolled in classes at the University of Chicago in the fall of 1917, just months after the United States entered World War I.

The only housing Tom and Nora could afford while living in Chicago was a small inner-city apartment. They took with them two daughters, Zada and Gay, and Nora never felt safe taking her two young children outside the apartment without her husband. Except for enjoying her associations at church, she found her time in Chicago very difficult and lonely.

Leaving Idaho to attend law school deepened Tom's resolve to remain active in the Church. In his personal history he wrote: "After observing that many students who went away to school became lukewarm in the faith and that inactivity was the primary cause, I made up my mind to be active. I have never regretted that decision. My marks may not have been as high as some, but even though I devoted the entire Sabbath day to Church work and a study of the Gospel, I did pass all the courses of Law that I undertook." Soon after arriving in Chicago, he was called to serve as the first counselor in the university branch presidency.

Tom was well above draft age, but many students and instructors at the University of Chicago Law School were called into service to their country. Because of Nora's unhappiness and the uncertainty of rail transportation (the federal government had assumed operation of the railroads), they decided to return to Idaho at the end of Tom's first year of law school. While in Idaho they arranged for Tom to transfer to Stanford

Law School, which had lost fewer of its outstanding law professors to military and government service.

In late 1918, prior to his last quarter of instruction at Stanford, Tom received an offer from Rexburg's mayor, John L. Balliff, to become the city attorney. Tom decided to accept the position and leave Stanford without his degree. About the decision, he said: "Diplomas meant little to me. I had earned two and lost the last one before I had a chance to read it. . . . I was nearly thirty-four and had a family of a wife and two children to support. It seemed a wise thing to do. My school days were over."

While serving as Rexburg city attorney, Tom contracted rheumatic fever. The doctor recommended that Tom be taken to Lava Hot Springs, about 110 miles to the south, where he could soak in the springs to relieve his pain. Nora complied with the doctor's recommendation, but she also knew her husband's life was in God's hands. She sought to understand God's will, but after receiving insufficient comfort from her prayers, she contacted the bishop of the ward in Lava Hot Springs to ask him to direct her to the most spiritual man in the ward. The bishop suggested an old farmer, and Nora went to him to request a priesthood blessing for her husband. Arrangements were made, the farmer and the bishop administered to Tom, and they promised him relief from the disease. In only a few days, Tom was able to return to Rexburg and resume work.

Tom's bout with rheumatic fever, however, left permanent physical damage—a weakened heart valve. But it did not seem to hold Tom back; he was a hard worker both physically and mentally throughout his life. His doctor recommended a single lifestyle change for Tom—a daily forty-five-minute nap after lunch. Tom set aside time to nap in the middle of the day, and Nora ensured that the house was quiet and that her husband was not disturbed.

Before Tom was taken to Lava Hot Springs, the student leaders at Ricks Academy heard about his disease, and they were understandably concerned. Tom was a former Ricks Academy valedictorian, former faculty member, and, as city attorney, a pillar of the Rexburg community. The student leaders wanted to honor him, and they decided to dedicate the class of 1920 Rixida yearbook to him. The deadline to submit the yearbook to the printer, however, came during the few days Tom was recovering at Lava Hot Springs, and the student leaders were not notified of his miraculous recovery. Assuming the worst, they dedicated the yearbook in Tom's memory. The inscription read, "We dedicate this book to L. Tom Perry, L.L.B.,[5] Lawyer, Humorist and Orator, First Alumnus and present Professor of Law, whose life and accomplishments are an inspiration to us."

Tom enjoyed telling the story of the 1920 Rixida yearbook throughout his life. Typically, he ended the story with the words of Mark Twain, the great American humorist: "The reports of my death [were] greatly exaggerated."[6]

Rexburg's civic leaders decided to issue bonds to upgrade the city's sewer system and roads. Hyrum Ricks & Company offered Tom a salary of $275 per month to prepare and manage the issuance of the bonds. It appeared to be a golden opportunity, and Tom decided to leave his job as city attorney to assume the position. His contract with Hyrum Ricks & Company, however, required Tom to invest a thousand dollars in a new hotel and to purchase a new home. The hotel proved to be a total loss, and eventually Tom traded his shares for a lifetime Shaffer fountain pen. This placed the Perrys in serious financial difficulty.

Tom was by nature cautious and conservative, and now he was weighed down by financial pressures in Rexburg. An offer came in the spring of 1922 from Nora's parents to live rent-free in the small house they had built next door. Tom decided to trade the equity in their Rexburg home for an automobile and move the family to Logan. His intent was to establish a private law practice there.

The Birth of a Future Apostle

Only months after the Perry family's arrival in Logan, while they were living at 472 North 100 West, Nora gave birth to a baby son. Lowell Tom Perry was born on August 5, 1922. The Perrys considered the birth of their first son to be the fulfillment of Nora's patriarchal blessing.

Nora had experienced difficulty bearing children. The pregnancy and birth of her second daughter, Gay, had been particularly hard, and she had not been able to become pregnant for several years. She visited their patriarch, Andrew J. Hansen, and requested a blessing. In the patriarch's blessing, Nora was promised that she would "bring forth in safety the souls of the children of men, even sons and daughters, preachers of righteousness, and leaders in the affairs of men."[7] A few years later, Nora became pregnant and carried baby daughter, Mignon, to full term. Continued fulfillment of Nora's blessing came with the birth of healthy Lowell Tom and then two more sons, Theodore (Ted) and Robert.

Eliza Sonne, Nora's mother, had been ill for several years, and relatively soon after the Perrys arrived in Logan, Chris suffered a stroke that left him partially paralyzed. Because the new baby in the Perry family would eventually require another bedroom, and given Eliza and Chris's declining health and their challenges maintaining a large home, it did not take long for the two families to decide to trade houses. Technically, the Sonnes owned both houses, but the home at 466 North 100 West in Logan became the Perry family home.

CHAPTER 5

THE GARDEN AND PASTURE

Leslie Thomas Perry wrote in his personal history, "As a lawyer measured by any fair financial standard, I was a failure." His private law practice was never lucrative, and it certainly wasn't an overnight success. Tom and Nora Perry kept copious financial records, and during the first six months of practicing law in Logan, Tom earned only $290.

Of necessity the Perrys were penny-pinchers. When they arrived in Logan in the spring of 1922, they were close to penniless, and Tom made barely enough to pay the utility bill and clothe the children. They made ends meet because they didn't pay rent, and they put to full use a very large garden plot and pasture behind their house.

Nora's parents had originally owned the entire city block just west of Main Street between 400 and 500 North in Logan. Alma Sonne had a home on the northeast corner of the block, and on the west side of the block were three homes in a row—Nora's parents' home, the Perry home, and the home of Emma and John Holmgren, Nora's older sister and brother-in-law. All of the land behind the three homes was tended by the Perry family. There was a large barn and a pasture in which they grew alfalfa. The Perry children tended Aunt Emma's bean field behind her home, and their family garden was behind the other two homes. They also used the corral behind Uncle Alma's house.

The Perrys kept a cow for milk and raised a pig for meat and chickens for their eggs. Nora's background in home economics and production came in handy in the family's ongoing struggle to keep food on the table. They lived off the garden in the summer, and Nora canned produce for winter. Moreover, their faith and willingness to pay a full and honest tithe brought the promised blessings of the Lord, either through miraculous means or a neighbor's kindness.

Eliza Sonne did not live long after the two families traded houses, but one of my father's earliest memories is of her dressed in a bathrobe and coming out on her back porch to give him a cookie. Lowell, as he was called, was usually playing with Mignon, who was just older than he, when his grandmother would treat him. Inexplicably, Eliza gave cookies only to her grandson and never to her granddaughter.

On February 10, 1924, eighteen months after Lowell was born, his father was sustained as the bishop of the Logan Ninth Ward. This began eighteen years of uninterrupted service as bishop, which meant Tom was often involved in Church service in the early evening when the Perry family cow needed to be milked.

Nora had grown up on a farm and was an expert milker, but she was a proud woman who didn't want her neighbors to see her going to the barn dressed in overalls to milk their cow. All three of Lowell's sisters were older, but his mother believed that milking the cow was not a job for her daughters. Her solution was to dress up Lowell in a pair of overalls large enough for her to wear. One can only imagine how Lowell looked in the overalls with the legs rolled up as he waddled out to the barn carrying a milk bucket. Once he arrived at the barn, he was instructed to close the door behind him, remove the overalls, unroll the legs, and lay the overalls over the milk stool. Nora would wait for a few minutes and stroll out to the barn in her dress, giving the impression she was going to check on her son's progress with the milking. Once she closed the barn door, she quickly put on the overalls and milked the cow. Then she would remove the overalls, dress Lowell in them, and walk back to the house. Lowell was instructed to wait a few more minutes and then trudge back to the house with the filled milk bucket. Nora would watch for him coming toward the house and rush out to help him the rest of the way with the heavy milk bucket.

Eventually, Lowell learned to milk the cow by himself, but long before he did, the neighbors thought of him as a prodigy at milking a cow. He received many looks of amazement and pats on the head at Church as his reputation grew among ward members for being the youngest milker in Logan.

There was something else neighbors noticed about the Perry family cow—she often got out of the pasture and wandered around the neighborhood. There were many days when Lowell was called out of school to chase the cow back into the pasture. One neighbor, Sister Strong, was especially afraid of the Perrys' cow. After being called home from school one day, Lowell found the cow standing by a tree on Main Street. Up in the tree, cornered by the cow, was Sister Strong yelling at the top of her lungs. It was a challenge for Lowell to herd the cow back into the pasture because he was laughing so hard.

Lowell's father did most of the milking—it was something he enjoyed doing in the early morning and evening when he wasn't involved in Church service or out of town. Lowell, however, was expected to do everything else for the cow, such as feeding her and cleaning the barn. Nora inspected the barn's daily cleaning and often supervised the weekly cleaning. Cow droppings were to be removed immediately after the cow was returned to the corral, fresh straw had to be laid on the floor every day, and the milking stall had to be washed with warm water so there was no danger of contaminants getting into the milk.

Lowell was also responsible for feeding the chickens and collecting their eggs, and when they were fattening a pig, he fed it. All the Perry children were relied upon to plant, tend, and harvest the large garden. Lowell's favorite crop was corn because there was little bending down involved with taking care of it. Having a large garden was not an optional activity that Tom and Nora Perry did to teach their children the joy of honest labor. Certainly it fulfilled that purpose, but their garden was a necessity—they depended on it for food. As the man of the house when his father was away, Lowell felt a deep sense of responsibility from an early age for the Perry family garden and pasture.

After School

At the April 2010 general conference, my father paid tribute to his mother for her teaching in the home. He recalled:

"I used to think some days as I ran home from school that I was through learning for the day, but this illusion was quickly destroyed when I saw my mother standing at the door waiting for me. When we were young, we each had a desk in the kitchen where we could continue to be taught by her as she performed household duties and prepared supper. She was a natural teacher and far more demanding of us than our teachers at school and church."

Lowell did not enjoy school and books as much as his siblings. He developed his poor attitude toward books partly because whenever he wanted to play with Mignon or Ted, they wanted to read instead. He also found it difficult to keep his mind focused in a classroom. He liked to look out the window at what was happening outside. Accordingly, Lowell received special attention from his mother during her daily after-school interrogations. When his mother asked him about what he had learned at school, only specific answers were accepted. Moreover, she kept abreast of teachers' lesson plans, so she knew if any of her children were reporting on the current or a previous day's lesson. Lowell soon realized that his mother could not be tricked, and he paid better attention at school. He was never at the top of his class, like Mignon and Ted, but by holding him accountable for what he learned at school, his mother turned her least-willing learner into an above-average student.

Learning was an integral part of almost everything the Perry family did. Even vacations to different state and national parks were opportunities for the former school teacher to teach her children. Nora was not inclined to waste time at idle chatter. There was always a purpose to a conversation. She believed the mind did not need to relax while the body was engaged in physical work. While she was ironing, she would help her children memorize the multiplication tables and the Articles of Faith. As she washed dishes, churned butter, played ball, or thinned beets in the garden, she was constantly asking a child a question, and neither an incorrect nor ill-thought answer ever passed muster.

Nora also instilled in her children the desire to learn through her example of scholarship, especially her gospel scholarship. At the April 2010 general conference, my father showed a visual aid—a notebook his mother had filled with notes as part of her preparation for teaching her class in Relief Society. Ted Perry recalled that her teaching routine began in the bedroom, where she kept her Church books. Ted could hear his mother in her bedroom practicing her lesson material out loud. She would ask herself questions and then answer the questions based on the lesson material. Next, she moved her lesson materials to the dining room, where her preparation became a family activity. In the dining room the interrogator became the interrogated as her husband, children, and even visitors would be invited to ask her questions on the topic of her lesson. Sometimes Nora and Tom disagreed on what was the correct answer to a gospel question. In fact, this was not an unusual occurrence because both Tom and Nora were former college debaters.

Fortunately, the Perrys had an able judge and tiebreaker. Because Tom had spent several years living at the Beehive House, he knew the Joseph F. Smith children well, including Joseph Fielding Smith. Tom would call Elder Smith and ask him the question he and Nora were debating. The Perrys were always willing to accept Elder Smith's answers as the gospel truth and thereby maintain peace. There were a few occasions, however, when Elder Smith admitted he had not considered the issue Tom and Nora were debating. Each time this happened, he called them back a few hours later with the answer he had obtained from studying the question.

On several occasions my father has publicly expressed gratitude to his parents for the spiritual training they gave him as a boy. He once said, "I guess my earliest recollection is being at Mother's knee before we went to bed. She was a woman of great faith." When he was older and shared a room with his brothers, his mother would go upstairs with them every night and wait outside the door long enough to be sure her sons had said their personal prayers. At one meal each day, Nora would turn the backs of the chairs to the table, and the family would kneel in prayer before eating. My father recalls, "As we would kneel in family prayer and listen to our father, a bearer of the priesthood, pour out his soul to the Lord for the protection of the family against the fiery darts of the wicked, one more layer was added to our shield of faith."

My father has also said, "Growing up in the home I was in, it was hard not to have a testimony; it was woven into our lives by our parents."[1]

Saturdays

Nora Perry lived the motto "Cleanliness is next to godliness," and she taught her children to live it too. Saturday morning was a time set apart for house cleaning, and everyone participated. First the bedrooms were dusted, swept, and vacuumed, and then the rest of the house received a thorough cleaning. Ted Perry recalls that he was frequently assigned to clean the cold air vents in the house. They were made of wood, and each vent had what seemed like a hundred tiny rectangular holes. His mother insisted that each hole be dusted, and she would spot-check several of the holes to make certain her instructions had been followed.

During the October 2000 general conference, Elder L. Tom Perry applied the lessons he learned from the family's Saturday morning cleaning routine to spiritual cleaning. Speaking of his mother, he said:

"Her instructions to us had been learned from her mother: 'Be certain you clean thoroughly in the corners and along the mopboards. If you are going to miss anything, let it be in the center of the room.'

"She knew very well if we cleaned the corners, she would never have a problem with what was left in the center of the room. That which is visible to the eye would never be left unclean.

"Over the years, my mother's counsel has had enormous application to me in many different ways. It is especially applicable to the task of spiritual housecleaning. The aspects of our lives that are on public display usually take care of themselves because we want to leave the best impression possible. But it is in the hidden corners of our lives where there are things that only we know about that we must be particularly thorough to ensure that we are clean."[2]

There is also a lesson of gratitude and loyal stewardship embedded in Nora Perry's efforts to involve her children in keeping their home immaculate. The Perry home had been remodeled, but it was the home in which she grew up. It was her parents' home, given so selflessly because her family's need for additional space was greater than her parents' need to stay in their home. Nora remained deeply grateful to her parents for the home in which her family lived, and she converted the gratitude she felt into visible action. The home became her stewardship when her parents moved out and her family moved in. She cleaned the home as thoroughly as she believed her mother would clean it. She recognized both the temporal and the spiritual implications of the scripture that says, "For of him [or her] unto whom much is given much is required."[3]

When the Perry children had completed Saturday morning cleaning assignments, it was time for their father to arrive home from work. He typically worked half a day on Saturday, and his arrival home was always greatly anticipated by the children. Nora and Tom Perry, although they highly valued work, realized that family bonds were also strengthened by play. During the winter months, the Perrys had to be creative in their choice of Saturday afternoon excursions, and sometimes they simply played parlor games such as Chinese checkers or

Rook. During the summer, however, the family would nearly always spend Saturday afternoons in Logan Canyon, where they could fish, hike, pitch horseshoes, play softball, and eat the fruit and vegetables of their labor from the family garden.

It was in Logan Canyon during a family excursion that young Lowell suddenly announced an important decision to his family. Like his father, he wanted to be called by his middle name, Tom, instead of Lowell. What was the reason behind the sudden announcement? His younger brother, Ted, was just beginning to speak, and he was unable to pronounce *Lowell* correctly. The younger L. Tom Perry was tired of hearing his brother call him "Wo-Wo."

Tom as a Young Boy

The population of Logan, Utah, changed little during the decade of the 1920s. The 1920 census records reported a population of 9,439, while the 1930 census reported 9,979, an increase of 5.7 percent. Logan was a moderate-sized town by Utah standards, and like many Utah towns, its citizens were predominantly Latter-day Saints. Logan was an idyllic place, where children could grow up in safety. Because of Prohibition, the decade of the 1920s was a dangerous, unruly time in many U.S. cities, but in Logan it was a peaceful period.

The block on which the Perrys and Sonnes lived was on the outskirts of town in those days. Beyond 500 North were mostly fields and few houses. One of Tom's earliest friends was Orson Bankhead. Orson had a Shetland pony that he would ride to Tom's house. Young Tom would hop on the pony with Orson, and they would ride together around the pasture in back of the Perry home and, as they grew older, venture out to ride alongside the roads north of Logan. These were mostly summer rides, of course. During the school year daily life was family centered. There were enough things to do on a daily basis that hanging out with friends was not part of the scheduled routine.

Tom had two sets of friends growing up—his school friends and his Church friends. Orson was a school friend, along with Joe Anderson. Joe Anderson became a lifelong friend, but Orson's family moved away during junior high schooL. Tom's early Church friends were Ariel Burtsen and Boyd Jacobsen.

During the summer months, one of the favorite activities of the Perry children and friends in the neighborhood was to play in sandpiles in the backyard. The Price family,[4] who lived nearby, and the Perrys both had large sandpiles. The Prices' sandpile was especially conducive to summertime play because it was protected by an awning constructed of wood and chicken wire. Vines would grow up the chicken wire, protecting builders of sand castles and cities from the heat of the summer sun.

In addition to their Saturday afternoon excursions to Logan Canyon, the Perrys took vacations to Bear Lake and Yellowstone National Park during the summer. Somehow the entire family figured out how they all could squeeze into the family car for trips to Logan Canyon and Bear Lake, but the trips to Yellowstone were too far for the entire family to go together. Accordingly, Tom and Nora took their children to Yellowstone in shifts, two children at a time. The two eldest daughters were the first to go, then it was Mignon and young Tom's turn, and, finally, the two youngest sons accompanied their parents. The trip to Yellowstone was the highlight of the summer for all the Perry children.

The Onset of the Great Depression

On August 3, 2002, during my father's eightieth birthday celebration, we checked into a motel that had been built on the land where the Perry family garden and pasture used to be. My father used this stop to teach us about the inevitability of change and particularly the need to accept and even embrace it. My father has seen many changes during a life that now spans ninety years, but perhaps no change in his life was as dramatic as the October 1929 stock market crash, the catalyst of the Great Depression.

His father had a private law practice, but his primary and steadiest source of income came from his position as the attorney for the First National Bank of Logan. Fortunately, the banking system, though wounded by the stock market crash, did not collapse for over three years, when decisive action had to be taken by newly inaugurated U.S. President Franklin D. Roosevelt, and a weeklong bank holiday was declared. Except for the week the banks were closed—March 6 through 13, 1933—his father was among the fortunate ones, remaining gainfully employed throughout the Great Depression. As a husband and father, the senior L. Tom Perry often acknowledged this blessing from the Lord. For the most part, he was spared from deep concern over his family's economic welfare. This freed him to focus his attention on the needs of others.

As the bishop of the Logan Ninth Ward, he had more than enough needs in his eight hundred-member congregation to keep him fully engaged mentally, emotionally, and even physically until late 1941, when he was released. It is interesting that Bishop Perry's release coincided with the event that most experts link to the end of the Great Depression—the beginning of World War II. He had been released on November 2, 1941, only a month before the Japanese bombed Pearl Harbor on December 7.

CHAPTER 6

Logan Ninth Ward Chapel

During the 1920s and 1930s, the Perry family income improved from the $290 the senior L. Tom Perry made in his first six months of practicing law in Logan but not dramatically. He averaged only about $200 per month of combined income for the first fifteen years of practice, and this included the salary he received from the First National Bank of Logan. In his personal history he made special note of the blessing it was to be allocated $30 a month by the Church for his expenses as bishop. Some months, he said, it "kept the wolf from the door."[1]

The other saving grace for the Perry family was Nora's careful management and frugality. My father has often called his mother the ideal Depression-era wife and mother. When he took out the garbage, he always noticed how little his family threw away compared to other families in the neighborhood. Ted Perry once commented about how he and his brothers were proud of the patches his mother sewed on their trousers. He claimed they actually improved their appearance.

The Perry family's careful management over the decade before the Great Depression in many ways immunized them against it. It also set an example for the members of the Logan Ninth Ward when the economic shockwaves hit. The Perrys, out of necessity, had learned to discern between wants and needs. This allowed Bishop Perry to teach the members of his flock ideals he and his family were already living.

The Logan Ninth Ward Building Project

Bishop Perry felt overwhelmed by the destitution left in the wake of the first waves of the Great Depression. Thirty percent of the heads of families in his ward were unemployed. Many of them were skilled craftsmen from the building trades. Bishop Perry decided to submit a request to the General Authorities to add a chapel onto the cultural hall in which the Logan Ninth Ward met.

The leaders of the Church agreed to allow Bishop Perry to move forward with the building project but only if he could first raise all the money. He accepted the challenge, and he started to canvass the ward, asking for donations. He asked everyone to contribute, and he promised blessings if they did. The largest donation was eight hundred dollars, and the smallest was ten cents. Even in the depths of the Great Depression, members of the Logan Ninth Ward rallied and donated the funds needed to complete the chapel addition. They also contributed their time and talents during various fund-raising projects.

Sharing a common purpose helped pull the ward members together. They sacrificed together and worked together. Some of the skilled craftsmen in the ward were hired for the project and paid by the building fund. The project lasted only eighteen months, but it provided hope to these men and their families. Their raised hopes equipped them for the lean years that followed.

The Perrys had little in the way of temporal wealth, but they had more than most families in the ward during that difficult period. As a point of reference, my father recalls that his fourth-grade teacher gave his class the homework assignment to ask their parents, "Do you earn more than five thousand dollars per year?" He recalls that less than a handful of students reported that their parents did. Bishop Perry earned approximately half that amount, but he was confident about his family's ability to live frugally. This led him to exercise his faith even further on behalf of the craftsmen in his ward who were hired to work on the Logan Ninth Ward chapel. As mentioned earlier, Bishop Perry also hired them to remodel his home so that when they weren't needed on the chapel project, they would have other employment.

I began hearing stories about building the Logan Ninth Ward chapel when I was very young, and I have since concluded that the experience affected my father deeply and permanently. Many of my father's unique strengths as a leader can be traced to lessons learned from his father as he led the members of the Logan Ninth Ward during the chapel-building project. My father learned about faith, compassion, and unity of purpose.

Building the chapel must have been an ongoing topic of dinner conversation in the Perry home from the time my father turned six until he was nearly eight years old. I'm not sure young Tom fully understood the faith required by Bishop Perry's ward stimulus package, but he understood enough that it made a lasting impression. Aspects of Bishop Perry's proposal to build a chapel could have seemed naive to the Brethren in Salt Lake City. It was clear how building a chapel would provide employment to the underemployed craftsmen in the Logan Ninth Ward, but it was not clear how the ward leaders would raise the funds to do it. The Brethren might have asked themselves, "How is a ward hit squarely between the eyes by the Great Depression ever going to raise the money from its struggling members to build a chapel?" And yet, they must have been impressed, even inspired, by Bishop Perry's initiative and faith. Clearly, Bishop Perry's faith preceded many miracles, both large and small, that kept the efforts to fund and build the Logan Ninth Ward chapel on track.

Bishop Perry also exhibited an unwavering resolve to care for his flock. He was clearly a wise and compassionate steward. Young Tom was invited by his father to assist in his compassionate service. For example, for Christmas 1929 Tom received a red wagon as a Christmas gift.[2] The wagon became a common sight within the boundaries of the Logan Ninth Ward because his father often assigned him to use it to deliver welfare items to needy members. When Tom arrived home from school, he knew to check his wagon in the garage to see if it was filled with food items. Often, Bishop Perry would accompany his son. These were precious times together between a busy father and son. There were also times when Tom made the deliveries of flour, sugar, wheat, and other commodities alone, following a list prepared by his father. It was so common for Tom to be out making deliveries pulling his red wagon behind him that he earned the nickname "Bishop" from some of his friends. Instead of being embarrassed by his nickname, Tom aspired to live up to it.

Nora Perry also enlisted the Perry children in compassionate service. About his mother, my father has said: "She went around all the time helping people who were having difficulty, and she liked to take us with her. She would put us to work washing windows, dusting, vacuuming rugs—things children could do without causing any difficulty."

Activities in the Perry home were often interrupted by a member of the ward ringing the doorbell in hopes of seeing Bishop Perry. In those days most homes did not have family rooms, and the living room was the center of family activities. When members showed up at the front door, the Perry children did not need to be told to move to the dining room. They knew the drill. The living room was the only place for their father to speak privately to a member of the ward.

While Tom was usually tolerant of these frequent disruptions, at least once he took countermeasures. Until his father and mother caught on and discontinued the practice, young Tom would sometimes disconnect the doorbell before he went to bed at night so his sleep would not be interrupted by an early-morning visitor.

One little old man was especially guilty of interrupting Tom's sleep. He had lost his wife, and his grief and loneliness had diminished his mental soundness. Whenever he became lonely, he would go to the Perry home to see Bishop Perry. It didn't matter whether it was ten at night or five-thirty in the morning, Bishop Perry would always welcome him, listen to his concerns, give him some food, and then drive him home.

When the man passed away, he left behind a letter addressed to "My friend, Bishop Perry." It was a final expression of gratitude to his bishop and friend—perhaps the only person who had taken any interest in him as the sun set on his life. Tom watched his father's reaction to the letter—tears rolled down his cheeks as he read it, and Tom understood a little better what it means to serve God and His children.

Among his siblings, Tom's disposition to serve others was both recognized and admired. Ted Perry relates the following account to compare his attitude toward service in the ward welfare garden to his older brother's:

"My memory of summers was rising with my brother early in the morning and going with our father to the ward's garden plot. There [my father] would give us our assignment of weeding and irrigating. This was in addition to our regular household chores. I recall I would judge from the height of the sun when my father had left for work, and then I would sneeze and go home to take care of my hay fever. My mother would let me read a book inside the house, but my brother, Tom, continued to work. Dad would reward him for his efforts by permitting him to take the produce to needy families in his wagon in the evenings. As a result of my eagerness to read instead of work, I never saw the happiness in the faces of the people who received the food they needed so desperately. But I am sure the happiness in the faces of those who received food from my brother made him the unselfish person that he is."[3]

Tom was also involved in maintaining the Logan Ninth Ward chapel once it was completed. It became a second home to members of the Perry family during the time their father and husband served as the bishop. Tom learned how to mow the lawn by mowing meetinghouse lawns first. He shoveled coal into the stoker, and he washed down the walls when they became discolored by soot. Tom even helped his mother with ward financial records and reports because during Bishop Perry's eighteen years of service, it was not standard practice for wards to call financial clerks.

The experience of watching his father lead the efforts to build the Logan Ninth Ward chapel, and also participating in that effort, helped Tom appreciate the unifying benefits of working to accomplish a common purpose. About the Ninth Ward building project, my father said: "Something happened to the ward during that period. Every activity was a fund-raising activity. We had fun. More creative talent was brought forth than I think has ever been displayed in any ward I have had the opportunity of being a part of. It was a very difficult time, but with the Spirit of God in us knitting our hearts together in unity and love (see Mosiah 18:21), we found a way to work through it."

My father both led and participated in many other meetinghouse building projects during his life—for example, on the island of Saipan and in Nagasaki, Japan, as a soldier, and in Sacramento, California, and Weston, Massachusetts, as a local Church leader. Consistently, he was able to draw on the lessons learned from his father, who, with strong faith and unfailing compassion, led a ward united by the common goal of building the Logan Ninth Ward chapel.

President Heber J. Grant Dedicates the Logan Ninth Ward Chapel

As the completion of the Logan Ninth Ward chapel approached in early 1930, Bishop Perry invited President Heber J. Grant to travel to Logan to offer the dedicatory prayer. President Grant accepted the invitation. At the time the Church was relatively small, and it was common for a member of the First Presidency to dedicate a new chapel. Still, it was exciting news for the entire Logan Ninth Ward congregation but especially the Perry family. For seven-year-old Tom, it was his first opportunity to meet the prophet face to face.

President Grant was invited to join the Perrys for dinner at their home before the dedication. In anticipation, Tom and Ted stared out the window for hours before President Grant's arrival. Finally, President Grant's car pulled up in front of the Perry home. Tom and Ted watched him get out of his car and walk toward the front door. At this very moment, Nora Perry tapped her sons on the shoulder and escorted them to the kitchen, where she had set plates for them. She had not informed them until that moment that they would not be eating with President Grant and the rest of the family in the dining room. She gently explained to them that their table manners were not yet ready for them to dine with the prophet. She, however, did leave the door between the kitchen and the dining room open a crack so Tom and Ted could hear the conversation, even if they could not watch the prophet eat his dinner.

After dinner, Nora invited President Grant and her husband to take a short nap. Again, this was a daily ritual for Bishop Perry, and after his long drive, it was also an invitation welcomed by President Grant. Bishop Perry retired to one of the upstairs bedrooms, and President Grant to the other. Tom was sent ahead to save seats for the family at the chapel.

Nora, her three daughters, and Ted arrived early for the meeting and took the seats Tom had saved near the front of the chapel. As the time to start the meeting approached, President Grant and her husband still had not arrived. Nora became nervous and instructed Tom to run home to find out what was keeping them. When Tom arrived home, he found his father and President Grant still asleep. First he awakened his father, who was so embarrassed that he sent Tom into the other bedroom to wake up the prophet.

At a devotional given at the Missionary Training Center in Provo, Utah, on August 15, 2000, my father shared his experience of waking up President Grant:

"Imagine, I was seven years old, and I had the assignment of going in and telling the prophet he was late for a meeting. I will never forget how kind he was. He sat up on the edge of the bed, pulled me down by his side, and for the next five or six minutes a little seven-year-old boy was alone with the prophet of God. I can't remember much of what was said, but I do remember the kind look he had in his eyes as we sat together. President Grant became my hero from that time on. To me, he is the special prophet of my youth."

Bishop Perry rushed to the meeting, and Tom and President Grant drove to the chapel together. A congregation of 525 people stood in unison as the prophet and Tom arrived. When President Grant sat down next to Bishop Perry on the stand, he said, "Bishop, you should have held the dedication in the Tabernacle. There would have been more room."

Bishop L. Tom Perry recorded in his personal history a few of the remarks he made before President Grant stood to speak and then dedicate the new chapel. Bishop Perry said:

"This is the test of the new chapel. Will the sermons preached in this stately chapel cut deeper into the lives of the young people than those preached seventy-five years ago in a green forest or in mud-plastered log cabins? Will the youth come out of this beautiful chapel more God-fearing men and women than those who walked down dirt roads, over cobbled rocks, or used stones for steps? Will the men and women who come out of this chapel take their place standing with the early pioneers? This is the test of a new chapel."

Bishop Perry Etches a Permanent Memory

Bishop L. Tom Perry was first and foremost a teacher. One of the lasting lessons young Tom learned from his father was how to etch permanent memories. The Tuesday following the dedication of the Logan Ninth Ward chapel, Bishop Perry reinforced in the minds of the Primary children the significance of the dedication of their new house of worship. He led a tour of the new chapel, pointing out many of its features and explaining their deep meaning.

First, Bishop Perry pointed to the back of the hall, where the beehive emblem had been painted above the back doors. He explained that the beehive was the emblem of industry for the early pioneers. He said:

"The bees are ever busy bringing honey and sweetness into the hive. The beehive is the center of a bee's life in the same way our chapel should be the center of our lives. We painted a beehive on this wall to be a reminder of the importance of being industrious each day and gathering the good things of this world and bringing them to be shared as we worship in our Sunday services."

Next, Bishop Perry pointed to a large painting in the front of the hall depicting the entry of the pioneers into the Salt Lake Valley. He reminded the children about the sacrifices the pioneers had made to gather in Utah, and how they further sacrificed to build cities in the Great Basin. At the centers of their cities they constructed places of worship. He explained that in Logan, the pioneers had built both a temple and a tabernacle and dedicated them to the glory of God.

Bishop Perry discussed two other paintings, one on each side of the large painting of the pioneers. The painting on the right was of the Prophet Joseph Smith, and the one on the left was of the prophet Brigham Young. Bishop Perry counseled the children to worship Heavenly Father and Jesus Christ but to always reverence the sacred calling of a prophet of God. He noted how special it had been to have President Grant in their midst only two days earlier. Their chapel had been dedicated or given to the care and keeping of the Lord by His prophet. Bishop Perry impressed upon them the uniqueness of such an experience and challenged them to remember throughout their lives how they felt when they were in the prophet's presence.

Bishop Perry then explained the motif that ran around the entire chapel. It was an egg and a dart repeated over and over again. He discussed why this motif was selected—the egg signified new life, and the dart represented the end of life. The egg was a reminder of our mortal birth and the time we have to be taught and trained in the ways of the Lord, to be obedient to His will, and to partake of the sacred ordinances that will qualify us to return to His presence. The dart represented the time of transition from mortality to immortality. He reminded the children that if they proved themselves worthy, they would receive the greatest gift of God, the gift of eternal life.

Finally, and with special emphasis, Bishop Perry approached the sacrament table. He instructed the children about the purpose of the sacrament. Because Tom was approaching his eighth birthday, he was especially impressed to hear that the sacrament represents a renewal of baptismal covenants.

There were many reasons Bishop Perry wanted to etch in the memories of the Primary children the importance of the dedication of the Logan Ninth Ward chapel, but the principal reason was to increase their reverence at Sunday meetings. The lesson deeply impressed my father, and it was permanently etched into his character. At the October 1990 general conference, Elder Perry spoke about the lesson of reverence he learned from his father. He said:

"Witnessing the dedication of our chapel by a prophet of God and attending the tour guided by my [father, the] bishop, impressed me greatly. I realized that every time I entered the chapel I was entering a holy place. It was not difficult for me to be reverent at church because all around me there were reminders of the Lord, His servants, and His eternal plan for me. These reminders reinforced my reverent attitude, and reverent behavior followed. . . .

" . . . Perhaps the parents of the Church could increase the reverent attitudes of their children by finding a time to be alone with them in the chapel and explaining to them that this is a special place, dedicated to the Lord, wherein only reverent attitudes and behavior are acceptable to Him."[4]

My father has often stated that he cannot remember ever not having a testimony. Perhaps his experiences surrounding the building and dedication of the Logan Ninth Ward chapel explain why he has never been burdened by doubt. He witnessed miracles as his father exercised his faith leading the Logan Ninth Ward through a critical period when every member's faith was tested. He met a prophet of God, spent a few precious minutes of time with him, and felt his spirit. He remembered another lesson taught by his father about sacred worship. As an impressionable seven-year-old boy, he learned to worship reverently. When he was baptized and received the gift of the Holy Ghost after turning eight, the Holy Ghost became his constant companion. Because he had already learned about reverence, he knew how to listen to the quiet whisperings of the Holy Ghost's still, small voice.

CHAPTER 7

Logan High School

On August 3, 2002, the celebration of my father's eightieth birthday took us to the old Logan High School, which had become a junior high school. At that time the old Memorial Bridge, which was on the school grounds and which honored the forty-six former Logan High School students who lost their lives in World War II, was being restored. My father paused in front of the project to remember his friends and classmates who paid the ultimate price for freedom. He told his grandchildren about one of his friends whose name is on that list, Lyman W. Tarbet. Lyman had taken the time to teach him how to use a slide rule, a tool he eventually mastered and used throughout his professional career.[1]

My father had another message for his grandchildren. I watched their faces during his presentation as we all stood on the steps in front of the school, and it was obvious his message surprised them. He told them that he had not really lived up to his potential during junior high and high school. He was a classic underachiever. He explained that he was shy during this period of his life, and he was so afraid of making a mistake that he was hesitant to try anything that was initially difficult. He concluded that he had denied himself of numerous opportunities to succeed because he considered the risk of failure too high and the consequences of failure too humiliating.

Part of the problem for young Tom was being the only B student in a family of A students. In any other family he might have considered himself smart, but when he compared himself to his highly intelligent siblings, he didn't feel he measured up. The worst days of the year were the days he had to bring his report card home from school. Early on he tried to hide his report card from his mother, but he quickly learned that this was impossible. Next door he would visit Aunt Emma Holmgren, who had no children and who treated the Perry children as her own. His mother, however, always seemed to know where to find him. When he found her waiting for him at Aunt Emma's house after school one report card day, he realized this time his trick wasn't even going to work as a delay tactic.

Initially, it bothered Tom that his mother's attention was disproportionately focused on him every report card day. After a little while he discovered why—his sisters' and brothers' report cards were highly predictable, but his wasn't. This realization only added to his inferiority complex.

Tom's comparative disadvantages at school led him to emphasize other things, especially service to other members of his family and the Logan Ninth Ward. There are many indications that Tom's parents appreciated his unique strengths, and there are few indications that they dwelled on his weaknesses.[2] Moreover, his older sisters adored him, and his younger brothers considered him their role model. In spite of his supportive home environment, Tom struggled with a lack of confidence during his junior high and early high school years, and that held him back.

So what changed for Lowell Tom Perry between the beginning of junior high and the end of high school? How did he come to discover his unique talents? How did he gain the confidence to become a classic overachiever in life? That is the story he was eager to tell his children and grandchildren in front of the old Logan High School on August 3, 2002.

Benson Elementary and Logan Junior High School

The Benson Elementary School, the same grade school Tom's mother attended, was on the corner of 100 East and 400 North, less than a ten-minute walk from the Perry home. Tom walked to school with Ted and Mignon, and they would walk home most days for lunch. The lunchtime meal was usually the major meal of the day, and a light supper of homemade bread[3] and canned fruit was a typical pattern for the Perrys.

Tom served as a traffic monitor—basically, a student crossing guard—for his fourth-, fifth-, and sixth-grade years at Benson Elementary. This meant he would arrive at school thirty minutes early and stay thirty minutes late each day. The traffic monitors were organized like a small police force. There was a captain, lieutenant, and sergeants, who were in charge of the patrolmen for each of the three upper grades. They would wear armbands and carry a flag as they performed their duties. It was considered an honor to be selected to serve as a traffic monitor, which was deemed a position of high trust and responsibility. During the sixth grade, Tom served as the lieutenant of the traffic monitors.

Though Tom was not someone who excelled in the classroom, he was a cooperative, if somewhat uninvested, student. His teachers liked him and he liked them, but he didn't enjoy having his nose in a book as much as he enjoyed other activities. Perhaps part of the reason Tom was the way he was is that Mignon and Ted were both avid bookworms. He grew tired of them wanting to read when he wanted them to work or play.[4] His father was also very academic, and though hardworking, he was far better at thinking than doing. Young Tom was relied upon as the doer, even the handyman, in the Perry home. He also became an organizer at home, and his talent for leading and organizing carried over to school and church. This is where he has excelled throughout his life. It was where he naturally gravitated, but because of his shyness, it took time for him to recognize his strengths at leading and organizing. Tom's shyness was not acute, but it often held him back from trying out for something.

Tom did have a most-embarrassing moment in junior high school that hurt his confidence, at least for a while. He and another boy were assigned to raise and lower the U.S. flag at Logan Junior High School. In the morning all of the classes came to the east side of the building, where they could see the flagpole, and in unison they repeated the Pledge of Allegiance. One morning Tom and his partner discovered just as they prepared to raise the flag that during the night a prankster had climbed up the pole and tied the rope at the top of the pole. During the moment of indecision about what to do, the students began chanting for one of them to climb up the pole and free the rope. Tom, wishing to please, quickly complied. He climbed to the top of the pole and untied the rope. As the rope dropped, all the students applauded his heroic effort. Caught up in the moment, he decided that instead of inching down the pole, he would slide down in great style. He heard the glorious cheers of the entire student body all the way down until his pant leg got caught in the metal rope tie at the bottom of the pole and ripped his pants. Then the cheers suddenly turned into boisterous laughter.

The Aaronic Priesthood and Scouting

Even today, part of my father's charm is how consistently he downplays his achievements. Clearly, he enjoys heaping credit on others more than himself. My assumption has always been that his accounts of his boyhood in Logan are similarly downplayed—he consistently praises others and diminishes his role in early successes. While this is only a suspicion on my part, it is corroborated by Ted Perry's accounts of his older brother's boyhood, which consistently reveal a more valiant Lowell Tom Perry. Of course, Ted's memories of his older brother's heroics might suffer from an opposing bias. More than likely, they slightly inflate the truth.

The point is, nobody really knows, apart from the brothers themselves. What we do know, however, is that the opportunities that came from callings and assignments in the Aaronic Priesthood and Scouting helped my father recognize his God-given talents for leadership and organization. My belief is that my father has always been a natural leader, but he might not have discovered this talent nearly as quickly had he not magnified his callings and assignments in the Church from an early age. He was like so many young men I have observed, who, instead of reluctantly performing their duties in the Aaronic Priesthood and Scouting, embrace them and grow accordingly. One of the central lessons of my father's life, and a lesson he deeply wants others to learn, is that whatever any of us give up in service to the Lord is returned to us a hundredfold. The lesson is simple, and it is a lesson he may have first likened to his experience tending the Perry family garden. Seeds of service are multiplied because once we plant them, the Lord provides all the conditions necessary for them to grow.

Tom served as the president of both his deacons and teachers quorums. He also served as the senior patrol leader in the Logan Ninth Ward Scout troop. These young men attended Scout camp in Logan Canyon for a week in the summer, and they would often go without their Scoutmaster because he could not leave work. Tom, as the senior patrol leader, was expected to take charge of the other Scouts.

The Logan Ninth Ward troop seldom won any of the competitions at Scout camp except archery and softball. Without adult supervision, the boys usually ran out of food by Friday. Tom had learned from his father about the edible berries in Logan Canyon. To tide the troop over until they were picked up on Saturday, he boiled service berries. This produced a juice into which the boys would dip bread and fill their stomachs.

Brother Alvin Larson, who served for many years as Bishop Perry's second counselor, was the coal dealer in Logan. This meant he owned a large truck. Brother Larson's truck afforded the Logan Ninth Ward Aaronic Priesthood quorums the ability to travel all together on different outings. One time they went to Salt Lake City and shook hands with President Heber J. Grant and President David O. McKay in the First Presidency's boardroom. They also went on a camping trip to Mirror Lake. For Tom, the most memorable trip was to nearby Clarkston, Utah, where they met William Pilkington, who told the story of how he, as a young boy, had met Martin Harris.

The trip to Clarkston was during the summer that Tom turned thirteen. They drove Brother Larson's coal truck to the Clarkston Cemetery, where Martin Harris is buried. Martin's tall granite gravestone identified him as one of the Three Witnesses to the authenticity of the Book of Mormon. Then William Pilkington appeared, introduced himself, and shared his incredible story about meeting and living for a year in the same log home as Martin Harris, who at the time was ninety-two years old. William pointed his finger at the young men of the Logan Ninth Ward, just as Martin Harris had pointed his finger at him many years earlier, and recited the testimony Martin Harris had borne to him. He said: "I am Martin Harris, one of the Three Witnesses to the authenticity of the Book of Mormon—a man who had the privilege of standing before angels, a man whose eyes beheld the golden plates, a man whose ears heard the voice of God declare that the book was translated correctly and then command him to testify to all the world that it was correct."[5]

Twelve-year-old Lowell Tom Perry never forgot the moment when he shook the hand of a man who had shaken the hand of Martin Harris. Tom's testimony of the truthfulness of the Book of Mormon became more resolute and steadfast after that Aaronic Priesthood outing to Clarkston.

The All-Church Volleyball Championship

My father has an amazing capacity to accept mistakes and move on. He is a very present- and future-oriented person. When he talks about his high school years, however, he usually starts by listing things he didn't do. For example, he wasn't a student body officer and he didn't go out for varsity sports. It was neither the absence of accomplishments to brag about nor having missed a chance to be in the spotlight that bothers him. His only regret is he did not take advantage of what could have been an opportunity to grow. He suspects that if he had been less focused on his weaknesses, he might have discovered his unique talents sooner.

Tom, nevertheless, began to blossom during high school by participating in a variety of activities. Though he did not play varsity sports, he played on a highly successful intramural team—the Mormon Meteors[6]—which won the overall intramural championship at Logan High School for the 1939–40 academic year.[7] Many times with his high school buddies Tom also hiked the scenic Crimson Trail[8] up Logan Canyon. Tom played the sousaphone in the high school band. He was the drum major for the ROTC band, wielding a saber and leading the band as it followed the presentation of the colors in each pass in review.[9]

Tom began to date in high school. His father, judging his son as being too shy, encouraged him to go on dates by offering him use of the family car. He came to regret his offer because Tom soon monopolized the car on most Friday and Saturday nights.

Once again, a key turning point in Tom's life was a Church-related activity—the all-Church volleyball competition.[10] His experience as a member, and later the captain, of the Logan Ninth Ward team helped him discover his talent for being enthusiastic and multiplying the talents of others.

During Tom's sophomore year of high school, he tried out for the ward volleyball team. The Explorer Scouts in the Logan Ninth Ward had developed a strong reputation for playing championship-caliber volleyball. The previous year the team had finished second in the all-Church volleyball tournament. Tom was nervous when he tried out, and he did poorly. His heart was broken after the tryout because he was certain he would not make the team, but to his surprise, he was selected. Later, he discovered the reason—because he was the bishop's son, the leaders of the team figured they had a better chance of getting new uniforms if Tom was on the team.

The first year Tom was a benchwarmer. He played a few times, closing out a lop-sided match or two. He embraced his role on the bench, however, and showed more enthusiasm than anyone else on the team. He realized he could help fire up the team and the crowd while just sitting on the bench. Even if he wasn't good enough to play very much, he still felt he was making a valuable contribution to the team.

The next year Tom played more, but the team had three extremely strong players, and this meant his playing time was still limited. The team did extremely well that year. The Logan Ninth Ward reached the finals of the all-Church tournament but lost the match, again placing second.

The three strongest players on the team all graduated before Tom's senior year, when he was selected team captain. Absent the strong nucleus of the previous year, the team was not very good at first. They lost most of their early games, and the attendance of ward members began to slip. As the season progressed, however, the team began to gel under the tutelage of the coach and the enthusiasm of its team captain. The Logan Ninth Ward team surprised everyone—first by winning the stake tournament and then by winning the regional tournament. Then the team surprised itself by winning the area tournament. Again the Logan Ninth Ward had earned a berth in the all-Church tournament.

At the all-Church tournament, the team lost its first match and was moved to the consolation bracket in the double-elimination tournament. Surprisingly, they won the consolation bracket, allowing their return to compete in the championship bracket. They won all their matches in the championship bracket, and once again they found themselves in the finals of the all-Church tournament.

Tom's team lost the first game of the finals match by a lopsided score of 15 to 4. The team they were playing was clearly a more talented team. The coach called Tom aside between the first and second game to remind him that it was not their talent that had helped the team get this far in the all-Church tournament—it was their enthusiasm. He challenged Tom to return to the court and inspire his teammates. He wanted Tom to use his enthusiasm to convince his teammates they could win the match. That's what Tom did, and the second game proved to be a turning point in the match. The Logan Ninth Ward team won the second game 15 to 10.

The third game was a nail-biter: 1–1, 2–2, all the way up to 10–10. Then Norm Sonne, Tom's cousin, discovered that the middle player on the back row couldn't handle the spin on his serve—a weakness on the otherwise superior team. As a result, the Logan Ninth Ward team soon led 14–10.

Tom called a time-out, and the team huddled. Tom told Norm to hit the same spot, and the Logan Ninth Ward would finally be all-Church champions. This time, however, the player on the other team was able to handle the serve, and he hit an excellent set-up to his team's best player, who hit a vicious spike. Fortunately, the ball hit one of the Ninth Ward players in the chest and bounced off him toward Tom at a perfect angle for a spike. Tom moved a few steps, planted his feet, leaped toward the ball, and struck it with all his strength. The ball hit the floor on the other side of the net! All Tom remembers of that moment was his father running out of the stands, embracing him, and lifting him into the air. The Logan Ninth Ward volleyball team was the all-Church champion.

This was in February of Tom's senior year. Ever since, he has practiced the lesson he learned from this experience. My father is too modest to think of himself as someone of extraordinary ability. He is confident, however, that whatever he may lack in ability, he can make up with enthusiasm. As his unique talent has matured, he has learned more about the source of his enthusiasm—that it is a gift from God. Indeed, the word *enthusiasm,* derived from Greek, means to have God in us.

The Sixtieth Logan High School Class Reunion

My father attended his sixtieth high school class reunion in 2000. Upon returning from the reunion, he made an interesting observation. Several of his classmates surprised him, likely in much the same way he had surprised his father. In high school they had been much like him—mostly out of the spotlight, and yet, they had grown up to live remarkable lives. Other classmates, who had shared most of the spotlight in high school, however, disappointed him. He based his assessment less on their accomplishments than on the kind of persons they had become. He was a little put off by their self-absorption and by their tendency to focus so much on what they had accomplished so long ago. In many ways it felt to him as if they had never moved beyond high school.

My father used the metaphor of a flowerpot to explain what he had observed among his high school classmates. It seemed that a few of them had been content to remain planted in the same flowerpot. Perhaps they had the largest, most beautiful flowerpots during high school. Everyone else wanted to be them at the time. In time, however, they began to push against the limits of their flowerpots. The only way to continue to grow was to remove themselves from the protection of their flowerpots by replanting themselves either in a larger pot or outside. Instead of leaving their flowerpot, however, some of his classmates held onto it. It was more comfortable and safe to stay planted in the same flowerpot than to leave it. The problem, according to my father, was even the largest high school flowerpot was never going to be large enough for a lifetime of growth. So a decision to cling to one's flowerpot was a decision to limit one's potential.

Lowell Tom Perry may have been a late bloomer, but as his life unfolded, he did not cling to the same old flowerpot—the one that was the most safe and comfortable. Instead, he was always willing to let God replant him wherever he was needed most. Perhaps this is the principal reason he continues to surprise us. I'm quite sure he has even surprised himself.

CHAPTER 8

First National Bank of Logan

The Perrys established a fun tradition in their family. On the first birthday of each child, the family gathered in the living room and placed in the center of the room four objects: a bottle filled with milk, a toy, a savings bank filled with coins, and a Bible. The one-year-old was placed on one side of the room with the family on the other side. Family members encouraged the child to crawl toward the objects and make a selection. The theory was that the object the child grabbed first indicated what interested him or her most—food, play, money, or the word of God.

Tom and Nora always claimed that they never took the results of the test seriously. If Robert, their youngest child, had been the first participant, they might have ended the practice after the first try. Robert crawled over to the objects, sat on the Bible, put the bottle of milk in his mouth, and held the toy in one hand and the bank in the other. Then again, they always considered Robert their most well-rounded child.

One-year-old Lowell Tom chose the bank.

Tom's Paper Route

Tom received a bicycle on his twelfth birthday. His bicycle offered him a new sense of freedom. He lived on it. In the summertime he would ride to North Logan, Hyde Park, or the west fields. He loved to listen to the birds and the sound of the telephone wires. He would inhale the various smells of the farming community, such as the smell of freshly mowed alfalfa.

As the proud new owner of a bicycle, Tom could have a paper route. Six days a week he delivered the *Herald-Journal,* Logan's daily newspaper. This was an early morning paper route—Tom delivered newspapers from six to seven-thirty in the morning, and then he returned home to clean up for school.

During summer vacation, Tom, along with high school buddies Lou Hickman and Byron Turner, would ride their bikes up Logan Canyon to the Hickman family's cabin and spend a week fending for themselves. They would live like their pioneer grandparents—cook on a wood stove, pump water from a spring, catch a fish or two for dinner, eat berries, and explore.

Even when he was young, Tom was a saver. He kept in a glass jar in his bedroom the coins he earned from delivering papers. His mother had a practice of borrowing from his coin jar to purchase meat for the family. She always left Tom an IOU when she took money, usually only a quarter, from his coin jar. Eventually, Tom's father encouraged him to open a savings account at the First National Bank of Logan, which Tom did. Often, when he went to his father's office after school to use his typewriter to write a report, he would stop at the cashier's window and deposit a small amount of money just to add one more transaction to his account's ledger.

Tom's bicycle was stolen when he was fourteen. Because he needed a bicycle to complete his daily paper route, he asked for a new one for Christmas. His parents had already decided to buy Ted a new bicycle for Christmas, and they did not have enough money to buy Tom one too. They went to Tom and explained the situation. They thought it would make a wonderful Christmas if both he and Ted received new bicycles, but they asked Tom to use some of his newspaper money to pay for his Christmas present.

Tom readily agreed. He appreciated that his parents confided in him, and he naturally considered his younger brother's wants and needs above his own. Likely he also considered it his duty to make such a sacrifice. It was never difficult for Tom to understand the economic realities of the Great Depression. He saw the effects every day, and he felt blessed that his family seemed to suffer less than other families.

The Death of Grandpa Sonne

Christian Sonne died when Tom was thirteen years old, and in his will he left Tom the house at 472 North 100 West in Logan. Grandpa Sonne had a special love for his grandson, and the feeling was mutual. Grandpa Sonne, afflicted by a stroke many years earlier, was only a shadow of the man he once had been, but he was a hero in Tom's eyes. Tom marveled at his mammoth hands and broad shoulders, and he imagined him as a young man who could do the work of a team of horses. Tom loved to listen to his grandfather's stories as they sat on the front steps of his home, and it was mostly through him that Tom felt connected to the noble pioneers who had settled Cache Valley.

In two separate entries in his journal, Alma Sonne, Tom's uncle, reported the events surrounding his father's death. On March 21, 1936, he wrote:

"I am sad to record that my aged father (83 years old) today fell when getting out of bed & broke his leg. He is badly crippled on his right side, the effects of a stroke some 15 yrs ago. Father has been a powerful man physically, large of stature and weighing normally 200 lbs. He has probably walked for the last time, and it is not improbable that he will be confined to his bed during the remainder of his earth life. . . . He is in the Cache Valley Hospital, where he is receiving the best attention available. . . . Father has been a good man, & a wise father, ever honest, upright, unassuming, hard-working, firm but reasonable, practical, full of faith & integrity. A worthy example for any son. God bless him!"[1]

A month later Alma wrote: "Today at 9 o'clock a.m. my father died at the CV Hospital after being confined there 4 weeks & 3 days. His broken leg had not healed and he had steadily grown weaker since the accident. Father will be remembered as being solid, sound, honest, fair & square—good natured in his daily work and talk and deeply appreciative of all favors. He expected little or no help from anybody. . . . All the children were at his bedside when he passed away."[2]

Christian Sonne was a remarkable man—the father of one General Authority and grandfather of another. Together, Chris's son and grandson have served the Church as General Authorities for nearly eighty years, and, in the course of their service, they both exhibited his native goodness and cheerful, enthusiastic disposition. Throughout his life, he lived up to his given name—he was a true Christian.

Shortly before he died, Christian gave Tom several of his tools. With a twinkle in his eye, he told his grandson that he expected him to take better care of his tools than his father would. My father has always considered his grandfather's tools precious, and they have received special care. He still has most of them.

The home at 472 North 100 West is no longer owned by the Perry family. Given that he inherited it when he was thirteen years old, Tom was never comfortable about owning it. Aunt Emma's husband, John Holmgren, died in 1940, leaving her without any way to support herself. After consulting with his parents, Tom invited Emma to rent out the house and keep the proceeds for her support. As soon as he was able, Tom began to pay the property taxes on the house as a Christmas and birthday present to his aunt Emma. Because Emma remained a widow for thirty-seven years, this turned out to be a long-term commitment.

Tom's First Ten Shares of Stock

Despite an average monthly income of approximately $200, Tom and Nora Perry managed to purchase shares of stock from the First National Bank of Logan on a regular basis over many years. Investing in bank stock was at the core of the Perry family investment strategy.[3] It is not surprising, then, that Tom encouraged his oldest son to purchase shares of bank stock with his newspaper money. Using some of the money he had accumulated in his savings account, young Tom purchased ten shares. Then, given that Tom was a stockholder in the First National Bank of Logan, his father insisted that he attend every bank stockholders' meeting and vote his ten shares. He assisted his father by counting the votes for the election of officers of the bank. Tom also attended some of the bank's board meetings. This wealth of experience gave him an early, firsthand education in corporate governance.

In the mind of the elder Tom Perry, the purpose of his son's involvement at the bank extended beyond a pure investment play. He was preparing his son for a career as a banker. Logan's bankers were the pillars of the community. Tom's brother-in-law Alma Sonne was an officer at the First National

Bank of Logan[4] and served as a counselor in a stake presidency, as a stake president for several of the years Bishop Perry served in the Logan Ninth Ward, and later as a General Authority. Clearly, Alma Sonne was a man of great stature in Logan—near the top of any list of prominent citizens. Tom may have envisioned his son growing up to be a banker and a Church and community leader like Alma Sonne. His vision of his eldest son's future may have begun taking shape as early as his first birthday when he chose the bank instead of the Bible, bottle of milk, or toy.

But my father never became a banker. He accepted a more attractive offer in retailing, and though his intention was to return to banking, he never did. Still, he has always thought about business as a Main Street banker does. Over the course of his two careers—in retailing and in full-time Church service—he has always been particularly attentive to cash-management issues. He wants to keep capital working and earning a return, even for small amounts over short periods of time. He often quotes Albert Einstein when teaching about compound interest. Einstein once said, "Compound interest is the eighth wonder of the world. He who understands it, earns it . . . he who doesn't . . . pays it."[5]

Tom has never thought anyone needs to be as smart as Einstein to understand this simple and timeless principle. Rather, the missing ingredient for most people is discipline. While not all of my father's financial discipline comes from his early experiences at the First National Bank of Logan, they may partially explain why he has always seemed to have more than his fair share of discipline.

Alma Sonne as a Role Model

Early in his life my father began to view himself as more Sonne than Perry. He loved and respected his father deeply, but he didn't always identify with him. His brother Ted was far more like his father—bookish, frequently lost in thought, deliberate about taking action, and hesitant to display emotion. Alma Sonne was more naturally social and socially aware, more open with his emotions, usually more decisive and quick to act. Given that Tom was encouraged by his father to become a Main Street banker, it was natural for him to look up to Alma Sonne and see him as a strong role model.

His closest siblings, Mignon and Ted, preferred learning from books, but Tom learned more naturally by taking in what was going on around him. Given that he was initially shy, Tom learned more through observation than interaction. He had ample opportunities to observe and learn from his uncle Alma at the bank, in church, as a community leader, and inside the Perry home.

The time during which Tom would have been especially attuned to watching Alma Sonne at the First National Bank of Logan was a time of crisis in the banking industry. Many banks were closing, and simply keeping the doors of a community bank open during the Great Depression was a major accomplishment. Bank examiners were frequent visitors, and local bankers were under intense scrutiny to justify their loan decisions and bank policies. At the same time, Main Street bankers felt an obligation to the community and its economic welfare. They were the lifeblood of a struggling local economy, and bankers realized that without sufficient transfusions of capital, many local farms and businesses would never get off life-support. This meant that sometimes it was necessary to take the kinds of risks that bank examiners are trained to question and criticize.

Because Logan and the surrounding towns were primarily farming communities in the 1930s, most of the vexing loan decisions involved farmers. Alma Sonne and other local businessmen were appointed by Utah governor Henry H. Blood to the Farm Debt Adjustment Committee to serve the farmers of Cache Valley. Similar committees were organized in areas across Utah. A statewide conference of these committees was held February 23, 1940. In a speech given there by Alma Sonne, both the challenging nature of his work and his business wisdom are richly evident. He said:

"Like you I have been working with a committee of wise and experienced men whose motives cannot be questioned. They have faced the farmer in distress and discouragement; they have listened to his recital of misfortunes; they have analyzed his assets and his liabilities; they have itemized and scrutinized his current obligations such as delinquent taxes and interest payments, and they have appraised his property only to find that a cruel and heartless deflation has robbed him of equities that represent years of struggle and persistent endeavor. . . . It is our duty, if possible, to secure orderly cooperation between creditors and debtors, for mutual adjustment will preserve the integrity of the borrower and the continuance of business relations."[6]

On any given day at the First National Bank of Logan, Tom could have observed his uncle Alma reviewing loan applications, counseling harassed debtors, processing Federal Housing Authority (FHA) loans, refinancing distressed customers to avoid foreclosures, and mediating differences between creditors and borrowers. To Tom, Alma Sonne must have seemed like a man in constant motion and at the center of every important decision at the First National Bank of Logan.

Alma was called to the Cache Valley Stake presidency in 1935, and he later became the stake president. He became a member of the stake presidency while Tom was a deacon in the Aaronic Priesthood, and he was still serving in the stake presidency when his nephew received the Melchizedek Priesthood.

This afforded Tom frequent opportunities to observe his uncle Alma as a Church leader. Alma was a large man and a powerful speaker. Tom looked forward to hearing his uncle Alma speak. His rich, deep voice resonated with his impressionable nephew, especially as he bore his commanding testimony.

Something else Tom learned from watching his uncle Alma serve as a Church leader was an impatience for unnecessarily long meetings. Tom developed an appreciation for short, crisp meetings. Just as with his uncle Alma,[7] the meetings Elder Perry conducts are well planned, and participants are held to their allotted time.

Tom had less direct exposure to Alma Sonne's efforts as a community leader, but he must have heard about them at the frequent Rook tournaments held in the Perry home. Rook was the Sonne family game, and the Perrys would often set up two card tables in their living room to host the four Sonne siblings and their spouses for an evening of playing Rook. The Perry children did not play, but the theatrics of the Rook tournament were always interesting to observe.

The pairings at the two tables were consistent—it was always Sonne against Sonne and Perry against Holmgren. At the Sonne table where Alma and his wife, Geneva, competed against Ola and his wife, Bertie, the game was far more intense. Alma was the best player at the table, and he and Geneva typically won. Moreover, Alma was not always a gracious winner with Ola. He took delight in taunting and teasing his older brother. The parrying back and forth between the two competitive brothers was a constant source of entertainment to Tom and his siblings.

Uncle Søren Petersen

Rook remained a popular game among the Perry siblings, and a Rook tournament was frequently a part of their gatherings. Whenever the family played Rook, inevitably one of the siblings would recall playing the game with Uncle Søren. His uncanny ability to know where every card was in every hand of Rook was the stuff of Perry family legend.

Søren Petersen was Tom's great-uncle, the son of Søren and Elsie Petersen. [8] He served three missions for the Church and was an excellent salesman and a good public speaker. He was also a good family man and became a successful businessman in Portland, Oregon.

Søren was serving as a branch president in Portland when his life took a tragic turn. The exact timing and reasons are unclear, but somewhere along the road of life, Søren picked up two vices—alcohol and gambling. He accumulated a large gambling debt, and desperate to repay it, he embezzled Church funds. When his malfeasance was discovered, he was excommunicated from the Church. He was so embarrassed by his actions that he abandoned his family and never returned. His siblings did not know where he was for many years.

Søren's sister Josephine (Aunt Jo) never gave up hope of someday finding him. Finally, as a broken old man, he found his way back to Logan. Aunt Jo took him in, and the two of them lived together for years. One of their favorite pastimes was playing Rook, and they often invited members of the family over to play with them. Apparently, Søren never grew weary of winning against his outmatched rivals.

The story of Søren Petersen does have a happy, hopeful ending. It was an ending brought about by the miracle of forgiveness and the Savior's redemptive love, which Søren later told and retold in long and powerful testimonies. Søren repented of his sins by working with his priesthood leaders over a period of years, and he was rebaptized into the Church. At the time, Tom was a priest in the Aaronic Priesthood, and his uncle Søren was the first person he baptized.

CHAPTER 9

THE LOGAN TABERNACLE

At a special meeting held December 7, 1864, for members of the Church living in Cache Valley, Elder Ezra T. Benson, great-grandfather of future Church president Ezra Taft Benson, proposed building the Logan Tabernacle. It is likely that Søren and Elsie Petersen, who had arrived in Cache Valley approximately a year earlier, attended the meeting with their daughter Eliza.

The architect who designed the Logan Tabernacle was Truman Angell, who also designed the Logan and Salt Lake Temples. Construction on the tabernacle was delayed several times for a variety of reasons. The initial delay occurred after Elder Benson's death. Life in Cache Valley was hard during those early years. The Saints lived in a beautiful, fertile valley, but the growing season was relatively short, and there was an ever-present threat of attacks by Indians. Without Elder Benson, the visionary leader behind building the Logan

Tabernacle, it was natural for the project to take a backseat to the pressures of day-to-day survival. As a result, no significant progress was made in constructing the Logan Tabernacle until early 1873. Before work resumed, a decision was made to expand the size of the original design of the tabernacle by more than two thousand square feet.

The first lesson my father drew from the history of the Logan Tabernacle was the necessity of leadership. Until someone else stepped forward after Elder Benson's death and entreated the members of the Church to continue construction of the tabernacle, little progress was made on it. Proverbs 29:18 is one of my father's favorite scriptures: "Where there is no vision, the people perish."

The basement of the Logan Tabernacle was completed and dedicated on January 26, 1877, the date of the first Cache Valley conference. In May 1877, President Brigham Young presided over a meeting at the Logan Tabernacle at which he organized the Cache Valley Stake—a stake that encompassed members of the Church living in Idaho, Oregon, Montana, and Western Canada. By this time the upper story of the tabernacle, constructed mostly of sandstone and limestone, was nearly completed.

My father taught us a brief lesson about the stakes of the Church that coincided with his history lesson about the creation of the Cache Valley Stake. He quoted another of his favorite scriptures, from Isaiah 54: "Enlarge the place of thy tent, and let them stretch forth the curtains of thine habitations: spare not, lengthen thy cords, and strengthen thy stakes."[1] My father wanted us to appreciate that the formation of a stake is a significant milestone for any area of the Church. A stake is strong enough to stand on its own, while it also lends support to the entire Church. My father firmly believes that the Church is only as strong as its stakes, and a significant theme of his ministry has always been the strengthening of stakes and stake presidents, who provide vision and leadership for the members under their stewardship.

In the early 1950s, President Leslie Thomas Perry of the Cache Valley Stake was charged by Church leaders in Salt Lake City to supervise the remodeling of the Logan Tabernacle. My grandfather noted in his personal history that the tabernacle, after being used for many years, was antiquated and in need of repair.[2] Exterior improvements included painting the stone and landscaping the grounds. Inside, the tabernacle's pews were replaced, and the pine floor was covered with asphalt tiles. The hand-stenciled ceiling was covered with acoustic tile, and other changes were made in accordance with the style of the day. Finally, the Logan Tabernacle organ was revoiced.

Remodeling the Logan Tabernacle was among my grandfather's important achievements during his tenure as stake president, but most of the changes were eventually undone during a four-year restoration project completed in 1989. As a member of the Quorum of the Twelve, my father had to decide whether he supported the Logan Tabernacle restoration project. This challenge taught him an important lesson about revelation.

He taught his children and grandchildren that one of the most important features of the Lord's plan for leading His Church is ongoing revelation. Just as building styles and preferences change, circumstances change and require new revelation. At the same time there are core, lasting truths that will never change. Perhaps these eternal truths are like classical architecture. While respect for classical architecture varies over time, the fact that it is classical means it has stood the test of time.

My father explained to us that after thinking and praying about it over several days, he became one of the strongest supporters of the Logan Tabernacle restoration project. He received comfort knowing that the changes his father supervised had been correct for their time. The proposed restoration project did not diminish his father's achievement because the results had served the members in Cache Valley well for nearly forty years. Perhaps that remodeling was always intended to be an interim solution. This was something about which my father decided not to try to read the Lord's mind. What really mattered, and what he focused on, was determining the current will of the Lord. If the current will of the Lord was to undo the changes to the Logan Tabernacle that his father had supervised, then that was the decision he should support.

A Unique Premission Interview

After Tom graduated from high school, he enrolled for his freshman year at the Utah State Agricultural College. Because at the time he aspired to be a banker, he knew that business, accounting, and finance courses were in his future, but during his freshman year he took mostly general education courses. Tom's grades were neither stellar nor terrible. As he had done in high school, he seemed to aim for the middle of the curve.

Tom lived at home during his freshman year, and except for the more challenging college classes, his life changed very little. He attended the Logan Ninth Ward, where his father was still the bishop, maintained the same group of friends, and continued to do many of the chores he had always done around the house.

Before Tom's freshman year in college, he had seldom spoken to his parents about serving a mission. Tom's father had not served a mission, and he regretted not having had the experience. In fact, he devoted an entire paragraph in his personal history to his feelings about missing this important piece of his preparation to serve as a stake president. Somewhat apologetically, he wrote:

"By this time you may be wondering why I have not listed missionary service as one of the necessary ingredients in the making of a Stake President. There was a time when I was deeply moved to go on a mission, and, in fact, I told the Bishop that I would like to be the first missionary sent from the Rudy Ward, and my father was consulted. He thought I was too young. After I moved away from [the] Rudy Ward my recommend was in Salt Lake City. My father was now financially able to support me, but it was out of his power. So I missed the missionary experience. . . . I have often felt that void when as a Stake President I was with a body of men, all of whom had served a mission. I felt that I had missed something. But church responsibility, supporting a family, seemed to put missionary service out of the question until I was too old to serve."[3]

Although he expressed these thoughts late in life, they reveal the kind of regret that forms and grows in the back of one's mind for a long time. Part of the reason he didn't speak a lot to his sons about serving a mission was that he had no full-time missionary stories to tell them. Still, it was an experience he wanted each of them to have, and he hoped that Tom would set an example for his younger brothers.

Tom also received encouragement from his mother. Nora's brother Alma had served a mission to England, and she had seen how much the experience had done for him. She saw many of the same characteristics in her son Tom as she saw in her older brother, and she sensed that a mission would affect Tom in much the same positive way it had affected Alma.

Tom's parents wanted him to earn some of the money necessary for his support as a missionary. Accordingly, Tom worked through the summer and fall of 1941 at Squires Cleaners, saving most of the money he earned for his mission.

During the summer and fall of 1941, the likelihood of the United States entering the war in Europe grew with each passing week, as the Axis Powers were overwhelming the Allies in Europe. Moreover, Japan had aligned with the Axis Powers, and it was taking aggressive actions in the Pacific and Asia. President Franklin D. Roosevelt was hesitant to enter the war. The painful memories of World War I—the massive loss of human life, in particular—were still recent memories. Moreover, the U.S. economy, while showing signs of recovery from the Great Depression, was still healing from the injuries it had sustained.

While Bishop Perry badly wanted Tom to serve a mission as soon as he had saved a little more money, he also wondered if, as was the case in his life, the timing would not be right. Given that a declaration of war was imminent, he suspected time was running out quickly. If war was declared, Bishop Perry knew his patriotically minded son would not hesitate to join the military before he was drafted into service. Because Tom had been active in the Reserve Officers' Training Corps and served as a cadet officer, he was eligible for Officer Candidates School, after which he would receive a commission as a second lieutenant.

Bishop Perry prayed about what he should do, and then something unexpected occurred. Elder Alma Sonne had been serving as a General Authority for seven months after being called as an Assistant to the Twelve Apostles in the April 1941 general conference, but he still had not been released as the president of the Cache Valley Stake. When the stake reorganization occurred on October 26, 1941, Bishop Perry was called and sustained as the second counselor in the new stake presidency. He was released as bishop the next Sunday, but for a week he served in both positions. The first thing Bishop Perry did was issue himself a temple recommend as both the bishop of the Logan Ninth Ward and as a member of the stake presidency. At that moment he realized he had received an answer to his prayers about what to do concerning Tom's mission.

During the week of October 26, 1941, Bishop Perry invited Tom to be interviewed to serve a mission. After receiving satisfactory answers to his questions, Bishop Perry walked out of his office for a few minutes to shake the hands of some of the members of his ward. The members were excited about his new calling as a member of the stake presidency after his eighteen years of service as the bishop of their ward.

After speaking briefly to everyone in the hallway, Bishop Perry excused himself and returned to his office, where Tom was waiting for him. He had Tom trade seats with him to denote the change in his role. He was now President Perry, and as President Perry he was interviewing Tom about his worthiness to serve a mission. President Perry asked Tom the same questions he had asked as Bishop Perry, and Tom gave essentially the same answers. Given that President Perry was concerned about slightly different issues than Bishop Perry, some of the probing associated with the questions was more in-depth with his second interview than with his first, while other probing was less in-depth. In other words, Bishop/President Perry was trying to do his best to conduct two different interviews using the same standard set of questions asked of prospective missionaries.

Once the two interviews with Tom were completed, he was excused, and for the rest of the evening Bishop Perry tried to tie up loose ends and prepare to transfer keys to a new bishop while attempting to learn his new calling. Something Bishop Perry completed before the evening ended was Tom's missionary application, and the next day he mailed it to Church headquarters.

An interview with a General Authority was also required before Tom could be formally called and assigned to a specific mission. Elder Alma Sonne was assigned by the First Presidency to interview Tom, and the future Elder Perry was asked the same set of standard questions by another member of the family.

Near the end of November 1941, Tom received his call to serve in the Northern States Mission. He was instructed to report to the Mission Home in Salt Lake City on January 5, 1942. Tom was especially excited about receiving a call to the Northern States Mission because his sister Gay, with her husband, Albert Kowallis, lived in Wisconsin, which was part of the mission.

"A Date Which Will Live in Infamy"

Tom was already receiving instructions and materials for his mission before Sunday, December 7, 1941. The news of the early morning bombing of Pearl Harbor that decimated the U.S. Pacific Fleet did not reach the Perry family until well after their morning Church meetings. Word soon spread around Logan neighborhoods, and families turned on their radios to listen to the sad, shocking news. Eight U.S. battleships had been damaged, with five sunk. Three light cruisers, three destroyers, and three smaller vessels were lost along with 188 aircraft.

Casualties, which were still being counted, would eventually climb to 2,335 servicemen and 68 civilians killed and 1,178 wounded. On the *USS Arizona* alone, more than a thousand crewmen lost their lives.

It was a fast Sunday, and as the fast continued, it assumed deeper significance. The evening's testimony meeting was a somber occasion, and the themes of faith, patriotism, love, and concern for family members and gratitude to those who were serving in the armed services dominated the many brief testimonies. Everyone at the meeting seemed to sense this was not a time for long-winded, unfocused testimonies. Because everyone at the meeting was thinking the same thoughts and feeling the same emotions, it was more a time for as many as possible to be heard. Nobody wanted to deny anyone else the opportunity to stand and be counted, so every testimony was brief and similar, like a parade of Primary children bearing their testimonies with childlike faith.

The next day, President Roosevelt appeared before Congress and asked for a declaration of war against Japan. He called the previous day "a date which will live in infamy."

War with Japan, Germany, and Italy had been brewing for a long time, and the official declaration of war was a galvanizing event for all Americans. For Tom, the month before he entered the mission field must have felt strange, even isolating. He was not enlisting in the U.S. armed forces, as were most of the young men his age. He was about to join God's army as a missionary. His path, at least for the next two years, was completely different from the path being taken by all his friends. More than seventy years later, while reflecting on this period in his life, my father cannot recall anyone from among his high school classmates who served a mission.

Tom's brother Ted felt compelled to enlist in the navy two years later, when he was only seventeen.[4] Ted's decision was motivated by a strong sense of patriotic duty, but there was another reason behind his abrupt decision. He wanted to defend the Perry family honor. Because Ted was three and a half years younger than Tom, his military service coincided roughly with Tom's military service. Still, by enlisting early and before his older brother had returned from his mission, Ted was trying to send a message. It was instinctive on Ted's part—perhaps a concern he might have dismissed had he thought about it longer—to protect both his father's and older brother's reputations. While it might have been unnecessary, it was a truly selfless act.[5]

The concerns that led Ted to enlist before he turned eighteen never crossed Tom's mind.[6] My father did not react the same way as Ted did, the result in part of a blessing nearly all newly called missionaries share: They become incredibly focused on the final preparations for serving their missions. Another partial explanation was Tom's ability to become fully committed to what he was asked to do, especially in this case, when he knew he was on the Lord's errand. As soon as he received his mission call, he directed all of his heart, might, mind, and strength to fulfilling it.[7] Tom may not have been immune from second-guessing himself, but he had learned never to second-guess the Lord.

January 5, 1942

The time arrived for Tom to enter the mission field. His parents drove him to the Mission Home on State Street in Salt Lake City on Sunday evening, January 4, 1942, and he reported for his mission. Because the Church had by then stopped calling young men as missionaries who were eligible for military service, Tom was in the last relatively large group to enter the mission field—a group of approximately fifty missionaries.

At the end of the day, all the new missionaries retired to a long dormitory room equipped with camp cots. Tom was exhausted. He stretched out on his camp cot while the other missionaries prepared for bed, and he immediately fell asleep.[8] His sleep, however, was interrupted by a feeling of being surrounded. As the fog of sleep lifted, he heard a prayer being said. He opened his eyes to see all the other missionaries kneeling around his cot. He quickly closed his eyes, acting as if he had never woken up. He was too embarrassed to get out of bed to join the other missionaries midway through the prayer. He stayed awake and thought about the adventure before him until he could hear some of the other missionaries snoring. He got up briefly to take off his missionary suit and put on his pajamas.

The first official day of Tom's mission was Monday, January 5, 1942. He received training for four and a half days at the Mission Home in Salt Lake City. The standard missionary training for the day included memorizing a few key missionary scriptures, learning how to teach the key doctrines of the Church—for example, the mission of the Savior, the Apostasy, and the Restoration—and receiving lessons on etiquette and how to lead congregational singing.

On Friday morning, Tom's parents again drove to Salt Lake City, this time in a blinding snowstorm, and they were present when Tom was set apart as a missionary by Elder Alma Sonne. The final good-byes were said, the final packing was completed, and Tom, along with three other elders and two sister missionaries, boarded a train bound for Chicago on Friday evening.

CHAPTER 10

NORTHERN STATES MISSION

Tom and the five missionaries who traveled with him arrived in Chicago on Sunday evening, January 11, 1942, after two full days on the train. They were met at the train station by two elders, who were the assistants to the mission president, and taken to the Northern States Mission home on North Sawyer Avenue.[1] President Leo J. Muir knew the new missionaries would be hungry, so he had arranged dinner for them. After dinner, President Muir interviewed each of the missionaries. Tom was interviewed last. Before Tom's interview, the other missionaries were instructed to retire for the night and were shown where they would sleep. After Tom's interview, however, he was driven back to the train station and placed on a train bound for Columbus, Ohio.

After spending that night and another full day on the train, Tom arrived at the Columbus train station on Monday evening. He was met by three missionaries—Elder Bennett, Elder

Kasteller, and Elder Tolman. The three missionaries escorted Tom to a boarding house on 22nd Avenue in Columbus, where the missionaries lived on the fourth floor. Their quarters were actually a finished attic, furnished with one dresser, two double beds, and four desks.

Elder Bennett was the senior missionary of the group. Because President Muir had not assigned Tom to a specific companion, Elder Bennett decided Tom and Elder Wendell Tolman should be companions. Elder Tolman had arrived in the mission field only three weeks earlier. Elder Tolman was from Idaho. He was the son of a butcher—a strong young man who had grown up working hard. He knew very little about missionary work, but he was eager to get to work with his new companion.

After morning study on their first day as companions, Elder Tolman and Elder Perry decided to go tracting door-to-door. They looked at a map of Columbus and decided to tract an area close to their boarding house. They reached their first house and decided that Tom would make the door approach. Just before Tom knocked on the door, he turned to Elder Tolman and asked, "What do I do?" Elder Tolman's response astonished him. He said, "I don't know. I've never done this before."

After taking a long, deep breath, Tom knocked without having a clue about what he should say if someone answered the door. A woman appeared, and she seemed genuinely delighted to see them. Before Tom could say a word, she invited the two missionaries into her home. The unexpected success buoyed the confidence of the two new missionaries, and they excitedly followed her into her living room and sat down. For a few moments, their expectations were limitless. They belonged to the only true Church. They were missionaries of the Lord Jesus Christ. Even if their delivery lacked practice and refinement, their message was still unmistakably true. Surely this woman would be their first convert.

Unfortunately, their lofty expectations quickly fell back to earth. The two missionaries, both raised their entire lives in predominantly LDS communities, were about to learn their first hard lesson of missionary service—members of other churches have strong beliefs too. The woman who invited them into her home was a devoted Southern Baptist who was well versed in the Bible. She thoroughly enjoyed the visits from the Mormon missionaries who lived just around the corner from her. Usually, they were new missionaries because the more seasoned missionaries knew that the homes around their living quarters had already been tracted many times. Perhaps new missionaries were not the most satisfying challenge, but they were easy prey. Elder Perry and Elder Tolman left the woman's home a few hours later thoroughly discouraged by their inability to defend their faith.

The following day of tracting was much the same, except that the next woman who invited them into her home was a Methodist. On the third day the two new missionaries left a home of converted Lutherans. Tom was so discouraged he began to think about whether he should give up and go home. After three unsuccessful days in the mission field, it was clear to him he was not cut out to be a missionary.

As Tom knelt in prayer at the end of the day, the words from a verse in section 38 of the Doctrine and Covenants came into his mind: "But if ye are prepared ye shall not fear."[2] He realized that though he had a strong testimony, he lacked confidence as a missionary because he had never been a serious student of the scriptures. He resolved to use his morning study time more effectively, and he decided to study every night for an additional hour before going to bed. While he regretted not having started earlier, he recognized that it was not too late to prepare to preach the gospel. He was behind where he should be, but through concerted effort he could still catch up.

The next evening as Elder Tolman prepared to go to bed, Tom explained to his companion that he was going down to the kitchen to study for another hour. Tom had decided that what he needed to study first were the first principles and ordinances of the gospel. He resolved that each of the next four nights he would prepare short talks about faith, repentance, baptism, and the gift of the Holy Ghost.

As Tom studied about faith, he noticed a plump mouse scurry across the kitchen counter, pick up a few crumbs, and race back to its hole. He decided the mouse could serve as the audience for his short talk about faith. He went to the cupboard, took a cracker out of a box, broke off a piece, and placed it on the counter near where the mouse had retrieved the crumbs. Eventually, the mouse smelled the cracker, and it again came out of its hole. As soon as the mouse approached the cracker, Tom began to teach it about faith. The mouse looked at Tom for only a moment, grabbed the piece of cracker, and ran back to its hole. Tom completed giving his short talk about faith absent an audience.

The next night Tom returned to the kitchen at bedtime, and he studied the doctrine of repentance. When he had finished his short talk, he once again placed a piece of cracker on the counter to draw the mouse out of its hole. Again the mouse smelled the cracker and came out. This time the mouse chose to eat the cracker on the counter, hearing part of Tom's message about repentance. As soon as he had finished the cracker, however, the mouse ran back to its hole.

On the third night, Tom went down to the kitchen, filled the dishpan with water, and washed some dishes before preparing his talk about baptism. Much like the previous nights, he prepared a short talk. Then he placed another piece of cracker on the counter and waited for the mouse to appear. This time the mouse approached the cracker but did not start to eat it. In fact, it seemed uninterested in the cracker, as if it had come out of its hole for a different reason. Tom began to preach about baptism, and the mouse seemed transfixed by every word he spoke. At the conclusion of the talk, the mouse turned around and walked back to its hole, leaving the cracker untouched.

The next morning when the missionaries went down to the kitchen to prepare their breakfast, they noticed that Tom had not emptied the dishpan of water the night before. At the bottom of the pan they found the mouse—drowned. Tom felt sad that his rodent investigator had died, but its death bolstered his confidence as a missionary. Here was definite proof that it had taken to heart the previous night's lesson. The mouse had sought baptism by immersion. If Tom could convert a mouse, he could convert anyone.[3]

Identifying with Joseph and Daniel of the Old Testament

As Tom continued to study the scriptures, he not only obtained the knowledge he needed to teach more clearly and powerfully as a missionary, but he also found new role models and heroes. Given that Tom had recently left the only home he knew and was living among people with different traditions and beliefs, it was natural for him to identify with Joseph and Daniel of the Old Testament. Their courage and unwavering faith in the face of adversity were an inspiration to him.[4]

Tom began to strive to be more like Joseph and Daniel as he met the day-to-day challenges of missionary service. No matter how bad the situation got, he tried to make the most of it just as they had always seemed to do. The crucial lesson he learned from the lives of these two biblical heroes was that he could embrace a challenge instead of being overwhelmed by it.

Beginning in the early weeks of his missionary service, whenever Tom felt overwhelmed by a new assignment, a trial, or any of a number of obstacles placed in his path, he would think of Joseph and Daniel. Their lives embodied a principle Jesus taught: "With God all things are possible."[5]

Another lesson Tom learned from the examples of Joseph and Daniel was that he would stand out in any crowd if he held to his core beliefs. He would be respected for living according to his beliefs, even among people who believed differently. As long as he was true to himself and his beliefs, he could be comfortable in any situation. In fact, it was likely that the best of all situations was when someone recognized there was something unique about him. Tom realized that even a young man from Logan, Utah, who was as common as dirt could lead an uncommon life when those around him recognized that he was "a man in whom the Spirit of God is."[6]

Marion, Ohio

Elder Tolman and Elder Perry served together in Columbus for only a month, but it was a month of enormous growth for both of them as they embraced challenges far beyond their natural abilities and training. They did not baptize anyone, but they experienced moments when the Spirit flowed through them, and they were both teachers and learners.

In those days of missionary work, there were few teaching aids beyond the scriptures. Missionaries, however, were equipped with a big black box that contained a record player and a set of records titled *The Fulness of Times.* When they chose to take the black box with them as they tracted, Elders Tolman and Perry walked side by side with a broomstick between them on which they carried it. Because Elder Tolman was considerably shorter than Tom, the broomstick was seldom level, and most of the weight of the big black box shifted to him.[7]

After a month of serving together, Elder Tolman and Elder Perry received an assignment from President Muir to take a bus to Marion, Ohio, on a Saturday, stay overnight with the Knudsen family, and then conduct Sunday meetings in their home. The Knudsens were members of the Church who had lived in the West until Brother Knudsen, an engineer, accepted employment at one of the war production plants in Marion. Because of the war effort, Marion had become a boomtown, producing tanks and other military equipment. It was attracting several Western transplants, and this created missionary opportunities.

Elders Tolman and Perry reported to President Muir that the Sunday meetings in the Knudsen home went extremely well. In addition to the missionaries and the Knudsens, a young family of four, the meeting was attended by the Carbridges and the Baileys. The Carbridges and the Baileys had met each other at a Civilian Conservation Corps (CCC) camp in the West and had convinced each other to go to Marion to work in one of the factories. Brother and Sister Carbridge were both inactive members of the Church, and Brother Bailey, a nonmember, had married Sister Bailey, an inactive member of the Church.

After receiving their report, President Muir decided to reassign Elders Tolman and Perry to Marion, Ohio. The Knudsens had an extra bedroom in their home for the missionaries, and Sunday meetings could be held in their living room until the membership of the Marion Branch outgrew it.

As it turned out, the Marion Branch outgrew the Knudsens' living room after only a few months. The first baptism Tom performed in Marion was the baptism of Sister Marty Jenkins. She was baptized in the Little Scioto River, which flows just west of Marion. Many years later, Elder L. Tom Perry spoke about this sacred experience at the October 2001 general conference. He said: "I remember the shock of wading into the cold river while encouraging my investigator to follow me. The coldness of the air and the water, however, soon vanished as I administered the ordinance of baptism. Seeing the radiant face of the individual who came up out of the waters of baptism is an image I will never forget."[8]

Elder Tolman and Elder Perry taught and baptized five families, one of them a part-member family of six—in short, it was a fruitful period of time. Some of the success in Marion hinged on these two dedicated missionaries taking their work seriously and seeking inspiration. Elders Tolman and Perry more than compensated for their lack of knowledge and experience by being humble and hardworking. More than the story of the success of two full-time missionaries, however, the story of the Marion Branch was about members catching the spirit of member-missionary work. The Knudsens planted the seeds of member-missionary work first by reaching out to the Carbridges and Baileys. They, in turn, reached out in friendship to others. The principle lesson learned from the growth of the branch was how simple and natural missionary work can be when the members became involved.

Soon it was necessary to move the Sunday meetings of the Marion Branch to a larger meeting place, so the branch rented the Marion Elks Lodge Hall. Because the Saturday night activities at the lodge were quite different from an LDS Church service, the missionaries had to go there early Sunday morning to sweep and air it out. Still, the lodge offered ample room for the Marion Branch to grow.

After ten months of serving with Elder Perry in Marion, Elder Tolman received a transfer. Tom missed him after he left. They had grown extremely close as they worked hard together helping the Marion Branch take hold and start to grow. Tom's new companion was an older missionary, Elder Mariner Jensen. The members in Marion, mostly new to the Church and extremely attached to the two young missionaries who had converted and baptized them, were slow to embrace Elder Jensen. The fact that he was the senior companion created an awkward situation. Tom loved serving in Marion, and he wanted Elder Jensen to feel included in what turned out to be his last proselyting area. Tom expressed some of his feelings in his weekly letter to President Muir, and within a few weeks he was transferred to Champaign, Illinois. The members in Marion, Ohio, soon embraced Elder Jensen and his new companion, and they formed strong bonds with one another.

Converting Elder Kidd's Family

With only a few new missionaries entering the mission field during World War II, it was difficult for mission presidents to maintain an even number of missionaries so they could serve two by two. During his entire time in Champaign, Illinois, Tom was assigned to serve in a threesome. The three missionaries tried to make the best of the situation, and Tom grew close to one of his companions, Elder Parkin. Still, the situation was not ideal, and they experienced little success during Tom's time in Champaign.

The next assignment President Muir gave to Tom was to serve as the supervising elder over the East Iowa District.[9] Tom and his new companion, Elder Ralph Kidd, were initially assigned to work in a small branch in Waterloo, Iowa. Waterloo was the home of the Fighting Sullivans—five brothers who had enlisted in the U.S. Navy and were granted special permission to serve together on the same ship. Their ship, the light cruiser U.S.S. *Juneau*, was sunk on November 13, 1942, in the Battle of Guadalcanal, and all five brothers perished. This tragedy was fresh in the minds of Waterloo's residents when Elder Perry and Elder Kidd arrived, and the people were quite hostile toward the two healthy young men who were not risking their lives at war but were instead serving as LDS missionaries. After only a few weeks of serving in Waterloo, they were reassigned to Cedar Rapids.

As the supervising elder, Tom spent a few days each week traveling to the other branches in the East Iowa District and working with other missionaries. Of course, Elder Kidd always traveled with him. Elder Kidd had served longer than Tom in the mission field, and Cedar Rapids was his last area. He had grown up in a non-LDS home, and as Tom and Elder Kidd became closer, they decided to set a goal to convert Elder Kidd's parents before he returned home. They began a letter-writing campaign to achieve that goal.

Elder Kidd was from Tustin, California, and a major benefit of launching the letter-writing campaign was that Elder Kidd's parents often responded by sending fresh citrus fruit—oranges, grapefruit, and lemons—to their son and his companion. Tom enlisted his parents in the letter-writing effort, which helped greatly because they were close to the same age as Elder Kidd's parents. The two missionaries even enlisted the help of the Cedar Rapids Branch members. After a few months of concentrated efforts involving many in the long-distance proselyting campaign, Elder Kidd's parents finally agreed to be taught by the missionaries in Tustin. They were baptized before Elder Kidd returned home, and approximately a year later, L. Tom and Nora Perry served as escorts when Elder Kidd's parents received their endowments in the Logan Temple.[10]

When Elder Kidd returned home, Elder Ray Davis was assigned to serve with Tom. During their service together, Elder Perry and Elder Davis baptized Sister Kuchera and her two daughters. They also taught Brother Kuchera, but he chose not to be baptized at the same time as his wife and daughters. The Kucheras ran a beef ranch five miles outside of Cedar Rapids. The elders would walk out to their ranch one evening each week to have dinner with them and to teach them. After the lesson, Brother Kuchera would drive them back to their apartment in town.

The Cedar Rapids Branch met in the old Roosevelt Hotel. A member of the branch presidency during this time was Lowell Durham, who later became a professor of music and dean at the University of Utah. He also served as a member of the Sunday School General Board. He once said about Tom, "Not only did Elder Perry impress us with his physical stature, but he immediately found a place in the hearts of all for his forthrightness, enthusiasm, naturalness, and obvious honesty and conviction of what he was doing."[11]

Tom saw his mission president only twice during his mission—when he arrived as a new missionary and at a district conference prior to President and Sister Muir's release. In a letter to his sister, Gay Kowallis, Tom wrote about President Muir's last conference:

"We had conference in Rock Island on the eighth. . . . It was President Muir's last with us. The new mission president won't be out for another month so we haven't seen him, yet. The conference was one of the best I have ever been to. I had to talk in the afternoon meeting and since I had been off visiting [other missionaries] I hadn't prepared anything, but I guess I got away with it all right because I received more praise than usual. President Muir got up and spent the first five minutes of his talk talking about my missionary work and my voice. They always talk about my voice in conference. He gave two very fine talks. One was on the Bible and the other on sweetness."

In the same letter to Gay, Tom wrote about his impending release: "As for thinking about coming home, the time has gone by so fast it doesn't seem that my time is about up. I am almost afraid to leave the mission field, though. They have such fine people out here and they are so close to each other that it will really be a change to come back and live in a ward again. . . . I haven't made any plans as to what I will do when I return, but I guess Uncle Sam will take care of that for me. Going into the army doesn't worry me at all after coming on a mission. I am almost looking forward to it in a way. Even though conditions will be different in a way, it will be like going on a second mission."

Tom and his last companion, Elder Clayton "Tiny" Wilkinson,[12] a former star basketball player at the University of Utah, spent the Christmas of 1943 with the Barton and Durham families. A few weeks later, Tom received a train ticket and his release certificate in the mail from his new mission president, David I. Stoddard. Two years after arriving in the mission field, he was returning to Logan but only for a short period of time.[13]

CHAPTER 11

The Marine Corps

When Tom arrived home from his mission, he realized that Logan was a very different place from the town he had left two years earlier. All of the young men were gone to war, and he felt oddly out of place in the only place he had ever called home.

Nevertheless, it was wonderful for Tom to be reunited with his family. Even Ted was home. He had been able to secure a short leave after completing basic training so that he could see his older brother for what would be the only time for another two and a half years. The Perrys had decided to delay their Christmas celebration for two weeks so that both Tom and Ted could be included. It was as if a ceasefire had been called at 466 North 100 West in Logan while the rest of the world was at war.

Until he received his orders to report for military service, Tom wanted to stay busy. Ted had worked at the grocery store on Main Street in Logan until he joined the navy, and when the owner heard that Tom had returned home from his mission, he quickly hired him. As soon as he hired Tom, the owner became seriously ill. After only a few days of training, Tom was asked to take over the operations of the store. He and the butcher then ran it until the owner recovered. This was Tom's first retail experience, and he discovered he had a natural gift for operating the store. It was the first time he entertained the idea that he would pursue something else instead of banking as a career.

Wendell Tolman, Tom's former missionary companion who had been released only three weeks before he had, was in the same awkward situation of being at home waiting for Uncle Sam to call. He decided to travel down from Idaho and visit Tom for a few days. The two former companions went on several double dates together during Wendell's visit.

Wendell and Tom also reminded each other of the commitment they had made while serving together as missionaries to join the navy upon being drafted. They knew the odds were small, but they still hoped that if they joined the same branch of the service at approximately the same time, they might have an opportunity to serve together. Asking for the blessing of serving another mission together was something they both had made a subject of prayer.

The interim between Tom's two missions proved to be only six weeks. He received his draft notice to report to Fort Douglas, Utah, at the end of February 1944.

Tom arrived at Fort Douglas with every intention of volunteering for the navy until he saw some men dressed in navy uniforms. In a rare moment of vanity, he imagined himself, with his long legs, wearing a uniform with bell-bottomed trousers. When a marine recruiter walked into the room and stood before the recruits, Tom could not help but be impressed by his sharp uniform. Suddenly, he was waffling on his commitment to Wendell Tolman. The recruiter asked for seven volunteers to join the U.S. Marine Corps, and Tom was the first to step forward.[1]

Tom was placed in charge of the six other recruits, but they were all granted liberty for the night. They were ordered to be on a train the next morning bound for California to report for basic training at the San Diego Marine Corps Base. Tom arranged to spend his last night as a civilian with his former missionary companion Ray Davis, who was from Salt Lake City. Ray set Tom up with a date, Maxine Moulton, and they went to a dance together. Tom and Maxine had such a good time that evening that they faithfully corresponded for the next two and a half years.

Tom felt rather important leading the small unit of recruits as they rode the train to San Diego. His sense of self-importance, however, lasted only until the seven men reported to a marine sergeant at the base. The sergeant asked who was in charge, and Tom stepped forward and handed him their papers. The sergeant took the papers and then gruffly told Tom to step back in line with the other recruits. The seven men, still in civilian clothes, were led to a room where everything they had brought with them was taken from them and placed in a sack to be mailed home. Then the recruits were issued their uniforms and everything else they needed. It mattered little who they were or what they had done before. They had a new identity now. They were United States Marines.

The San Diego Marine Corps Base

Once again Tom found himself in a new situation. The contrast between the mission field and U.S. Marine Corps basic training was stark; basic training was like a treatment of shock therapy. The transition, however, was made easier for Tom by a Mormon battalion of marines who had completed basic training just before he arrived. They had made a positive impression on everyone at the San Diego Marine Corps Base. Because of their example, to be a Mormon was a mark of distinction. In Tom's mind, LDS marines had a responsibility to polish—not tarnish—the Church's sterling reputation.

Tom also took courage from his biblical role models Joseph and Daniel. He decided if he was going to be a marine, he would become the best marine possible. He learned quickly, to enjoy the physical rigor of basic training. Moreover, he had several advantages over the other recruits. He was older and more mature, but most important, he was a Mormon following in the footsteps of the Mormon Battalion. He never experienced the classic in-your-face dressing-down from his drill instructor—the standard practice with all new marine trainees. In fact, Tom's drill instructor tried to watch his language when Tom was around because he had been impressed by the goodness of the Mormon squad he had just finished training. He chose Tom as the squad leader and quickly shifted responsibility to him. He knew he could trust Tom to maintain discipline among the trainees in his squad, and Tom did not want to disappoint him.

As part of their basic training, Tom's squad participated in forced marches. Loaded with packs on their backs and rifles over their shoulders, they set off on 10-mile hikes over the hot desert terrain of Southern California. Following the long columns of marine platoons would be a Red Cross truck to pick up those who could not make it. In the *semper fi* culture of the Marine Corps, to have one of your squad members picked up by the Red Cross truck was considered a disgrace. As the squad leader, Tom was the first to offer assistance if a member of his squad began to fall behind. Tom would carry the squad member's rifle or hike beside him and lift the weight of his pack off his back. If his relief was insufficient, he would enlist others to help. A few times early in their training, squad members had to be carried the final miles of their forced march while other members of the squad carried their rifles and packs.

One experience at boot camp impressed upon Tom the reality of the Lord's protection. His platoon was delayed as it conducted a training exercise in the field. Upon their return they were directed to the mess tent, where they were served dinner several hours after it had been prepared. As was his normal practice, Tom bowed his head and said a blessing on his food before eating his meal. In the middle of the night the men discovered, in many cases quite painfully, that the food they had eaten was spoiled. Everyone in Tom's platoon except him became violently ill with food poisoning.

As Tom became stronger with each day of training, he also became more competitive. He tried to outdo the rest of the men in his platoon in physical exercises, and he wanted his squad to be the best in the platoon. He drew close to the men in his squad and learned about their strengths and weaknesses, and they respected his leadership.

On his first Sunday at the base, Tom attended church, and among the many new faces he saw was a familiar face—that of Wendell Tolman. The two avowed navy recruits had both decided to join the marines. They had seen each other only weeks earlier, but it was a joyous reunion. They appeared destined to serve another mission together. Tom and Wendell belonged to different platoons, but their paths crossed often—in the mess hall, on the rifle range, and, of course, every Sunday at church. More like Daniel than Joseph, Tom was able to adjust to the strange new world of military service with a trusted companion.

At the end of boot camp, Tom took a test. Based on the test results, he was assigned to remain at the base in San Diego to receive communications training. He was granted a short leave between boot camp and the beginning of his training, and he returned home to Logan. He had already earned all the credits necessary to graduate from the LDS Institute of Religion, so while he was home he graduated from the Logan Institute with one other marine and eighteen young women.

Tom completed his communications training, but there were no communications openings, so he was reassigned to a large contingent that included Wendell Tolman. The contingent was to receive artillery training at nearby Camp Pendleton. Upon completing that training, Tom's unit was assigned to specialized artillery training at San Clemente, at the northern tip of Camp Pendleton. Wendell's unit was assigned to another part of Camp Pendleton.

While stationed at San Clemente, the trainees had evenings off, and they were granted liberty on weekends. There were no LDS men at the facility, and Tom was drafted by a group from his unit to go with them on liberty to Los Angeles, primarily so he could drive them back. Tom went along, but when they arrived in Los Angeles and he observed how the men in his group were acting as they traveled by streetcar, he realized he had joined with the wrong group. He began to move toward the back of the streetcar, away from the others in his group, when a young lady asked him if he knew anything about the Mormon Church. He quickly struck up a conversation with her and then joined her and her LDS friends at a dance at the Adams Ward meetinghouse in Los Angeles. The young men in the group invited Tom to stay overnight with them. While Tom was stationed at San Clemente, he joined them every weekend he had liberty.

The Battle of Saipan

The Battle of Midway and the Guadalcanal Campaign had been fought and won by U.S. forces while Tom served as a missionary in Ohio and later in Illinois. By the time Tom reported to Fort Douglas, the United States had captured Eniwetok, an atoll in the Marshall Islands. Capturing Eniwetok Atoll was an important strategic victory for the United States because it provided an airfield from which to launch air attacks on the Mariana Islands. Saipan, the largest of the Mariana Islands, was of great strategic importance to the United States because of its proximity to Iwo Jima and Okinawa.

At the end of specialized artillery training at San Clemente, Tom's platoon was awakened at midnight and transported to San Diego Harbor. They boarded a troop transport destined for Eniwetok. Traveling by troop transport for that distance was extremely uncomfortable. The men slept in canvas bunks that were stacked five or six deep in tight quarters. They were ordered to remain in their bunks most of the day and night and allowed only brief periods to breathe fresh air on deck. The troop transport made one brief stop in Hawaii. The men were taken off the ship for a few hours to conduct calisthenics, walk, and stand in close proximity to the ship. Then, it was several more days before they arrived at Eniwetok.

As Tom's platoon gathered on the deck of their troop transport at Eniwetok and prepared to disembark, they looked around and realized they were part of a major military campaign. Surrounding their transport was a small armada of ships that were using Eniwetok as a staging area from which to launch the Battle of Saipan.

As Tom stepped off the ship and his feet touched land for the first time in several days, he looked up and saw six marines walking toward him. One of them was Wendell Tolman. It was a Sunday, and the six men were on their way to church. Tom asked for and received permission to join them.

The next day, Private Perry received his orders. He was initially assigned to be a clerk/typist in the headquarters and service battery of the 10th Marines in the 2nd Marine Corps

Division. Private Tolman was the company clerk of the Second Battalion of the 2nd Division. Both returned missionaries were assigned to fight the war with their typewriters.

The Battle of Saipan began on June 13, 1944, as fifteen U.S. battleships bombarded the southwestern shores of the island to soften Japanese defenses. The landings started at 7:00 a.m. on June 15 and were led by the 2nd and 4th Marine Divisions. More than three hundred tracked landing vehicles landed eight thousand Marines and their equipment on the beaches of Saipan. The 2nd Marine Division invaded a several-mile swath of the island just north of the landing of the 4th Marine Division.

After several days of combat, the Japanese army retreated to the center of the island and its defensible, mountainous terrain. The mountains of Saipan were dotted with caves, which served as hiding places for the Japanese soldiers. The U.S. forces would initially blanket with artillery an area that might include several caves, and then ground forces would clear out one cave at a time using machine guns and flame throwers.

On July 7, the last three thousand able-bodied Japanese soldiers launched a final suicidal banzai charge against the U.S. forces.[2] It was the largest Japanese banzai attack of the war, and the fighting was fierce. Still, it was a hopeless fight for the Japanese, and the island was declared officially secured late in the afternoon of July 9. After twenty-five bloody days, the Battle of Saipan was over.

Once the island was secure, the headquarters staff, including Tom and Wendell, landed and set up offices. Over the twenty-five bloody days of battle, 2,949 American soldiers had been killed and more than 10,000 had been wounded. Nearly all of the 30,000 Japanese soldiers who were garrisoned on Saipan lost their lives.

Several months after the Battle of Saipan, Tom was promoted to corporal and was assigned to the personnel classification headquarters and service battery of the 2nd Division. In a December 14, 1944, letter to his parents, he described his life on the island in his usual upbeat and reassuring way:

"Say, this overseas life isn't half bad. Even though the office keeps me very busy, I still enjoy it. This work is a great deal of fun. I don't know how long I will have the job, though. Certain they can find someone else who knows more about office work than me. But as long as I have the job I will enjoy it. . . . By the way, the personnel section is in the rear echelon. They are the last to ever go anyplace. So don't worry about me. I am just as safe as if I were sitting in dad's office."

Once their respective offices were up and running, Tom and Wendell turned their attention to organizing the LDS military men on Saipan. An LDS chaplain, Gerald Erickson, was assigned to the U.S. Air Corps on the island. He called Wendell and Tom to serve as group leaders. In the same December 14 letter, Tom also described Church activities with his former missionary companion:

"By the way, Elder Tolman is still here. He lives about a block from me, and we are together very often. Last night we walked two and a half miles to an M.I.A. [Mutual Improvement Association] meeting at one of the other camps. We have a lot of Mormons on the island and hold a number of meetings. Tolman and I are back holding meetings together again.

"The Lord has really blessed me. I am certain that he has called me here to do a great work, and I will be home again just as soon as I have finished it.

"I'm well and happy, and, by the way, this is a very healthy island."

With the help of Chaplain Erickson, Tom and Wendell obtained a tent in which they held Church services. They fashioned benches, a pulpit, and a sacrament table from scrap lumber to furnish the tent. Under the sacrament table they kept a green footlocker filled with sacrament supplies—a wooden plate, a wooden water tray with several boxes of sacrament cups, and a card with the two sacrament prayers.

Tom and Wendell worked regular hours—8 a.m. to 5 p.m.—six days a week, completing reports and typing orders. They devoted two nights a week to their Church duties. They set another night aside for writing letters, and they regularly pulled guard duty one night each week. This left three nights free each week, and Tom and Wendell used two of those nights to hold companionship study. The other night they would watch a movie. In a letter to his sister Gay, Tom explained their system for selecting their movie night. Each week he and Wendell would look at the movie schedule. The night when the best movie was showing would become their movie night, and the other nights were gospel-study nights.

The two former missionary companions used the Church tent on their study nights. Saipan was secure throughout their fourteen months on the island, but there were occasional air raids by Japanese aircraft. After some time the air raids took their toll on the Church tent.

In the October 2001 general conference, Elder L. Tom Perry reminisced about those study sessions with Wendell Tolman. He said: "I recall many companion study sessions under the light of a Coleman lantern in a shrapnel-scarred tent. Several times our reading of the scriptures was interrupted by the sound of an air raid siren. We would quickly turn off our lantern, then kneel together and close our study class with a prayer."[3]

On Saipan, Tom and Wendell's gospel study together strengthened them spiritually, much as it had in Ohio during the ten months they served together as missionary companions.

One night as they were praying to conclude one of their study sessions, the Spirit spoke to them. They realized that the lessons they had learned in Marion, Ohio, about the power of member missionary work were just as applicable in their current situation. They began encouraging the other LDS servicemen to share the gospel with their fellow marines.

The results of member missionary work among the servicemen stationed on Saipan were miraculous. Tom and Wendell's second mission proved even more fruitful than their first, and there were many baptisms held at Red Beach[4] that were either the direct or indirect result of their efforts as group leaders. Moreover, the more the LDS servicemen shared the gospel with others, the more strongly they became bonded together in brotherhood.

A Mother's Prayers for Her Son's Safety

Remarkably, Tom's younger brother Ted, who served in the Pacific Theater on a troop transport vessel, had also been involved in the Battle of Saipan, but neither brother knew the other's whereabouts at the time. They were both writing home, of course, but the mail moved too slowly to alert them. Even if they had known, it is unlikely they could have arranged a meeting because Ted's ship was constantly on the move assisting on several battlefronts during those critical months of war.

Tom's efforts to reassure his mother of his safety were partially motivated by his realization that she had two sons at war to worry about. Moreover, given that he was the older brother and his clerical role kept him mostly out of harm's way, he preferred that Ted receive a disproportionate benefit from their mother's prayers. This is not to suggest that Nora Perry overlooked Tom in her prayers, but sensing danger for her children as only a mother can, she likely prayed harder for Ted.

It was only after Ted was safely home that he fully understood the benefit of her prayers on his behalf. By comparing the timing of Nora's strongest impressions to Ted's experiences aboard ship, they realized that the two times Nora prayed most mightily for Ted's safety were the same times he was in the gravest danger.

The first time coincided with a submarine attack on Ted's ship. The second time involved one of the most perplexing tactical decisions made by a Japanese naval commander during the entire war. It happened on October 25, 1944, during the Battle of Leyte Gulf off the coast of the Philippines.

The Japanese navy had devised a brilliant strategy to inflict severe casualties on the U.S. forces landing on the island of Leyte. First, they were able to draw the U.S. Navy's 3rd Fleet, commanded by Admiral William Halsey, away from the Leyte Gulf with a decoy northern force. Second, they moved the central force, commanded by Vice Admiral Takeo Kurita, under the cover of nightfall through the San Bernardino Strait to attack U.S. ships in the Leyte Gulf from the north. Finally, a southern force approached the Leyte Gulf from the south, and when it spotted the U.S. 7th Fleet, under the command of Vice Admiral Thomas Kincaid, it turned around to draw it away from the landing forces. The effect of the strategy was to leave the landing forces defenseless against the central force.

The Japanese plan worked to perfection. The central force, led by the super battleship *Yamato,* met determined resistance from the remaining U.S. ships in the Leyte Gulf, but the Japanese forces greatly outnumbered the Americans. The Americans were losing badly when, inexplicably, Vice Admiral Kurita gave the order, "All ships, my course north, speed 20." He retreated back to the San Bernardino Strait and missed a golden opportunity to alter the course of the war.

Military historians have debated Kurita's ill-timed decision. In the heat of battle, the intelligence he received was limited, and he was rightly concerned about the return of Halsey's 3rd Fleet. Still, there was very little standing in the way of him accomplishing his mission, and had he accomplished it, the Japanese would have dealt a major setback to the U.S. assault on the Philippines. Perhaps it was not one mother's prayer on behalf of her son that changed the course of the Pacific War, but on that fateful day of October 25, 1944, Nora Perry was one of thousands of American mothers praying for the safety of their sons.

Building a Chapel on Saipan

In April 1945, the 2nd Marine Division was deployed to Okinawa as a decoy force for the invasion.[5] Nearly every soldier in the division was taken by troop transport to the southeastern side of the island to confuse the Japanese about an invasion planned for the southwest beaches. As the war in the Pacific moved farther west, the strategic importance of Saipan diminished, and so only about twenty members of the 2nd Division headquarters staff were left behind as the rear echelon. Tom was among the men assigned to the rear echelon; Wendell Tolman was not.

The round-trip to Okinawa and back to Saipan took approximately a month. During this period, there was little to do for the men left behind on the island. Tom spent a lot of time in the Church tent alone reading his scriptures and thinking. April is usually part of the rainy season on Saipan, and April 1945 was no exception. The shrapnel-scarred Church tent proved to be inadequate protection from the intense downpours common to Saipan's rainy season.

By the time Wendell returned from Okinawa, Tom had an idea. He remembered what building the Logan Ninth Ward chapel had done for member unity while his father served as the bishop during the Great Depression. He proposed building a small chapel on Saipan in which LDS servicemen could hold Church services. A chapel-building project was exactly what the servicemen stationed on Saipan needed to strengthen their brotherhood. Moreover, their Church services deserved better than the leaky, undersized tent.

Tom and Wendell approached Chaplain Erickson with their proposal, and he called all the LDS servicemen group leaders together to discuss it. Eventually, they approached the lead Marine Corps chaplain with a formal proposal to build a small LDS chapel on Saipan and received his approval.

It was a pretty outlandish proposal, given the conditions on the island. Moreover, most of the servicemen had little experience as builders, and they had few tools and no building materials. Still, they had a vision and the faith that a group of priesthood holders could accomplish anything.

The three branches of the service assigned to the island—the air force, marines, and navy Seabees—each embraced the challenge of gathering everything needed to build the small chapel. The Seabees supplied the tools, and the marines and air force provided the building materials. They found a marine who had helped his father build a barn, and they assigned him to oversee the design and construction of the chapel.

Each evening after completing their regular duties, the men would assemble and begin working at the construction site. Day by day, one nail at a time, the beautiful little chapel began to rise. Even more impressive than the building itself were the effects on the spirits of the servicemen as they worked together. Less-active LDS servicemen, who had been reluctant to attend church on Sunday, joined the project. Even several nonmembers, upon seeing the spirit of brotherhood generated from the project, asked to join the effort. Some of them became interested in learning more about the gospel; others did not, but they were all drawn toward the spirit of unity created by the project.

One evening as the light of day was fading and the men were hammering the last nails to secure the roof, the whole harbor below them lit up as all the ships in the harbor shot tracers into the air. At first the men on the chapel roof were concerned about an enemy invasion, but they soon learned that the end of the war had just been announced. Briefly, the men hugged each other and shook hands, and then they returned to finish their work on the chapel.

Wendell Tolman conducted the Saipan chapel dedicatory service on September 9, 1945, and Tom led the singing.[6] The lead Marine Corps chaplain spoke. Chaplain Erickson also spoke and offered the dedicatory prayer. By this time the men of the 2nd Marine Corps Division had already received new orders. They were to begin loading troop transport ships the next day and go to Nagasaki, Japan, to be part of the U.S. occupation forces there. Accordingly, they were able to attend only one Sunday service in the new chapel, which had taken the spring and summer of 1945 to build. They left behind a building they had labored long and hard to build, but they took with them to Japan the memories and the spirit of building it together.

Nagasaki, Japan

From September 10–27, Tom got very little sleep. This was an extremely busy period for a headquarters personnel staff member because so many men were on the move. Tom worked all day in the office updating records and completing reports, and he was also expected to take his turn at night loading the ship. He reported in a September 28, 1945, letter to his parents that the only sleep he'd had during the previous few days on

Saipan was while riding in a cargo truck between the camp and the ship.

Tom's time aboard the troop transport was equally demanding. Fortunately, the headquarters staff had an office on the ship, so he was not confined to a bunk as he was during his trip from San Diego to Eniwetok. Still, his days were filled with work, and he had four hours of watch duty every night. His hearty spirit and incredible resilience, however, were evident in the same September 28 letter to his parents. He wrote, "I was just about dead last night from the lack of sleep, but after a good night I feel swell again."

Tom could never forget what it was like to see Nagasaki the first time. Perhaps it was the greatest shock of his life. He saw devastation he could not have possibly imagined unless he had seen it firsthand. Another excerpt from his September 28 letter captures this poignant moment in his life:

"Needless to say we were all very anxious to see just what the city looked like after the raid. As we pulled into the harbor we were all at the rail looking the place over. I would never have believed the place could have been as completely destroyed if I hadn't been there to see it.

"The harbor was just hit by fire raids, and there wasn't a building left standing except for part of the framework. I certainly saw the results of this war on the Japs' homeland. We all thought the harbor district was bad, but as we got on the trucks to ride to our camp, we had to pass through the end of the atomic bomb district. There wasn't one thing standing there—just a leveled city. The Japs still hadn't been able to bury all of the dead and Marine road equipment was in there covering up the bodies to get rid of the smell. I never hope to see anything quite like that again."

Initially, all of the 2nd Marine Corps Division was housed in a former Japanese Air Corps base in Isahaya, about fifteen miles outside of Nagasaki. In a few weeks, however, the 2nd Division headquarters staff set up offices in the Nagasaki Port Authority building. There were some openings, and Tom arranged for Wendell to join him on the headquarters staff, allowing them to work and serve more closely together.

Tom had an experience while the headquarters staff was setting up the offices in the Port Authority building that dramatically altered his view of the Japanese people. Staff members were being assisted by Japanese workers in moving sheets of glass to place on top of their desks to provide a protective cover for their personal photos. Two Japanese men were carrying a sheet of glass up a staircase for Tom when they accidentally hit a post and shattered the glass.

Initially upset by their clumsiness, Tom grabbed the arm of one of the men, ready to reprimand him for his ineptitude. But upon grabbing his arm, Tom realized the man was trembling. It was startling to Tom to suddenly perceive that his enemy was neither a monster nor nameless. He released his hold on the man's arm and attempted to reassure and comfort him. Using hand gestures to communicate, Tom asked the men to go find another piece of glass, and he would find a broom and clean up the broken glass. When Tom had arrived in the Nagasaki Harbor, like other servicemen he called the people "Japs," but after feeling the Japanese man's trembling arm, he learned to call them by name, and his former enemies became friends.

Nagasaki was a uniquely Christian Japanese city. Its Christian roots reached back to the 1500s, when Jesuit priests played a profoundly influential role in Japanese politics. As the Jesuits lost power and were either executed or expelled, Nagasaki prefecture became the only safe haven for Christians in Japan. It was where most of Japan's Christians gathered and built churches.

Like nearly every other building in Nagasaki, the Christian churches needed to be rebuilt. Tom and Wendell approached their division chaplain to request permission to help rebuild a few of the Christian churches, and it was granted. Because of government restrictions during World War II, most of the Christian churches had ceased to function. The first thing Tom and Wendell needed to do was track down the surviving Catholic priests and Christian ministers and convince them to return to their pulpits. Working with the local clergy and their parishioners, Tom and Wendell organized a group of mostly LDS marines to repair and replaster chapels during their off-duty hours so Christian congregations could resume meeting together.

Another way Tom and Wendell found to serve was to assist Nagasaki's orphans. In a letter to his sister Gay, dated January 24, 1946, Tom described how this work started:

"We found a little boy on the streets the other day just about out of his mind from hunger. We took him back to our quarters, fed him, and cleaned him up. We then found one of the interpreters to see if we could find out where his home was. He used to live in the atomic bomb area, and all of his family were killed as a result of the bomb. Since that time he has been wandering around by himself eating and sleeping where he could find a place. We fixed up a place for him to stay out in the buildings behind our barracks and have been saving part of our chow for him. Today some of the other fellows found another. Now we have two and are wondering how many more are wandering around homeless." Eventually Tom and Wendell helped local clergymen open orphanages for some of the displaced children.

By early summer 1946, Tom and Wendell had finally made it to the top of the list to return home. They were instructed to board a train to Sasebo, where they would embark and travel by troop transport back to the states. In the *Special Witnesses of Christ* video, Elder L. Tom Perry described the tender moment at the Nagasaki train station:

"As we were boarding the train that would take us to our ships to return home, we were teased by a lot of other Marines. They had their girlfriends with them saying good-bye to them. They laughed at us and indicated that we had missed the fun of being in Japan. We had just wasted our time laboring and plastering walls.

"Just as they were at the height of their teasing, up over a little rise near the train station came about 200 of these great Japanese Christians from the churches we had repaired, singing 'Onward Christian Soldiers.' They came down and showered us with gifts. Then they lined up along the railroad track, and as the train started down the tracks, we reached out and just touched their fingers as we left. We couldn't speak; our emotions were too strong. But we were grateful that we could help in some small way in reestablishing Christianity in a nation after the war."

Because replacements for them could not be found, Tom and Wendell were kept from boarding the first transport vessel home. They were stationed in Sasebo for over a month, performing their duties and waiting for the next troop transport to arrive. Tom and Wendell were both promised rank advancements if they would reenlist. Tom was even told that his previously submitted application to Officers Candidate School had been accepted. By this time, however, both Tom and Wendell were eager to put their military careers behind them and return home. Appropriately, they took the same troop transport home and organized Sunday Church services while en route.

CHAPTER 12

UTAH STATE AGRICULTURAL COLLEGE

The ship on which Tom and Wendell returned home arrived in San Diego Harbor, and the moment they were granted permission to leave the ship, they had completed their two-and-a-half-year military commitment. They both felt an overwhelming sense of gratitude and joy to be back on U.S. soil. Moreover, it was the first time in four and a half years that they were not fulfilling a long-term commitment, either to the Lord as missionaries or to Uncle Sam as soldiers.

The time had also arrived for Tom to make the two most important decisions of his life: (1) What to make his life's work? (2) Whom to marry? Tom pondered these two questions during the long bus ride home. He believed he had pretty good answers to both questions. In one case, he was right, but in the other case, wrong.

Tom's bus took him to the Salt Lake bus station, where his parents picked him up and drove him home to Logan. As a returned missionary and Marine Corps veteran only a few weeks away from turning twenty-four years old, he was no longer a Logan boy. In the faraway places he had been, Tom had become a man.

Provo vs. Logan

Tom was not the only one in his family who had experienced significant changes in his life. His father was now the first counselor in the presidency of the Cache Stake. Moreover, he had recently completed a unique assignment. Between October 20, 1945, and June 1, 1946, the senior L. Tom Perry had served as temporary stake president while President William W. Owens attended the University of California to further his education. Tom's father noted in his life history that he contracted mumps in early June 1946 and that President Owens returned just in time to resume his duties. President Perry was bedridden for a couple of weeks with the disease, which can be severe when it afflicts adults.

Tom's mother had also changed. The worries of having two sons serving in the Pacific Theater during World War II had aged Nora Perry. She looked noticeably older to Tom, even since the time he had returned from his mission. She had always been a high-energy person, and it was a shock for her son to see how much she had slowed down.

In a letter written on January 24, 1946, to his sister Gay, Tom had shared his plans for civilian life after his return from war. First, he expressed his interest in Maxine Moulton, his date on his last night in Salt Lake City before he left for the San Diego Marine Corps Base. Maxine had faithfully written Tom throughout the war, and he fully intended to follow her to Provo, where she was attending Brigham Young University. He wrote:

"My plans for civilian life seem to be improving with each bit of news I receive from the states. Maxine suddenly decided to attend school at BYU this quarter. She will be there to break me into college life again when I return. The only thing I had against the 'Y' was the fact that I would be a stranger in the school as I started in. Now that problem seems to be settled. She is certainly fond of the school. If I ever had a doubt in my mind about attending the BYU it has been removed through the last few letters I have received from her. She has certainly sold me on the school.

"My problem of courtship has also been cleared up. I can now do my courting on the campus instead of having to make it during the weekends."

Before he arrived home from Japan, Tom had been accepted to BYU and had paid a deposit on the fall semester tuition. When he saw his aging parents, however, he changed his mind. The realization that he had been away from home for four and a half years suddenly hit him. He decided going to Provo was not a good idea. He needed to live at home and attend the Utah State Agricultural College.

Tom's decision made dating Maxine Moulton impractical. She had come to the Salt Lake City bus station when Tom's bus arrived, and she was working in Salt Lake during the summer. Tom and Maxine had shared a wonderful long-distance relationship, but they both found their face-to-face meeting a little awkward. Tom dated Maxine a few times in Salt Lake before she returned to Provo, but the serious relationship they had frequently discussed in their letters never gained traction.

Tom arrived home just before the Pioneer Day celebration in Logan. Only a year before, in a letter written July 17, 1945, to his sister Gay, Tom had written about the Pioneer Day celebration he and the other LDS servicemen were planning on Saipan:

"Right now we are in the middle of our plans for the twenty-fourth of July. Even way out here we are going to celebrate. We are all planning on meeting together for an afternoon of ball games and stuff, and in the evening have an island meeting for the Mormons. It sounds like a great day and to add to the enjoyment of it, we are arranging for the rare items of pie and ice cream for our evening meal. With such to look forward to, I am sure of a good time."

As Tom ate ample portions of pie and ice cream at the Logan Pioneer Day celebration in 1946, the previous year's celebration and everything that had happened since flooded his mind with memories. He was inexpressibly grateful to the Lord to be back in Logan and reunited with his family to celebrate and honor his pioneer ancestors. He felt especially close to his departed Grandpa Sonne, who, more than anyone else in Tom's early life, embodied the great Utah pioneer spirit.

Between the 24th of July and Tom's birthday on August 5, four of the Perry siblings—Mignon, Tom, Ted, and Bob—took a trip to Yellowstone National Park. The four of them, who had each been to Yellowstone several times with their parents, had never gone to the park all together because their family car could comfortably seat only four people. It was delightful for Mignon and Tom to share the memories of their trips together and for Ted and Bob to do the same as they navigated the upper and lower loops of the park. Tom decided during their trip that Yellowstone National Park would be a great place for a honeymoon, if and when he convinced some young woman to marry him.

Tom also took a road trip in August with his boyhood friend Lou Hickman. Lou had been stationed in Oklahoma City during part of the war, and he had a girlfriend there. The two recently discharged soldiers thoroughly enjoyed hitting the open road together. The trip gave them a sense of freedom they had not felt for a long time.

A Twenty-Four-Year-Old College Sophomore

Tom had matured a great deal since the last time he cracked a college textbook. He had learned about his unique strengths, and he had overcome some of his earlier weaknesses. Financial support from the GI Bill paid most of his expenses,[1] which afforded him the luxury of not needing a part-time job, at least initially. All this helped Tom become a more serious and focused student. He soon decided to major in business administration, a subject in which he had both interest and natural ability. Methodically, he began to raise the mediocre grade-point average he had earned as an eighteen-year-old college freshman, and he started to be noticed by his professors.

In addition to acquiring improved study habits through his experiences as a missionary and a marine, Tom had also gained both the desire and the ability to contribute more to making a positive difference around him. There is ample evidence that by this time Tom had become a talented public speaker. For example, in a letter to his parents written October 26, 1945, Tom told about his first day taking a speech class offered for college credit to the servicemen in Nagasaki, Japan:

"Did I tell you that I had started taking a class in speech? We held our first last Tuesday. As they usually start any class in speech, they had all of us get up and talk for three minutes on any subject. After I was through, the teacher asked me where I had all of my experience in public speaking. The greater part of the rest of the class I was telling him about my mission. After I was through, the teacher said that he was ready to turn the class over to me. Everything he would do after that he would first ask me what I thought of it. It looks as if I will do the greater part of the talking and teaching in the class. I don't know why. I have only had one class in speech in college. I will have a little fun showing off."

Tom's impressive physical stature also meant he stood out in any crowd. Leadership came so naturally to him that others began approaching him to seek his counsel and gain his support. This was the case soon after Tom joined Delta Phi, a fraternity of LDS returned missionaries. He was approached by the president of the Delta Phis, Farris Nyman, about a problem on the Utah State campus. During the war, in order to accommodate the servicemen on campus, the college had operated a temporary union building. Alcohol was served in this building, and across campus smoking was allowed. This did not seem to bother the fraternities and sororities on campus. In fact, they preferred the college's increased permissiveness. Many of the LDS students who attended Utah State, however, were appalled by how much the acceptance of alcohol and tobacco on campus had changed it.

Tom was asked to run for president of the Independent Students Association (ISA) and to rally the students unaffiliated with the fraternities and sororities to reclaim their campus. He won the election, and with the backing of Delta Phi, Lambda Delta Sigma, and the LDS Student Association, the ISA successfully lobbied the college administration to ban smoking and drinking on campus. Tom was such a successful leader that he was reelected ISA president for the 1947–48 school year.

Tom ran for student council while serving as ISA president, but he lost by six votes to his boyhood friend Joe Anderson. Tom did not take the defeat very hard, and perhaps he didn't even devote his full attention to the campaign. Between the time he decided to run for student council and the election, he had met a young woman from Hyde Park, Utah—Virginia

Clare Lee—and his focus suddenly changed. In the 1947 Utah State yearbook, the *Buzzer,* Tom is highlighted as one of the better-known campus leaders. His caption reads, "Is a likeable, friendly Delta Phi . . . became a campus landmark between classes waiting for Virginia . . . is looked up to by almost everyone . . . was ISA prexy [president] for this year and re-elected for next."

Virginia Lee

My father is a devoted Utah State Aggie. He has learned to cheer for BYU when it plays Utah State in football and basketball, but he is loyal in every other way to his former school. In addition to his 1949 bachelor of science degree in commerce, he received an honorary doctorate in 2008. He was also honored by Utah State in 2006 when he was given a Distinguished Alumnus Executive Award by the Huntsman School of Business.

Other family honors include the Nora Sonne Perry and Mignon Perry Scholarship and the Theodore S. Perry Scholarship, granted by the Huntsman School and named in honor of my father's mother, sister, and brother. In addition, the Sonne Board Room on the top floor of the Utah State University Inn is named in honor of Elder Alma Sonne.

Still, when my father took his extended family to the main quad on the Utah State University campus on August 3, 2002, as another stop on his eightieth birthday celebration, he mainly had one thing on his mind. He said: "There was so much going on at this time of my life, but my courtship of Virginia became the most important thing. When this time comes to each of you [grandchildren], it affects everything that you do. Make it precious and special."

Before Tom was discharged from the Marine Corps, his father wrote him and told him he would have a new Church calling when he arrived home. He would be the activity counselor in the stake Young Men Mutual Improvement Association. While serving in this calling, Tom stood behind the pulpit to take attendance at a stake MIA board meeting in December 1946. He called for the attendees from the Hyde Park Ward to rise to be counted, and two beautiful young women stood up. When Tom saw Virginia Lee for the first time, he temporarily lost his train of thought. All he could do was smile at her. When he was about to regain his composure, she smiled back at him, and he briefly lost it again. For my father, a trained accountant, correct counts and accurate records have always been very important, but to this day he doubts the accuracy of the attendance count from that fateful stake MIA board meeting.

Tom found Virginia after the board meeting, introduced himself, and walked her to her car. The next Sunday he assigned himself to make an official stake visit to the Hyde Park Ward, and after the morning meetings, he walked Virginia home. At the time, Virginia had a boyfriend, but he had gone home for Christmas break. This meant she was able to accept Tom's invitation to the stake New Year's Eve ball. Their first date must have gone extremely well because when her boyfriend returned to Logan a few days later, Virginia broke up with him.

Virginia Clare Lee was born December 24, 1923, at home—120 West Center Street in Hyde Park. A Christmas Eve baby, Virginia was considerably younger than her three brothers and three sisters. When she was born, her mother, Hattie, was almost forty-four years old, and her father, John E. Lee, was fifty-six. Her older sisters Jessie and Maud were out on Christmas Eve dates the night of Virginia's birth. When they brought their dates home, they excitedly took them into the parlor, where their mother's bed had been moved for the birth. Hattie was lying in bed holding their new baby sister and, according to Jessie, their dates quickly became very embarrassed.

Virginia was named after her father's first wife, who was Hattie's older sister. Virginia May Reeder Lee had died on January 2, 1901, three weeks after giving birth to a second son, Victor, who was born December 14, 1900, and died eleven days later, on Christmas Day.[2] John, who was left alone to raise their first son, Ernest, later married Hattie, with whom he raised six more children.[3]

John Lee doted on Virginia. She was his pride and joy, and he always called her Dolly. Jessie remembers her father wanting to hold baby Virginia on his lap evening after evening, and he was always willing to babysit her when the rest of the family had other plans.

As Virginia grew older, she remained an easy child to love. Her disposition was constantly bright, cheerful, and warm. Even as a child, she had a gift for putting people at ease and listening to them. Perhaps it was because the attention of others came to her naturally that she never demanded it. In fact, she preferred it when others were the center of attention.

Virginia's sister Jessie became almost a second mother to her. When Jessie married Vernal Seamons, they built a home next door to Jessie's parents, and Vernal ran a Texaco gas station on the corner of 100 West and Center Street. Jessie recorded a memory of watching Virginia as a young girl in the yard between the two homes. She wrote: "I could look out my window and see Virginia when she was just a girl standing out on the lawn with her arms down at her side, chin up, shoulders back, marching back and forth. She always had good posture."

Virginia was both confident and shy. She became embarrassed easily, but she usually regained her composure quickly. She was able to laugh at herself when she became flustered, and with a reflective smile, she regathered herself. She made friends easily because others quickly sensed her kind nature.

Virginia was also an excellent student. She attended Hyde Park Elementary School, and she later rode the streetcar to North Cache Junior High School in Smithfield, Utah, and to North Cache High School[4] in Richmond, Utah. She loved to read. She inhaled the beautiful words of classic literature as if they were fresh mountain air. She enjoyed reciting poetry and reading a good story. Public speaking frightened her, but she was gifted enough at it to win speech contests in high school.

When Virginia graduated from high school in 1942, she wanted to attend college, but her family could not afford to send her. She worked as a secretary for two and a half years at the Utah Mortgage Loan Corporation, earned enough money to go to school while living at home, and enrolled for fall semester 1945 at Utah State. She decided to major in Portuguese at the encouragement of a professor. Virginia said: "I had a professor in college who encouraged seven or eight of us to prepare ourselves to go to Brazil to teach English. It sounded daring and adventurous. For this purpose I decided to major in Portuguese."[5]

Virginia's intent to go to Brazil led her to join and become actively involved in the Portuguese Club. She was also a member of the Phi Chapter of Lambda Delta Sigma. And, like Tom, she was a college sophomore at the time they started dating.

By the time Tom noticed Virginia at the Cache Stake MIA board meeting, she had already noticed him walking across the Utah State campus. Her sister Jessie remembers Virginia mentioning him as having made quite an impression on her. But before Virginia met Tom, her mother had noticed and mentioned him, having heard Tom speak at a sacrament meeting in the Hyde Park Ward. Hattie told Virginia, "The most magnificent young man spoke today in church."[6] Virginia learned as much as she could about Tom, and then she patiently waited for him to notice her.

April 19, 1947

Tom and Virginia dated each other exclusively after their New Year's Eve date, and their love for each other deepened during winter semester 1947 at Utah State. A special three-university (Brigham Young University, University of Utah, and Utah State) Delta Phi conference was scheduled on the BYU campus for April 19, 1947. Tom invited Virginia to attend the conference with him, and they drove to Provo together. The conference concluded with a big dance. Both Tom and Virginia loved to dance, and they spent a wonderful evening together on the dance floor.

Between dances, Tom gazed into Virginia's eyes. He knew what he wanted to accomplish that evening, but Virginia's glowing countenance unnerved him. Finally, in the middle of one of the last dances of the evening, he asked her to leave the dance floor—he had something he wanted to tell her in private. They went to Tom's car, and they sat without speaking a word for several minutes. Finally, Tom found the courage to turn and look straight into Virginia's eyes, but he was dumbfounded by her beauty. He could not form the words he so much wanted to say. Finally, he pulled his Delta Phi pin from his pocket and pinned it on Virginia's dress, still unable to explain his intentions. Virginia lifted her eyes after watching him fumble with the pin and asked, "Do you love me, Tom?" He nodded, and then he was able to ask Virginia to marry him.

They returned to the dance floor and announced their engagement to all their friends. Even many years later, Virginia delighted in teasing Tom—who seldom seemed at a loss for words—for not being at his best on the evening of their engagement.

The few months Tom and Virginia were engaged were mostly uneventful. With their paychecks they began to purchase items to use once they were married, such as a vacuum and a radio. Tom picked out a ring for Virginia and gave it to her. In a letter he wrote to her on May 28, 1947, he mentions it: "I'm glad everyone liked the ring. I was just interested in it meeting the approval of one very special person. If you're satisfied, then that's all I want."

The reason Tom commented about the ring in a letter instead of in person is that when he wrote the letter, he was taking his turn with the mumps.[7] He was recovering quickly but was still unable to see Virginia because she had not had the disease. In the letter, Tom explained why, thirty-nine days earlier, he was tongue-tied when he asked Virginia to marry him. He was thoroughly smitten by her. He wrote: "Boy, do I miss you. The mumps aren't so bad, but this staying away from you is slowly killing me. Of course, I would like to have you come and see me if I thought that it was the right thing to do, but under these conditions I don't want to take any chances with anyone as wonderful as you. I'm recovering fast now anyway. One side of my face is almost back to normal. I'm sure I'll be back to school Monday."

Perhaps the awkwardness of expression is part of the letter's charm. Regardless, Tom seemed to draw courage from the thought of seeing Virginia soon.

CHAPTER 13

The Logan Temple

Between the time I was three and a half until I was eleven, we lived in a small suburb of Sacramento, California. Our vacation each year was to drive to Logan and spend a week with my father's and mother's families. We drove through the Sierra Nevada Mountains, the Nevada desert, and Utah's Bonneville Salt Flats until we reached Salt Lake City, where we stayed overnight at the Travel Lodge Motel near Temple Square. We always ate breakfast and lunch at Dee's Restaurant, toured Temple Square and other Salt Lake historical sites, and then jumped back into our car and drove to Logan. As we descended out of Sardine Canyon toward our destination, our excitement would peak. We knew that very soon, perhaps around the next turn, the road would straighten, and we would see Logan in the distance. All of us in the car—my father, mother, sister, and I—wanted to be the first to shout, "There's the Logan Temple!"[1]

July 18, 1947

Tom and Virginia were married July 18, 1947, in the Logan Temple. Shortly before the wedding, the following announcement appeared in the Logan *Herald Journal* under the headline "Miss Virginia Lee Is Making Plans for a July 18 Wedding":

"Mr. and Mrs. John E. Lee of Hyde Park, announce the engagement of their daughter, Virginia, to L. Tom Perry, Jr., son of President and Mrs. L. Tom Perry, of Logan. The marriage is being planned for July 18, in the LDS Temple.

"Miss Lee is a graduate of North Cache high school and seminary, where she was an honor student and prominent in school activities. She has been attending the USAC for the past two years where she is affiliated with Lambda Delta Sigma. Prior to that she was employed by the Utah Mortgage Loan Corporation.

"Mr. Perry is a graduate of Logan Senior high school and seminary and the LDS Institute of Religion at the USAC. He has filled an LDS mission in the Northern States and spent 30 months in the U.S. Marine Corps—23 of which he served in the Central Pacific and Japan. Since his return from service, he has continued his studies at the USAC, where he has been prominent in school affairs. He is president of the Independent Students Association, and a member of Delta Phi. Mr. Perry is also active in church and civic organizations.

"The young couple is planning a honeymoon in Yellowstone National Park, after which they will make their home in Logan at 472 North First West. Mr. Perry will continue his scholastic studies at the USAC."

Entering the largest of the eleven sealing rooms of the Logan Temple was not an entirely unfamiliar experience for Tom. He had attended the Logan Temple with his parents several times before his mission. Although he was far away from an LDS temple for several years during his mission and military service, he had resumed his practice of regular temple attendance since returning to Logan in July 1946. Moreover, during the past year he had joined with family and friends in witnessing the sealings of other couples for time and eternity.

While his thoughts were focused on Virginia on his wedding day, he could not keep himself from doing something he always did inside the Logan Temple. He carefully studied the beautiful woodwork in the sealing room, and in his mind's eye he imagined his Grandpa Sonne hauling logs by sleigh down Logan Canyon in the winter as he helped build the temple. He was connected to the Logan Temple as to no other temple because his Grandpa Sonne had helped build it.

For Virginia, attending the Logan Temple, participating in temple ordinances, and entering a sealing room was a completely new experience. Everything about it was unfamiliar, except the family members and friends who surrounded her, the sealer—ElRay L. Christiansen, a former member of her stake presidency who was now the Logan Temple president—and, of course, the young man kneeling on the other side of the altar who was about to become her husband. Attending the temple, however, was something Virginia had prepared to do for as long as she could remember. One of her cherished memories was of her mother pressing her temple clothes. Virginia reported: "She handled them with tender care. That made such a wonderful impression on me."[2]

Like Tom, Virginia also had a very special familial connection to the Logan Temple. To help with the building of the temple, her grandfather Christen Christensen Lee had hauled many tons of rock from the Hyde Park quarry in Logan Canyon. In his journal, Christen made this entry on December 9, 1878:

"Cloudy and somewhat cold today. I hauled from the Hyde Park rock quarry one load of rocks for the Logan Temple,

47.17 lbs.[3] . . . I hauled [since] the latter [part] of September, 21 4/6 ton of Temple rocks. The canyon is froze with little snow; very slippery today. The work is now closed on the Temple for this season."

Like the Sonnes, the Lees were early settlers of Cache Valley, and they were among the approximately two thousand five hundred people who sacrificed to help build the beautiful Logan Temple. The day of July 18, 1947, marked not only Tom and Virginia's eternal union but also the day on which a welding link joined two noble families, both richly blessed by their Utah pioneer heritage.

Christen Christensen Lee

Christen Christensen was the first son born to wealthy parents Christen Christensen and Dorthea Marie Jensen on October 20, 1833, on their North Lie estate, near Harristlev, Denmark.[4] Christen (Chris) wrote in his life history, "As we had a large farm I stayed and assisted in the work and in time became an expert farmer and was respected and had many friends and was also beloved by my parents."

Chris met Kristen Maria Jensen, they fell in love, and in 1851, when he was only eighteen, they became engaged. It was in 1851 that Chris also began to hear about the Mormons, and he was shocked to learn that his fiancée's family, including Kristen, was among the first converts in the area. Chris told Kristen that if she was going to belong to the Church, he would have nothing to do with her. She answered him, "All right, then I'll serve the Lord."

Christen tried to move on, but he eventually went to Kristen and told her that he knew she was right about the Church. He attended his first meeting on Sunday, May 23, 1852. Chris's father was strongly opposed to his joining The Church of Jesus Christ of Latter-day Saints, and he used both inducements and threats to try to stop Chris from investigating the Church. Chris's belief in the truthfulness of the Church only became stronger with time, and though he delayed his baptism in the hope that his father's opposition to the Church would soften, he eventually was baptized and confirmed a member of the Church on November 11, 1852.

Chris and Kristen wanted to go to America to join the Saints who were gathering in Utah. They obtained four hundred dollars for that purpose, but the brethren of the branch met and decided that their branch president, Brother Tahon, who wanted to emigrate to Utah with his large family, was more deserving.[5] Chris and Kristen accepted the decision, and the Tahon family was overjoyed and grateful to receive the money.

Upon hearing that his eldest son wanted to emigrate to America, Chris's father panicked. He needed his son's help on the farm, and, therefore, he struck a deal with him. If Chris would stay and work the farm one more year, his father would give him enough money to go to America. Chris accepted the terms, but he also insisted that he be allowed to leave the farm whenever he was called to Church service.

Chris did become heavily involved in Church service during his last year in Denmark. He was ordained a teacher on December 4, 1853, and assigned a companion, J. P. Jensen, to work with the members of the Harristlev Branch. A month and a half later, on January 26, 1854, Chris and Kristen were married by a magistrate.

During the winter of 1854, Chris labored as a missionary with J. P. Jensen, and he didn't return to North Lie until mid-April to help his father with the spring planting. Then, as soon as the crops were harvested, he returned to missionary service until November 2, 1854, when he returned to North Lie to settle with his father. At first, Chris's father did not want to honor their agreement, but the next morning he had a change of heart. They traveled to the town of Hjorring, and before a lawyer, Chris renounced his inheritance for a sum of two hundred dollars. He later wrote about the experience: "I got $200, a small sum compared with several thousand, which I could have had later on. But I know that all the riches in the world would not help me if I lost my soul and was glad and satisfied."

Upon receiving the money, the first thing Chris did was go to the branch president in Aalborg and pay his tithing. He also gave eight dollars to a poor sister who didn't have enough money for her journey.

Chris and Kristen, after making all the preparations, boarded the steamship *Cimbria* on November 25, 1854. Because of severe storms, however, the ship had to return to Denmark for repairs. Eventually, they were able to reboard the *Cimbria*, and they arrived in Hull, England, on December 24. They stayed in England briefly and set sail for Liverpool aboard the *James Newsmith* on January 11, 1855.

The *James Newsmith* journeyed to New Orleans, where the passengers first saw the coast of America on February 18. Chris, Kristen, and others journeyed up the Mississippi River, and they eventually landed in Weston, Missouri, near Kansas City. The money Chris had received from his father was sufficient to take them to America but not to Utah. It took Chris and Kristen two and a half years to save the $362.54 they needed to equip themselves to cross the Great Plains. It was sometime during this period that Chris and Kristen adopted the surname Lee, after the family estate in North Lie.

Finally, the Lees joined the Matthias Cowley company in Florence, Nebraska, in late June 1857, and they arrived in Salt Lake City on September 13. The Lees headed directly to Brigham City, where they intended to reunite with Kristen's parents to help with the fall harvest, finish building their house, and stay with them for the winter.[6] They, however, had arrived in Utah in the middle of the Utah War, which changed their plans when they arrived in Brigham City. Twice, Chris was called to join a militia to defend against the invasion of Johnston's Army. Because of early snow, however, Johnston's Army was forced to stay at Fort Bridger, Wyoming, for the winter, a direct conflict with the Mormons was averted, and Chris was able to return to Brigham City to spend the winter.

In the spring of 1858, Brigham Young, still concerned about the approach of Johnston's Army, sent the Saints in the northern valleys to Utah County. The Lees joined a company and moved to Spanish Fork, Utah, for the summer. A treaty ending the Utah War was signed in July, and the Lees moved back to a farm in Brigham City that Chris rented for two years.

In the spring of 1862, Chris bought a farm, and while the first harvest was meager, it was a start. Chris also began to build a house out of adobe, but he did not finish it in time for winter, which came early. Kristen became very ill, and they decided to go to the Salt Lake Endowment House to be sealed. Chris and Kristen were sealed on November 18, 1862. At the same time, Chris was sealed to a second wife, Sophia Madsen. Sophia was only sixteen and a half years old when she was sealed to Chris. She had been hired by the Lees the previous summer to help them produce butter and cheese to sell locally, and she had stayed with them for the winter.

Kristen did not recover from her illness, and she died on January 7, 1863. Chris and Kristen had been unable to have children, but a daughter was born to Chris and Sophia on November 11, 1863. They named her Mary Lorinda.

A year later the Lees sold their house and farm in Brigham City and moved to Hyde Park. Chris was blessed in his first summer of planting in Hyde Park with a harvest that was several times the size of what he had reaped from his Brigham City farm. He proudly reported a harvest of 319 bushels of wheat, 105 bushels of oats, 50 bushels of potatoes, and 10 tons of hay.

The summer of 1864 was eventful for another reason. On July 8, Chris was sealed to his third wife, Tomine Petersen.[7] Tomine was Kristen Lee's niece, the daughter of a sister who had died in 1855. Tomine was born on June 9, 1847, in Wensysel, Denmark, and she had arrived with her family in Utah earlier than Chris, in the fall of 1854. The first child born to Chris and Tomine was a daughter, Clara, on March 8, 1866. A year and a half later, on October 2, 1867, Tomine gave birth to a son, John Ernest Lee, who became the father of Virginia Lee Perry.

Chris Lee became one of the pillars of the Hyde Park community. He endured grasshopper infestations during the summers of 1867 and 1868. With four partners, he built a sawmill in November 1867. He worked briefly on the transcontinental railroad in the fall of 1868. Chris mourned when his third wife, Tomine, died after giving birth to another daughter, Tomine Kirsten, on August 1, 1869. The burden of raising twelve children fell on Sophia. Four children died in the diphtheria epidemic of 1876, including Tomine Kirsten. Two years later, a half-sister, Irene Prudence, died of the same disease.

Later in life, John described his stepmother, Sophia, in a loving way. He said, "No one could have had a kinder stepmother than I did. I felt that I was the favorite child." Sophia had promised John's mother on her deathbed that she would take care of her children. John recalled that when Tomine Kirsten died in 1876, his stepmother grieved over losing her even more than she had grieved the loss of her own children.[8]

Chris Lee helped organize the United Order of Hyde Park in 1875, and he was elected to its board of directors on November 4, 1878. In 1892 he purchased the Hyde Park Co-op Store on 47 North 100 West and operated it as the C. C. Lee

& Sons Store. C. C. Lee & Sons later established a creamery. The creamery purchased surplus milk from local farmers and made it into butter and cheese. The creamery is credited with launching the highly successful Cache Valley butter and cheese industry.[9]

Chris Lee's life was not an easy life. Like the Perrys and the Sonnes, he had many accomplishments and hardships that characterized the lives of all the early pioneers who settled the Great Basin. Given that his was such a challenging and busy life, it is all the more impressive that he found the time to haul many tons of rock from the Hyde Park quarry during the fall of 1878 through the summer of 1879 to build the Logan Temple.

The Parents of the Bride

Hattie and John Lee were beaming as they watched President Christiansen seal their youngest child, Virginia, to the worthy young man she loved, L. Tom Perry. It was the highlight of a perfect day—its central, defining moment—to be gathered as family and close friends in the sealing room of the Logan Temple to witness the beginning of a sacred, eternal union. Perhaps Hattie, now sixty-seven years old, and John, only a few months shy of his eightieth birthday, considered it the culminating moment of their life together. They both loved Virginia so much, and to see her so completely happy was the epitome of parental joy and reward.

Hattie and John had been married in the Logan Temple on October 1, 1903, a day before John's thirty-sixth birthday.[10] Hattie was a small woman, barely five feet tall, with beautiful long, black hair.[11] She was twenty-three when she married John, and she had helped with raising Ernest from the time he was one and a half years old, after her sister, Virginia, died. Ernest lived with Hattie's mother, Ellen, until he was ten, and then he moved back to live with his father and stepmother.[12]

John, Hattie, and their children shared a beautiful Victorian home in Hyde Park. It had high ceilings, a spiral staircase, several bedrooms, and a lovely parlor on the main floor. The parlor was furnished with velvet-upholstered furniture, and prominent in the room were a player piano and an early gramophone.

John was called by Bishop Charles G. Hyde to serve as a missionary in the Central States Mission in December 1907. John offered to support a younger, single man to serve instead, but Bishop Hyde told him he was the one called to serve. John entered the mission field with a companion, Frank Traveler, from nearby Richmond, Utah. Their missionary experience involved walking from one end of Kansas to the other, but they had no converts.

Most of the people they met were very poor. They lived in sod houses, barely kept food on the table, and lacked the means to move in search of better conditions. The two missionaries spent many nights sleeping in barns on haystacks, and as they served without purse or scrip, they were caught outside in many terrible Midwestern storms. Despite his mission being so difficult and unsuccessful, John mostly enjoyed his three years of service, and he and Frank Traveler remained close friends the rest of their lives.

John was nearly forty-one years old when he left on his mission, and he left Hattie with a six-week-old baby daughter, Jessie; another daughter, eighteen-month-old Maud; and a three-year-old son, Preston. He sold many of their possessions to leave Hattie with some money while he served, and he placed the money he received in the care of his half-brother, Francis (Frank).

John's call was both unexpected and extremely upsetting to Hattie. As a relatively new wife, she was suddenly being asked to assume the dual role of nurturer and provider for her family.

John's three years of missionary service were three years of tremendous loneliness for Hattie. Her closest companions were her three children, who were with her constantly.

Hattie revealed the strength and depth of her pioneer spirit as she coped with her difficult circumstances. Instead of feeling sorry for herself, she approached each day with purpose. She knew John had been called into the Lord's service to spread the light of the restored gospel of Jesus Christ. It was this belief that sustained her through each day of their separation.

When the High Creek Electric and Power Company brought electricity to Hyde Park in February 1909, it gave Hattie an idea about how she could properly welcome her husband home from his mission. Her goal over the final year and a half of John's missionary service was to save enough money by the time he returned home to have their house wired for electricity and connected to the new power lines. She wanted this to be his welcome-home surprise. According to Virginia, her mother envisioned that "every light would be shining against the dark as a beacon for his coming home."[13] When John, wearing a worn-out missionary suit, walked up Center Street in Hyde Park and saw for the first time in three years their two-story home at 114 West, it was shining with electric lights.

In her life history, Hattie's daughter Jessie wrote about how her mother had accomplished this feat. Jessie wrote: "My mother wanted to have the house wired, but Uncle Frank thought she shouldn't spend the money. Mother was quite determined. She had a large home, so she furnished room and board for some of the power workers. I have often wondered how she did it with three small children."[14]

Something that never ceased to bring comfort to Hattie was the scriptures. For much of her life, she tried to read through all of the standard works every year. She always sat in her favorite rocker and rocked while she read.[15]

John loved animals. He always kept cattle, cows, chickens, sheep, and horses. He was particularly fond of horses, and he enjoyed training them. One day while he was trying to train a horse, his life was spared in a miraculous manner. The event occurred before Virginia was born, during the winter of 1920, but she liked to tell the story as if she had been there. She said:

"The horse reared back, and the rope tied to him caught on father's leg. Father was roughly pulled over a four-strand, barbed-wire fence, and his new overalls were ripped to shreds. The family ran to my father, thinking he would be seriously injured, but he didn't have one scratch on his body. We knew our father had been protected by the Lord."[16]

One of the more interesting aspects of John and Hattie's marriage was their political allegiances. John was a committed Democrat, while Hattie was a committed Republican. To avoid contention in their home, they rarely discussed politics with each other. Still, both of them were extremely civic-minded individuals with impeccable voting records. Oddly, they always chose to go to the polling station together, fully aware that their votes were going to cancel each other out.

Both John and Hattie gave remarkable service to the LDS Church in the Hyde Park Ward. On January 28, 1923, the ward bishopric was reorganized. James W. Seamons was called to serve as the new bishop, and he chose John E. Lee as his first counselor. They served together for nearly twenty years, during the same period of time that my grandfather L. Tom Perry served as the bishop of the Logan Ninth Ward. Hattie served the ward for many years as president of the Relief Society and the YWMIA, and she was always a faithful member of the Hyde Park Ward choir.

Like his father, John became a pillar of the Hyde Park community. On Memorial Day in 1986, Elder L. Tom Perry spoke at the groundbreaking of Lee Park in Hyde Park. Beautiful Lee

Park was created on farmland donated to the city by Mae Lee, widow of Preston Lee, Virginia's older brother. It was a tract of land that Chris, John E., and Preston Lee had all farmed. Before Elder Perry spoke at the groundbreaking, the mayor of Hyde Park gave a short speech. He spoke mostly about Chris and John Lee—how they had built an irrigation system to channel water from the mountains; invested in the first culinary water system; created paths, then dirt roads, and later paved roads; and participated in building schools, churches, and the Logan Temple. He concluded with these words: "The beautiful Hyde Park community that we all share and love was built on the broad shoulders of men like Chris and John Lee."

CHAPTER 14

The Aggie Ice Cream Store

The final lesson my father wanted to teach to his children and grandchildren on August 3, 2002, was the importance of family traditions. He directed us to stop at the Aggie Ice Cream store, which used to be located on the Quad at Utah State University but later moved to 750 North 1200 East, a few blocks to the north.

Family traditions are extremely important to my father. Several times at general conference, Elder Perry has encouraged parents and grandparents in the Church to establish and maintain strong family traditions.[1] As a prophet, seer, and revelator, he sees many corrosive forces weakening families in our modern, technology-driven era. Building stronger family traditions is no longer optional—traditions form an essential protective barrier to guard families against the widespread corrosion of family values.

My father realizes that the time in which he grew up offered fewer options to families for spending time together, and, therefore, traditions formed more naturally through repeating the same, familiar activities. In a time when nearly limitless options exist, the natural tendency is to look for new experiences, as if repetition is tantamount to boring. Family traditions, however, bond families together slowly. They require repetition and become stronger through familiarity. They build cherished, shared memories each year and, therefore, cannot be fully appreciated until several years after a family has started them.

Our family's annual trip to Bear Lake has taught this powerful lesson. When we started going to Bear Lake many years ago, it was not my father's intention to continue the tradition for more than twenty years (and still counting). In the beginning, he would ask us each year if we should go to Bear Lake the next year or try out another place. He didn't want his sentimental attachment to Bear Lake to determine the vacation spot for everyone else. After the family went to Bear Lake for about five years, however, the issue resolved itself. Because of all the memories associated with Bear Lake, his grandchildren didn't want to go anywhere else. Not only was Bear Lake the place of some of their fondest memories, but it was also something they anticipated each year, such as Christmas and their birthdays.

My father has always had an expansive definition of family traditions. They range from daily rituals, such as family prayer and scripture study to weekly activities, such as family home evening and a Friday night date with one's spouse. They also include annual events, such as cherished holiday traditions, and marker events, such as baptisms and priesthood ordinations. As he did early on with our family's annual trip to Bear Lake, he believes in assessing whether a new family tradition is fulfilling its intended purpose. Still, like any successful long-term investor, he maintains a consistent investment strategy. He also diversifies risk by establishing and maintaining a wide variety of family traditions. He knows some traditions will have more staying power than others, but all of them are investments in an eternal family—one of only a few earthly treasures that "neither moth nor rust doth corrupt."[2]

There are other family traditions associated with Logan and its surrounding area that my father could have chosen to teach his final eightieth birthday lesson. For example, because it was a Saturday afternoon, we could have driven up Logan Canyon and stopped at one of the campgrounds closest to Logan, like Bridger or Spring Hollow. We could have driven all the way up and past Logan Canyon to Bear Lake. My father considered doing so because he knew how significant the annual Bear Lake trip has been for his grandchildren, but he decided the long and snaking drive was impractical, even a little dangerous, near the end of an already packed day. Or he could have waited to teach the lesson until our scheduled dinner at the Bluebird Restaurant—another favorite Perry family stop—and skipped the visit to the Aggie Ice Cream store. So, knowing my father as I do, I believe it's not unfair to assume he had an ulterior motive—he really wanted a double scoop Aggie Ice Cream cone for his birthday.

472 North 100 West

Soon after Tom asked Virginia to marry him, they decided that after their honeymoon they would live in the home that Chris Sonne had left Tom in his will. There were renters in the house at the time of Tom and Virginia's engagement,[3] but they were duly notified, and they vacated the house in time for Tom and Virginia to move in after they were married.

Tom was still receiving monthly benefits from the G.I. Bill, and he also had found part-time work as a bookkeeper for a malt shop and creamery in North Logan, a few of the Utah

State fraternities and sororities, and the firm that had contracted to paint the Logan Temple. So Tom could focus more of his attention on completing his degree than on supporting their family, Virginia decided to leave school and work full time as a secretary for the manager of the Federal Land Bank office in Logan.

Living at 472 North 100 West was a comfortable arrangement for Tom and Virginia. They had several sources of income, and they were living rent free. Moreover, since Tom had returned from Japan, he had helped tend his parents' large garden. Accordingly, Tom and Virginia had all the fresh produce they needed during the summer and canned fruits and vegetables for the winter. Given their limited fixed expenses, it was a time during which they had some discretionary income.

Their home, however, needed some modernizing. When they moved in, the house had an old coal range that served multiple purposes. Virginia cooked their meals on the stove, which was also the only source of hot water and heat in the little house. They saved their money and soon bought a new electric stove, a coal furnace, and a water heater.

Tom served another year as president of the Independent Students Association, but he delegated more of the workload during his second term. He also continued to serve as a counselor in the stake YMMIA presidency. The newlyweds stayed busy, of course, but not too busy. They faced the same adjustments and compromises all newly married couples face, but given the comfortable pace of life, they had sufficient time to talk issues out and form a new, distinctive set of family traditions by blending the traditions of their two families.

Living next door to Nora Perry allowed Virginia to learn how to prepare Tom's favorite dishes, such as rice pudding and pea soup. Hattie Lee was also a marvelous cook, and Sunday dinners at her house introduced new favorites into Tom's diet that Virginia was already an expert at preparing. Fortunately for Tom, his tall, skinny frame could support the weight he gained in the years following marriage.

Tom and Virginia adopted the Perry family practice of fall and spring cleaning before general conference. The way they spent Saturdays also emulated the Perry family—they worked in the morning and played in the afternoon. It was a weekly ritual to drive out to Hyde Park on Saturday morning to do laundry, which in the days of wringer washers and clotheslines was a job that took most of the morning. Then they spent Saturday afternoons in Logan Canyon with the Perrys. It was back to Hyde Park for most Sunday dinners with either Virginia's parents or her older sister Jessie and her husband, Vernal.

Again, learning from the Perrys, Virginia turned the chairs at their small kitchen table backward before one of their daily meals so they could kneel in family prayer. Like the Sonnes, one of Tom and Virginia's favorite pastimes was the card game Rook. Prepared to lose, they regularly went to Aunt Josephine's house to play Rook with her and Uncle Søren. A holiday tradition Virginia continued from her family was reading "'Twas the Night Before Christmas" on Christmas Eve, her birthday. Virginia also insisted on continuing another Lee family tradition—opening all her presents on Christmas Eve, except the ones from Santa Claus.

A Perry Family Christmas

As a homesick marine corporal writing from Nagasaki, Japan, Tom provided a description of the typical Christmas at 466 North 100 West in Logan. In a letter to his family dated December 10, 1945, he wrote:

"I will never forget the Christmas seasons I spent at home. It always seemed to open with the night they turned on the Christmas lights downtown. Even during the few years I found myself in bed, you always carried me out to the car and drove me through town. The other years found us at Aunt Jo's looking out her window at the hotel.

"The next big event was the trimming of the Christmas tree. I first remember the years Mignon and I found ourselves on our knees awaiting the dropping of an icicle so that we could add something to the tree. Then as years added height to my body I found that I was taking the place of the ladder, and I even rated placing the star on the top.

"Christmas Eve always meant sitting around the fireplace with the whole family. Even after I reached dating age I didn't feel like Christmas Eve was any time to leave home because I felt I would be missing a great deal if I wasn't with the family on that night. It was a night when Dad would always be at his best, and no one wants to miss out on Dad's humor when he is in a mood such as that.

"I guess my sisters will never forget the nights Ted and I would call in from our room about every fifteen minutes to find out what time it was. Six o'clock was certainly slow in rolling around when you knew that there was a real surprise awaiting you in the morning. Of course, the slowest minutes were after we were out of bed and awaiting the arrival of Uncle John, Aunt Emma, and Aunt Jo.

"The line to go into the tree brought another change as years passed by. I can remember when I was near the front. Now I am two inches in the rear of everyone else. (Correct me if the two inches is wrong, Ted. The last time we met you were only six feet two inches.)

"After finding ourselves the most fortunate family in the neighborhood on Christmas morning, we could settle down to a day of playing, and a day of eating the best food that could ever be found."

The Perry family traditions reached across the Pacific Ocean on Christmas morning in 1945. When Tom, Wendell, and the other LDS servicemen celebrated Christmas with the group of Nagasaki orphans they were helping support, they lined them up by height before they brought them through the door into a room with a little Christmas tree in the corner. Beneath the tree were presents sent from home—a toy or a doll for each child. These were the only presents the LDS servicemen had asked Santa to send them that year.

The tradition of lining up children by height on Christmas morning was not a tradition Tom and Virginia considered until the Christmas season of 1949. Even then, thinking about it was premature, but at least by Christmas Day 1949 there was a new member of the family who someday would stand in the line.

Barbara Lee Perry

In April 1949, approximately twenty-one months after Tom and Virginia were married, Virginia learned she was pregnant. The next month, Tom graduated from Utah State with a bachelor of science degree in commerce and took a job with the Utah State Extension Service as the administrative assistant to the director. The extension service offices were located on the Quad at Utah State, next to Old Main (the administration building). Tom's experience in campus leadership and the recommendation of one of his accounting professors had helped him get the job. He was delighted about his new job. He believed strongly in the mission of the extension service to offer both on-campus and localized in-service instruction in the areas of agriculture, family and consumer sciences, leadership development, natural resources, community and economic development, as well as sponsoring 4-H programs for youth. The pay was modest but adequate for him to support his family and allow Virginia to stay at home once the baby was born. Having a job at the college also meant he could continue to take classes tuition free. He completed several graduate finance courses while working at the extension service for the next year and a half.

Tom's job description at the extension service included supervising the small headquarters staff. Some of the specialists, who reported to the director, had personal secretaries, but most were supported by headquarters staff. Tom was in charge of all the accounting functions, including coordinating annual audits by federal agencies. He also managed several federal grants, and he reported on how funds were used and their results. Finally, he managed the operation of the extension service building, which functioned as an office but also as a motel for people who came to the college to attend short courses offered by the School of Agriculture. Learning his new job kept Tom busy, but when December arrived, he found it difficult to concentrate on work, given that fatherhood was imminent.

On December 20, 1949, Logan had a severe snowstorm. Tom was at work, and as the snow began to pile up around their home, Virginia began to feel contractions. They progressed quickly, and she called Tom to alert him. Tom looked outside and realized it was going to take him some time to dig out the car and drive down the hill. He called his father and asked him to take Virginia to the hospital, and he would meet them there. A few hours after Tom had arrived at the hospital, a new baby daughter was placed in his arms, and he carried her into Virginia. They named their new daughter Barbara Lee Perry.

Tom and Virginia adored Barbara. She had big, gorgeous blue eyes and a wonderful disposition. Neither Virginia nor Tom ever wanted to put her down. In time, Virginia's possessiveness of Barbara created a little tension between her and Tom's mother. Nora was used to having a significant role in caring for her grandchildren, and she was quite insistent about taking care of Barbara. Virginia, however, wanted to be independent, and she was reluctant to share Barbara with anybody except Tom and her mother. When Tom took Virginia on a date, for example, she would insist that they leave Barbara with her Grandma Lee in Hyde Park, not next door with Grandma Perry. Occasionally, Virginia's reluctance to share Barbara with Nora hurt her feelings. Nora, in turn, would irk Virginia by trying to monopolize Tom's time with her projects or sneaking him a piece of fresh pie or one of her giant cinnamon rolls while he worked in their backyard. There was never open hostility between the two women, but it was a challenge for them to adjust to living next door to each other for three and a half years.

The Decision to Leave Logan

In the summer of 1950, Virginia realized she was pregnant again. This was joyous news to Tom, but he also realized that their current home would not accommodate a family of four. The house had only one small bedroom, and Barbara, who wasn't yet a year old, was sleeping in a crib in the corner of their bedroom. For the first time since he and Virginia had married, Tom felt financial pressure. He decided one way for them to save money for the birth of their second child and a new place to live was to work in the evenings during the holiday season at C. C. Anderson's department store in Logan. When Tom applied and the store manager saw he had a background in accounting, he hired Tom to collect the cash and receipts and to balance and close the books each night while the store offered extended hours to holiday shoppers.

Tom's excellent work during his two months at the Logan store did not go unnoticed by C. C. Anderson's corporate offices in Boise, Idaho, and he was offered a job in the corporate auditing department. The offer involved considerably more money than Tom was earning at the extension service. Leaving Cache Valley and their families was difficult for both Virginia and Tom, but they concluded it was the best thing for their relationship and their growing family. Moreover, if the new job didn't work out, Tom was confident he could return to Logan and find another job, perhaps with the First National Bank of Logan.

Tom's father showed his support for Tom and Virginia's decision by offering to buy their house. He offered them enough that they could make a down payment on a new, slightly larger home in Boise. Later, his true intentions were revealed when he gave the home back to Tom as long as it would be used as a rental property to support Aunt Emma Holmgren.

Shortly after moving to Boise, Tom wrote a clever newsletter titled "Boise Newzee." It revealed the sense of humor and playful nature of a young man who was deeply devoted to his family and who was experiencing success early in his career but, at the same time, missing his parents. Tom reported:

> FRONT PAGE
>
> The big front-page news from the Perry Household is the current crime investigation being conducted by interrogator father on the crime of: Who stole daddy's slippers while he was taking a bath? The first witness called was mother. Her testimony was foolproof. She could prove by the cake that she had just baked that she was busy in the kitchen. The second witness called was young Barbara. The first question by the interrogator was, "Where were you at the time the slippers were taken?" The witness answered, "I do not wish to answer that question on the grounds that it might incriminate me." Miss Perry was held in contempt.

L. Tom Perry with the first of his two red wagons.

Tom at six or seven years old.

Tom and Ted.

Fishing, a favorite pastime.

Leslie Thomas and Elsie Nora Sonne Perry family portrait, about 1934.
Young Tom is standing, back left.

Detail from family portrait.

Tom at sixteen.

Logan Ninth Ward volleyball team, 1940. Tom is seated, center front.

Missionary in the Northern States Mission.

Tom (back row, second from left) with other missionaries and Church members at district conference in Marion, Ohio.

On missionary laundry day, Tom towers above the clothesline.

Missionary transfer day.

Newly enlisted in the United States Marine Corps.

Tom with Japanese children.

With friends in Japan.

Tom (third from right) with his office staff buddies in Nagasaki, Japan.

In Nagasaki.

Buzzer yearbook photo at Utah State Agricultural College after the war. Tom Perry was honored in the yearbook as a "*Buzzer* personality."

Calling for a date during his years at Utah State.

THE BOARD OF TRUSTEES OF

UTAH·STATE·AGRICULTURAL·COLLEGE·

ON THE NOMINATION OF THE FACULTY
HAS CONFERRED UPON

L. TOM PERRY, JR.

THE DEGREE OF

BACHELOR OF SCIENCE IN COMMERCE

TOGETHER WITH ALL THE HONORS, RIGHTS AND PRIVILEGES BELONGING TO THAT DEGREE. IN WITNESS WHEREOF THIS DIPLOMA IS GRANTED BEARING THE SEAL OF THE COLLEGE AND THE SIGNATURES OF THE CHAIRMAN OF THE BOARD OF TRUSTEES AND THE PRESIDENT OF THE COLLEGE.

CHAIRMAN OF THE BOARD OF TRUSTEES

PRESIDENT OF THE COLLEGE

GIVEN AT LOGAN IN THE STATE OF UTAH, THIS THIRD DAY OF JUNE IN THE YEAR OF OUR LORD NINETEEN HUNDRED FORTY-NINE AND THE COLLEGE THE SIXTY-FIRST.

At the fence between the two Perry homes in Logan, Utah.

Tom and Virginia, just home from their honeymoon, in front of Tom's parents' home in Logan.

Proud new parents Virginia and Tom with baby Barbara.

Virginia holding baby Lee.

Tom holding Barbara and playing with the dog, Tiny.

Certificate of Ordination
to the
Holy Priesthood

This Certifies that

L. Tom Perry

Of the Lewiston Ward in Spokane Stake

Was Ordained A High Priest

In the Church of Jesus Christ of Latter-day Saints

June 21 1953 By Elder Harold B. Lee

A Apostle In Said Church

State Office in Priesthood

President W. L. Jeaman Quorum

Attest F. E. Ericksen

Quorum Secretary

The Perry children with their father, New Year's Day, 1960.

With Allied Builders Club. Tom is at the head of the table.

At a business luncheon in Lewiston, Idaho. Tom is in profile at right.

Treasurer at R. H. Stearns in Boston.

Quorum of the Twelve Apostles, April 6, 1974. Clockwise from left:
Ezra Taft Benson, Gordon B. Hinckley, Thomas S. Monson, Boyd K. Packer,
Marvin J. Ashton, Bruce R. McConkie, L. Tom Perry, Howard W. Hunter,
Hugh B. Brown, LeGrand Richards, Delbert L. Stapley, Mark E. Petersen.

Tom and Virginia, October 1973.

L. Tom and Virginia Clare Lee Perry family photograph, April 6, 1974, the day Elder Perry was sustained as a member of the Quorum of the Twelve Apostles. Standing: Barbara Perry Haws, Terry D. Haws, Lee Perry, and Linda Gay Perry. Seated: Sister Perry and Elder Perry.

Sustained as an Apostle at the April 1974 general conference.

First official Church portrait of Elder L. Tom Perry as a member of the Quorum of the Twelve.

Elder Perry soon after his call as an Apostle.

LOCAL NEWS

Spring weather has at last arrived in this fair city. Saturday was a beautiful day. The Jaycees held their annual Easter Egg Hunt. Thousands of kids crowded Boise's Julia Davis Park to search for colored eggs. Among this large crowd, this correspondent noticed a young family of three off in one corner of the park by themselves. They didn't appear to be searching for eggs. The youngest member of the family was decked out in a new spring coat and bonnet. The proud parents were attempting to take a picture of the young miss, new spring outfit, and new Easter basket. Sizing up the shape things were in, I noticed that the mother was very camera shy. She was very certain not to be in the direction the camera was being aimed. The three were having great troubles. The daughter wanted to run through the park and the parents wanted to take a picture. The father would get into position, and the mother would hold the daughter until the father would say, "All set." With that command, the mother would run to the east and the daughter would run to the west, and father would take a beautiful picture of a little green pine tree they were using for a background. I believe one of two were good. You may see them later on this spring.

BUSINESS NEWS

C. C. Anderson's is happy to announce the appointment of L. Tom Perry as Internal Auditor—a new position just created to improve the figures that are being posted in their ledgers. The position brought no increase in salary for Mr. Perry, but he believes that this is surely a start in the right direction for advancement.

The new position will require a great deal of planning and work from the new appointee. He will be given a free hand in planning procedures and reports for the new position. The new position came as a result of the recommendations of an outside auditing firm which is just completing an audit of C. C.'s books. They believe that a number of errors could be eliminated if an immediate check could be made of all reports coming into the Central Office from the stores. The position means that Mr. Perry will have to gain working knowledge of the entire accounting procedure of the C. C. Anderson Company.

FARM AND GARDEN

Now that spring has arrived, the Perry family is greatly missing their neighbors from Logan. The replacement cost for items usually borrowed from their neighbors on the south has brought financial problems. Items such as wheelbarrow, lawn mower, rake, shovel, and hoe are all in need before spring work can get underway. Technological skill in the planting of lawn, gardening and building a fence are also needed at this outpost.

All is well in the northland.

Love,
Ginny,[4] Barbara, and Tom

The decision to move to Boise marked a significant change in my father's life. He had already left Logan twice for extended periods of time as a missionary and a soldier, but Logan had remained the place he called home. Boise was not a great distance away from Logan, but it was the first step in a journey that would take my father to the West Coast and then to the

East Coast until a Church calling brought him back to Utah. He would never return to live in Logan again. Still, in response to a letter from his sister Gay about the possibility of selling Grandpa Sonne's house to her,[5] Tom wrote in a letter dated November 12, 1968:

"Now for 472 North 1st West. I'll do anything that will help you out. I do want a stake in Utah for security. I have always thought that someday I would trade 472 in on a larger piece of land. . . . I would like to have a piece big enough to at least put food on the table, just as security. Would that be about 3 or 4 acres? You could use the land for a garden until we needed it. I have about $6,000 here in a savings account [that] I was planning to use for this purpose when I had time to get out there and find the right piece."

Nearly eighteen years after leaving Logan, my father, then a successful retail executive living outside Boston, still called Logan home. Even after he had transplanted himself and his family several times, the roots of his noble character remained planted deep in Cache Valley soil.

CHAPTER 15

Boise, Idaho

Tom and Virginia did not need a moving van to move to Boise. The only piece of furniture they took with them was Barbara's crib, which they packed with their other belongings in their 1950 Plymouth.[1]

They moved after Christmas, celebrated the new year of 1951 in Boise, and Tom started work on January 2. Only two months before, Tom had started as a part-time employee of C. C. Anderson's department store in Logan while working full time at the Utah State Extension Service. Suddenly, he was a full-time auditor at C. C. Anderson's headquarters in Boise with a substantial pay upgrade. Life had changed unexpectedly and dramatically for the young, upwardly mobile professional and his family.

As soon as Tom accepted the job in Boise, he called a friend, Conway (Con) Dunn, a fellow Delta Phi and member of the Independent Students Association at Utah State who had moved to Boise a year earlier. Tom asked Con to help look for a small house in one of Boise's newer developments that was near a bus line to C. C. Anderson's offices. Con narrowed the search to two homes, from which Tom and Virginia quickly made their selection—a new two-bedroom home at 2805 Palouse Street.

Tom and Virginia furnished their new home with new furniture—a card table and folding chairs in the kitchen, a bed in their bedroom, and a sofa and chairs in the living room. Virginia fashioned drapes and curtains out of bed sheets to cover the windows. Given that it was a new home, there was no landscaping, but there was plenty of room for a large lawn on which Barbara could play and an ample plot for planting a garden. Tom looked forward to spring, when he could plant grass and start the garden.

Tom and Virginia attended church on Sunday, and Tom discovered that their bishop was his former ninth-grade seminary teacher, Wilburn Talbot. Bishop Talbot recommended to the elders quorum president that Tom serve as his second counselor. Tom was called and sustained the next Sunday, and he immediately dived into improving ward teaching.[2]

Tom's biggest challenge was learning the ropes at his new job. C. C. Anderson's had been part of the Allied Stores retail conglomerate since 1937. At the time it was acquired by Allied, C. C.'s had twenty-one stores spread throughout Idaho, Colorado, Utah, Oregon, and Washington. The founder, C. C. Anderson, was a charismatic leader and retailing innovator. For example, C. C. Anderson's was the first U.S. retail chain to provide refunds to dissatisfied customers. The stores also operated with low profit margins and frequent turnover of merchandise.

Allied Stores was a national chain and one of the early consolidators in the retail industry. When Allied acquired C. C. Anderson's, it already owned The Bon Marché, a Seattle-based department store chain. Since they operated in the same geographical region, the two chains were merged within the Allied Stores system when C. C.'s was acquired. This meant the two chains continued to operate their stores independently, but they shared purchasing and distribution systems.

Tom had learned some of the Allied Stores and C. C. Anderson's accounting procedures while working at the Logan store, but there was still much to absorb. Fortunately, Tom made an immediate connection with his new boss, Bill Proudfoot, who was the manager of C. C.'s auditing department. Tom recognized in Bill someone who knew how to get things done at the corporate offices and who was willing to mentor him. Bill saw in Tom someone who could learn quickly and who was also loyal, honest, and hardworking. Both their strengths and personalities were well matched.

Not only did Tom and Bill make a strong team at work, but they also became close friends. An after-work activity that the two men bonded over was playing horseshoes. Tom had played the game often on Saturday afternoons with his family in Logan Canyon, but Bill was better. It probably was good for Tom's career that he was good enough to make the games competitive but that he regularly lost to his boss.

Bill Proudfoot was also better than Tom at networking. As soon as Tom received his first promotion to internal auditor, Bill began taking him to the corporate dining room and insisting he sit at the executive table with the vice presidents and directors. At first, Tom was uncomfortable and not particularly excited about the topics of conversation, which always focused on the retail business. Tom told Bill that if they couldn't convince the other executives to discuss sports instead of business, he would probably go back to eating by himself. With Bill's encouragement, however, Tom continued to eat at the executive table, and in time he came to enjoy talking about business almost as much as sports.

Shocking News from Logan

On February 6, 1951, while Tom was working in his office, Bill Proudfoot appeared in the doorway and told him that his uncle was on the telephone. It was Uncle Alma Sonne, who called to tell Tom that his mother had just passed away. Tom knew that his mother had aged during the years he and Ted had served in the military, but the news came as a complete shock to him. He returned to his desk, put away the work he'd been doing, and drove home to tell Virginia. They packed the Plymouth, awakened Barbara from her nap, and within an hour were on their way to Logan.

Nora Perry died of a heart attack only two weeks after her sixty-third birthday. Her funeral was held Friday, February 9, in the chapel built while her husband served as the bishop of the Logan Ninth Ward.[3] The *Logan Herald Journal* noted that the number of people attending her funeral could have filled the Logan Tabernacle, but it was more fitting for the funeral to be held in the chapel where she and her husband had served so faithfully.

Elray L. Christiansen, president of the Logan Temple, spoke at the service. About Nora he said: "If ever there was a person who stood for right, for decency, and for the highest qualities of life, it was Nora Sonne Perry, and her love, trust, and confidence in her Maker was unshakeable. She did not doubt, she did not argue. Her goodness, her smile, and her friendliness were indeed beautiful to behold. Her love and faith in her wonderful family were an inspiration to each one of them."

While Tom was serving with the marines on Saipan, he wrote a letter to his mother for Mother's Day 1945. In the letter, dated May 3, he revealed the depth of his gratitude and how much he missed his mother. He especially appreciated all she had done to mold his character by her example and the expectations she set for all her children. Tom wrote:

Dear Mom,

For the last three or I guess I should say four years I have had the great misfortune of having to spend Mother's Day away from you. Each year I have wanted to be with you and tell you just how I feel and how much I think of you, but since it is once again impossible I will have to do the next best thing and send my thoughts through the mail.

This year more than any of the other three I can see just what having a wonderful mother has done for me. First of all, I miss the little things you used to do for me. Whenever I got out of bed in the morning I never had to worry about whether I had a clean shirt and clean socks. All that I had to do is open a drawer and I would find them. At meal time I always knew that I would find something I liked prepared the best way possible. At night I always knew that I would find clean sheets on my bed and just the right amount of covers to keep me very comfortable. Living at home was really a great pleasure.

But deeper is the feeling for you because of the example you set for me. I was never told that I had to get out of bed Sunday morning and attend church, and, yet, I always did because I always knew that both you and dad would be going, and I was always proud to be seen with the two of you. When I came in late from a date, you didn't ask me what I had been doing. You always trusted me when I was away from home, and because of the trust you had in me I always tried to do the things you would have wanted me to do. I was never told not to drink and smoke, and, yet, I could see how much better you got along without them. Life was made so enjoyable for us as a family that we wanted to follow in your footsteps, to continue on through experiencing the same joy that had been ours in our younger days. You always found time to take the family into the canyon at least once a week, and we could count on you to do anything from climbing mountains to playing ball with us. You and dad were never going on vacations alone. The family was always with you. Why should we seek amusements of a lower class when you were supplying our fun for us? I was always looking forward to my Saturday afternoons because I knew that they would be spent with the family. Now that I am away from home I always like to talk about my home life because it was so enjoyable. I couldn't turn from your teachings now because my actions would reflect on your character. Life is a great challenge to me to be worthy to be called the son of Mrs. L. Tom Perry. I am very proud of this title, and I hope that I will always be worthy of it.

I must close now and get ready to attend our Thursday night meeting.

I hope that next year finds me with you to show you the good time I have been planning to show you on Mother's Day for the past four years.

May the Lord bless you for all the wonderful things you have done for this troubled world.

All my love,

Tom

Tom found it difficult to wrap his mind around his mother's death. Even when he was far away from home, she had been an integral part of his life. Moreover, except for his mission and military service, he had either lived at home or next door to her his entire life until the move to Boise only a month before her death.

Tom was concerned about his father, who seemed lost and visibly shaken by the death of his eternal companion. He was a strong man who had met many challenges and endured several hardships in his life, but he felt an indescribable emptiness without Nora by his side. As president of the Logan Cache Stake, he had the responsibility to "succor the weak, lift up the hands which hang down, and strengthen the feeble knees,"[4] but the prospect of doing it alone seemed impossible.

While peace and consolation came slowly to Tom's father, it did come with time. In his life history, he wrote briefly about the period following Nora's death:

"After her death on February 6, 1951, she often came to console me. I felt her presence as strong and as certain as I ever felt it during life. She prompted my thoughts and actions. I consulted with her more after death than I ever did in life and knew when she approved and disapproved of my acts.

"On one occasion soon after her demise, while seated with Zada's family in Mesa, Arizona, a sudden peace came over our gathering. It is impossible to describe. I knew her as I have never known another woman. I am positive she was with us. I could not have been mistaken."[5]

The Final Days of Virginia's Pregnancy

When Barbara was born, Virginia's obstetrician had been Dr. George Gasser, a young physician who had been in practice in Logan only a short time. Barbara's birth had been a good experience for Virginia, and when she became pregnant again, she returned to Dr. Gasser's care. The decision to move to Boise came in the middle of the pregnancy, and Tom and Virginia decided it would be better for her to return to Logan in time for the baby to be delivered by Dr. Gasser than to find a new obstetrician in Boise. An additional consideration made this the obvious course. Virginia had a rare blood type—she was AB negative. Barbara was born with a positive Rh factor with no complications, but the development of antibodies in the first pregnancy can make the second and subsequent pregnancies problematic. Today medical treatments have mostly eliminated Rh disease,[6] but in 1951, such treatments did not exist, and the situation was considered dangerous. This concern was central to Tom and Virginia's decision that she remain under Dr. Gasser's attentive care.

Virginia returned to live in Hyde Park in mid-April 1951, near the beginning of her ninth month of pregnancy. This separation began a series of letters between Tom and Virginia that are tender expressions of their feelings for each other, Barbara, and eventually their new baby. In his first letter to Virginia, dated April 19, Tom wrote: "It is a very sad man who is writing you tonight. I never thought that I could be so lonesome. I would be willing to trade this house for a tent tonight if I could have you and Barbara with me."

In the same letter, Tom shared the schedule of his typical day. He wrote:

6:00 to 7:00 Out working in the yard.

7:00 to 7:30 Prepare and eat a breakfast of 1 orange, one egg, a dish of cornflakes, and a piece of cake.

7:30 to 8:15 I get ready for work and run to the bus stop.

8:15 to 12:30 I am either riding the bus or working.

12:30 to 1:00 I eat at C. C.'s, costing between 55¢ and 65¢ depending on whether I have the vegetable plate or a piece of meat.

1:00 to 6:15 At work again.

6:15 to 8:30 I am either riding the bus or working in the yard.

8:30 to 9:00 I eat a bowl of bread and milk and two pieces of cake while I read the paper.[7]

Most of the rest of Tom's letter described his work in the yard planting grass and building a fence. He also noted, however, the significance of the day—April 19 was the fourth anniversary of the day he asked Virginia to marry him.

In Virginia's letter to Tom, also dated April 19, she offered a peek into what Barbara was doing:

"Barbara looks out the window every now and then and calls, 'Dad!' She went with daddy [her Grandfather Lee] to feed the chickens and gather eggs and came tripping back all excited with a small egg about twice the size of a robin's egg. She wouldn't give it up and for about an hour went bouncing around while we held our breath for fear she would drop it any minute. Finally, when we had begun to relax a little, she let it slip and cracked it. Daddy lets her throw the wheat to the chickens and they practically eat out of her hands."

In another letter, dated April 22, Virginia wrote these words to Tom:

"I realize how fortunate and privileged I am to have such a fine husband. It makes me feel all warm and secure inside. If we have a son this time, my fondest desire will be to have him grow up to be a man just like his father."[8]

"Push-shot" Perry

A baby son was born to Tom and Virginia on April 29, 1951, at 1:57 p.m. Tom answered the telephone on Saturday, April 28, at a little after 5:00 p.m. Virginia was on the other end of the line, and all she said was, "Come quick!" Tom boarded the 10:35 p.m. train to Logan, spent a mostly sleepless night in transit, and arrived at Cache Junction at 6:30 a.m., where Vernal Seamons, his brother-in-law, picked him up and drove him to the Logan LDS Hospital. When Dr. Gasser saw Tom and briefed him on Virginia's progress, he assured him that he had arrived in plenty of time. Seeing how tired the prospective father looked, Dr. Gasser escorted him to a small couch in his office and advised him to get some sleep. The next thing Tom was aware of was being awakened at slightly after 2:00 p.m. and being handed a new baby boy wrapped in a baby-blue blanket. Tom then took the baby to Virginia in her hospital room.

Tom needed to return to work in Boise, so he caught a train Monday evening, April 30. He worked all day Tuesday, May 1, but in the evening he wrote a letter to Virginia to share some of his feelings. He began the letter with these words:

"I have never been an overly sentimental fellow. I have always taken things as they would come without giving praise and credit to those who have brought so much joy into my life, but last night as I left my family in Logan I got so choked up inside I could hardly say goodbye. I wish that I had a wire recording of my thoughts as I rode on the train last night. Maybe then you would get a small idea of how much I think of my family.

"You will never know how much I hated to leave Logan last night and come to Boise alone. First it was saying goodbye to you at the hospital, and then in Hyde Park little Barbara seemed to know from the time I stepped into the door that I was leaving again. She would cry every time that I wasn't with her. It was a wonderful feeling to know that you have a wife and a child who want you near. Even though we are only separated for a short time, each day seems so long when we are not together. I surely love my little family. Words can't express my feelings for a wonderful wife who seems to have a heavenly influence radiating from her. May all of my children be blessed with the same sweet spirit of their mother."

The next night, Wednesday, May 2, Tom wrote another letter in which he recounted his experiences surrounding his son's birth. At the end of the letter he wrote: "A sign now stands in front of the little white house at 2805 Palouse. It reads, 'Wanted to buy a hoop, a basketball, and a garage to anchor them to. This is the future home of the famous Push-shot Perry.'"

Complications

In a letter to Tom dated Sunday, May 6, Virginia reported on Barbara's reaction to her mother coming home with a new baby. She wrote:

"Barbara squealed and hopped around when I brought the baby from the hospital, and then she was bound she was going to take him. When she wasn't allowed to do so, she was quite upset and didn't want me to hold him either. She is becoming better adjusted and more used to having him around each day. She likes to stand on tiptoe and peer over the side of his crib. Now, whenever he cries, she rushes to get hold of my finger and leads me to him."

Dr. Gasser went to New York after the baby was born to take an obstetrics/gynecology certification exam on May 2, and he left Virginia under the care of his older partner, Dr. Wendell. Dr. Wendell advised Virginia to wait a few weeks before returning to Boise, if possible. Because he was her doctor, he was concerned mostly about her health, but he also wanted to be certain the baby did not have Rh disease.

Virginia described early signs of the baby's demanding personality in a letter to Tom on Friday, May 11. She wrote: "Don't be expecting another nice, quiet baby like Barbara was because this boy really has a set of lungs and he doesn't hesitate to use them. He insists on having his nightly feeding right on the hour. He's really a fine boy, though."

Virginia wrote a long letter to Tom dated Tuesday, May 15, in which she tried to reassure him but also provided a detailed description of complications with the baby's health. She had noticed a few days earlier that the baby's color had turned slightly yellow—a sign of jaundice. At a scheduled appointment with the baby's pediatrician, Dr. Barlow, on Friday, May 11, he did not think it was anything to be concerned about. He believed it was too late for the development of Rh disease, and the baby was otherwise extremely healthy. He instructed Virginia, however, to watch him closely over the weekend.

The baby's color became worse over the weekend, and when Dr. Barlow saw him Monday afternoon, he agreed there was a problem. He tested the baby's blood, and the test confirmed Rh disease. He gave the baby a shot and some drops for his eyes, and he told Virginia to bring him back on Thursday if his jaundice had not cleared up.

Tom was expecting to pick up Virginia, Barbara, and the baby on the weekend and take them back to Boise, but those plans were delayed several weeks. The baby had to receive several transfusions in Logan, and still his symptoms persisted. Finally, in early June, Tom and Virginia decided their baby boy could be treated just as well in Boise as in Logan, and it was time for their family to be reunited. Tom drove down to Logan for a long weekend and brought his family home.

The pediatrician in Boise was able to turn around the baby's health quickly. On Sunday, July 1, the baby was well enough to be given his name, Lee Tom Perry,[9] and a blessing. Lee had gained so much weight by this time that Tom felt embarrassed about blessing such a large baby.[10] His embarrassment was short-lived, however, because it would be decades before he attended church again in Boise. He left after the evening service to drive upstate to Lewiston, Idaho, where he was expected to report to work at the C. C. Anderson store. Tom had been transferred out of the Boise office.

CHAPTER 16

LEWISTON, IDAHO, AND CLARKSTON, WASHINGTON

Until 1951 each of C. C. Anderson's stores had a store manager and an assistant store manager but not a controller. Most of the accounting function was managed centrally at the company's Boise headquarters. Soon after Tom went to work for C. C.'s, however, a decision was made to decentralize much of the accounting function and place controllers in each of the chain's stores. Tom was given several options, including returning to Logan, but he chose the Lewiston, Idaho, store. The communities of Lewiston, Idaho, and Clarkston, Washington, were about three hundred miles north of Boise, and the store in Lewiston was one of the largest in the C. C. Anderson chain.

Given all the commotion surrounding Lee's birth, the associated medical complications, and the suddenness of the transfer to Lewiston, Tom and Virginia decided it was best for her to stay behind in Boise for a few weeks. Tom could look at homes to buy in Lewiston while Virginia worked with a realtor to sell their home in Boise.

Tom left immediately after the fast and testimony meeting in which Lee was blessed,[1] and he drove to Lewiston with another C. C. auditor. The other auditor was going to help Tom set up a separate general ledger for the Lewiston store and then return to Boise. Tom knew setting up the separate general ledger and installing a new accounting system for the store would be a major undertaking, and he was happy to have another person to help.

Tom and Virginia had only one car, the 1950 Plymouth they had brought from Logan to Boise. The other auditor volunteered to drive his car to Lewiston, and Tom was happy to accept his offer so he could leave the Plymouth with Virginia. Tom learned after the first few miles of driving with the other auditor that he had just purchased his first car, and he was still learning how to drive. After about fifty miles of the three hundred-mile drive, Tom convinced him to let him take a turn at the wheel, and he drove the rest of the way to Lewiston. They arrived at 3:00 a.m. and checked into a motel.

Tom and the other auditor got only a few hours of sleep before reporting to work the next morning. Installing the new accounting system proved to be more challenging than expected. This, of course, was long before today's point-of-sale accounting systems that update financial information automatically with each customer transaction. The cash registers in the Lewiston store were not connected, and there was not a centralized database. The general ledger was a book, and with the assistance of an adding machine, someone would enter each line of sales information by hand. Reconciling the books was not automatic—it was done by adding columns and rows of figures with the hope of arriving at the same total.

With two people it was possible for one of them to focus on setting up the separate general ledger based on year-to-date information and the other to update the year-to-date information with the daily sales totals. There was also extensive training to do with the sales staff so they would follow the control procedures as defined by the new accounting system. Also, as problems arose, both men could tackle them together. When the other auditor returned to Boise, however, Tom was left with everything, and he found it extremely difficult to keep up. Because he was in Lewiston alone, he started a pattern of working a day, a night, and a day, before taking a night off, hoping he could get the system running as it should.

There was another challenge at the Lewiston store. The store manager and Tom's immediate boss was Frank Fish. Tom and Frank formed a close working relationship, but Frank had a drinking problem. Occasionally Frank would arrive at the store in the morning with a hangover. If it was a particularly bad hangover, he would sleep at his desk for much of the morning. Because his office had a large window overlooking the sales floor, he was in full view of both the sales staff and the store's customers. It is a tribute to Tom that he was able to raise this delicate subject with Frank and gently convince him that it would be better if he slept off his occasional hangovers in an empty office in the back.

Back in Boise, Virginia was able to find a young couple who wanted to buy their home, but the buyers did not have a down payment saved. The only way they could purchase the house was on contract. Tom and Virginia decided to accept their offer, mostly because they didn't want to be separated any longer. They knew that until they cashed out of the Boise home, however, they would be renters, not homeowners.[2] Tom stopped looking for a home to buy, and he found an apartment. Three weeks passed before Tom returned to Boise on a weekend to move his family and possessions to Lewiston.

Virginia did not like the apartment in Lewiston that Tom had found, and they quickly moved to an apartment in Clarkston. Tom told Virginia about his workload and his intention to continue his routine of sleeping at home every other night. Virginia was against the idea, mostly out of concern for his health. But she also wanted more help from Tom with moving in and caring for Barbara and Lee. In addition, she worried that Tom was working so hard that he was losing perspective and balance in his life.

The Lewiston Ward Bishopric

Tom and Virginia negotiated a compromise. Tom would come home every night for dinner with the family, and after helping put the children to bed, he would return to the store if needed. This was the arrangement the whole time they lived in their Clarkston apartment, although Tom gradually worked fewer late nights by the time they moved from the apartment to a rental home, also in Clarkston.

Soon after moving into the rental home, Tom was having dinner with the family, fully intending to return to the store later, when there was an unexpected knock at the door. Tom opened the door to a man who introduced himself as a counselor in the stake presidency.[3] He invited Tom to come out to his car for a brief visit. Inside the car was another man—David Barker. Tom recognized Brother Barker as a member of the Lewiston Ward bishopric. The counselor in the stake presidency informed Tom that there was to be a change in the Lewiston Ward bishopric the coming Sunday. Brother Barker had been called as the new bishop, and his first counselor was to be Cleon Seipert. Then the counselor in the stake presidency deferred to newly called Bishop Barker, who asked Tom to serve as his second counselor.

The call to the Lewiston Ward bishopric caught Tom completely off guard. He understood the demands of such a calling, given that his father had served as a bishop for eighteen years. He also knew he needed to accept the call, but with the demands of work and family, he did not know how he was going to squeeze it into his life. He knew he couldn't function on any less sleep, and the other hours of the day and night were packed.

The new bishopric was sustained on Sunday as planned. Afterward, Tom was ordained a high priest and set apart as the second counselor by Elder Harold B. Lee of the Quorum of the Twelve when he came to the area for a stake conference. In a letter to Tom's father, Virginia recalled the blessing given to Tom by Elder Lee. She wrote:

"He [Tom] received a most wonderful and inspirational blessing. It sounded so native to Tom, as though Elder Lee was very well acquainted with him. He spoke of his sense of humor and his ability to make friends. Tom was told that he would be a peacemaker and a means of bringing unity to the ward. . . . All in all, it was a wonderful blessing and one could not help but know Elder Lee was inspired. I was very grateful that the wives of the new bishopric were asked to be present."

Virginia also noted in the letter that as soon as Tom gave his name, Elder Lee said, "That sounds like Logan."

Bishop Barker may have sensed that Tom felt overwhelmed by his new calling. After all, he was feeling a little overwhelmed too. He started the first meeting of their new bishopric by sharing a leadership insight based on the Old Testament story of Jethro visiting his son-in-law, Moses, in the wilderness. Moses had lived with Jethro, a holder of the Melchizedek Priesthood, for forty years. Jethro ordained Moses to the greater priesthood and loved him like a son. As Bishop Barker explained it, however, Jethro was dismayed by what he observed the next day in the Israelite camp near the base of Mount Sinai. The people were coming to Moses early in the morning, with many of them waiting until evening, to inquire of God through Moses. The way Moses was leading his people befuddled Jethro. He asked his son-in-law: "What is this thing that thou doest to the people? Why sittest thou thyself alone, and all the people stand by thee from morning until evening?"[4]

Moses tried to explain, but a skeptical Jethro offered his feedback. He said: "The thing that thou doest is not good. Thou wilt surely wear away, both thou, and this people that is with thee: for this thing is too heavy for thee; thou art not able to perform it thyself alone."[5]

Then Bishop Barker taught his two counselors about the principle of delegation. It was the same simple idea that Jethro had shared with Moses—to organize with rulers of thousands, hundreds, fifties, and tens.[6]

Bishop Barker's insight was an epiphany for Tom. He embraced the principle of delegation, and he observed how Bishop Barker delegated responsibilities to him to learn more about the principle. The changes were not automatic—it was not as if a button were pushed and everything changed in an instant. Still, Tom recognized that he had not been an effective delegator, and he needed to learn how to delegate better to restore balance in his life. He recognized that he would "surely wear away" unless he shared more of his workload.

Evidence suggests that Virginia's encouragement also hastened Tom's transformation into an effective delegator. While Virginia was supportive of Tom's career, she was unwilling to allow him to sacrifice his health and family for it. For example, in a letter Tom wrote to his father on January 11, 1953, we see

Virginia asserting herself when her husband caught pneumonia. Tom wrote:

"I'm right in the middle of cleaning up a big December business and inventory, and year-end closing [is] only two weeks away. I have been forced to take a week's vacation. I caught a cold about three weeks ago when the Xmas pace was at its peak, and I couldn't take thc time to check it. After three weeks of trying to get rid of it, I went to the doctor to see if a shot would aid the process. He listened to my story, took an x-ray, and announced that I had been running around with pneumonia for three weeks. He wouldn't even allow me to go back to the office to clean off my desk.

"I feel good enough to be at work. It must be a very light case. Virginia is really up in arms about me staying on the job until I allowed myself to get in this condition. I don't know if she will allow me to go back to work again this spring. She is insisting that I do everything the doctor ordered, including getting us up every morning at 3:00 a.m. to take a handful of pills."

In the same letter, Tom even did some soul-searching about the demands of his job. He wrote: "This retail business is really a fight. It doesn't give you much time for anything else. If you ever make the grade, I guess there isn't a better field for getting a good return for your hours. Sometimes I wonder if it's worth all the demands it makes on your time. But then I always end up with the conclusion that there isn't such a thing as a job with a future that doesn't require many hours of hard work."

Church and Work

As Tom's capacity to manage a greater workload increased, he always seemed to be given more responsibility at the Lewiston store. Perhaps the retail business felt to Tom like the country the Red Queen described to Alice in Lewis Carroll's

Through the Looking Glass. She said: "Now, here, you see, it takes all the running you can do, to keep in the same place. If you want to get somewhere else, you must run at least twice as fast as that!"[7]

Just as Tom started to shorten his hours at work, C. C. Anderson's decided it could eliminate the position of assistant store manager in many of its stores and shift responsibilities to the store controller. On the mornings when Frank Fish was not at his best, Tom was left to run the store mostly by himself.

Although the times Tom was left to run the Lewiston store temporarily stretched him, they provided invaluable training that he was able to apply throughout his career in the retail industry. In Lewiston he gained firsthand experience with all store operations, from receiving and stocking merchandise, to hiring and training all store personnel to managing the office. More important, he learned how to build morale in a store that had a history of morale problems. He would challenge sales people to reach goals. He would ask the more successful sales people to share the keys of their success with others. He focused on teams of people working together to help the store perform better, and under Tom's leadership, it did. Something Tom especially liked about retailing was that a store's sales made it relatively clear whether the store was doing better or worse than it had been. The key to Tom's annual bonuses was beating last year's sales numbers, and the Lewiston store consistently did that during the three and a half years he was there.

Because he received little mentoring at work, Tom began to apply more and more lessons from his Church service to his job. For example, the delegating skills he learned from Bishop Barker as they served together in the Lewiston Ward bishopric were transferable to working with his direct reports at the Lewiston store. Tom also learned to apply the principles of stewardship and accountability when he met with department managers and talked about beating last year's numbers and reaching sales targets. There were still many aspects of the retail industry that Tom had to learn by trial and error, especially the details of store operations. Still, the success he experienced at the Lewiston store had far more to do with the human side of the enterprise, and the people skills he learned from serving in the Church became the cornerstones of his managerial style. It was a managerial style that emphasized multiplying the talents of individuals to improve overall performance.

A Family Man

As Tom learned how to better manage the demands of work and church, he devoted more and more time to his family. Certainly, Virginia's encouragement helped steer Tom in this direction, but it was also the examples of the other young couples in the Lewiston Ward. Tom saw the balance in their lives, and he decided he needed to do better in his own life. Moreover, Tom and Virginia loved being with the other young couples in the Lewiston Ward—the Barkers and Seiperts, of course, but also the Kilfoyles and Cashes. Not only did they do family activities together, such as ward picnics, but they also went dancing as couples.[8] This was the big band era, and all the great bands toured the country and played live music for dances, even in remote places like Lewiston, Idaho.

Tom also began to realize this was a critical time for him and Virginia to establish family patterns and expectations for the rest of their married life. Until they moved to Boise, they had lived too close to parents to become completely independent as a family. The time in Boise was too short and chaotic for them to settle into any kind of a routine. And though the Lewiston and Clarkston period brought all the demands of adult life, it also offered their young family three and a half years to settle down and find balance.

Also, their children were growing up and showing more and more of their personalities. For example, Tom described their 1952 Christmas in the letter he wrote to his father on January 11, 1953:

"We had a very enjoyable Christmas this year. The kids are becoming more fun each year. I got out of bed, first, Xmas morning and situated myself behind the tree in order to catch the first appearance of the children as they came from the bedroom. I sent Virginia in to send them out together. The plan didn't work the best. Lee had an idea that something was up, and as soon as Virginia set him on the floor he raced for the living room. The first thing that came into his reach was Barbara's doll. He picked it up and ran into the bedroom, gave it to Barbara and was back at the tree before Barbara and her mother made an appearance. I don't believe that I managed to get both of them in the same picture all morning."

Some family traditions did not work out as well as others. For example, Tom, following the example of his father, decided to purchase part interest in a dairy cow with a neighbor. When Lee was three, Tom tried to teach him how to milk the cow. Lee caught on quickly to the hand action of a fine milker, but his aim was not very good. Whenever Lee was left alone to milk the cow, the bucket did not get very full, and there was usually a large white puddle of milk around it. Lee, of course, was just as proud of the big white puddle he'd created as he was of the milk in the bucket.

Tom also tried to turn Lee into a gardener. He assumed three-year-old Lee had a height advantage for pulling weeds. Unfortunately, Lee was more interested in pulling young garden plants than weeds. Instead of a neat row of carrots, the result of Lee's weeding was a neat row of weeds. The carrot plants, after all, had more interesting orange roots.

Another frustration with Lee was he was difficult to get to sleep. While they lived in the Clarkston apartment, Tom would place Lee in his crib and sit in a chair while Lee cried himself to sleep. The window in Lee's bedroom that was opposite the chair in which Tom sat looked straight out onto the Clarkston High School football field. On game nights, Tom did not mind staying in Lee's bedroom for a long time while waiting for him to go to sleep. On other nights, however, there usually wasn't much activity on the field, and so Tom would try to crawl out of the bedroom as soon as possible without disturbing Lee's sleep. Any small noise seemed to wake Lee up, however, and Tom would need to return to the chair to stop him from crying.

There was another interesting issue related to living in an apartment complex across the street from the Clarkston High School football field. The football coach's name was also Tom Perry, and he lived in the same apartment complex. Whenever Clarkston lost, irate boosters and parents would often call Tom to complain about the game. There were two listings for Tom Perry in the phone book, but Tom's name and phone number were listed first, and most people did not notice the second listing. They naturally assumed he was the same Tom Perry they wanted to criticize for what they considered dubious coaching decisions.

Tom and Virginia enjoyed going to movies, and during the summer months they were always on the lookout for a movie they wanted to see at the drive-in theater. The beauty of drive-in movies is that Tom and Virginia didn't need a babysitter. They arranged a mattress in the backseat of their 1950 Plymouth for Barbara and Lee, who saw the beginning of a lot of movies but rarely the end.

An investment opportunity presented itself in the summer of 1954 that was exciting enough that Tom wrote home about it. The members of the Lewiston Ward bishopric decided to buy a small cottage at Lake Chatcolet, Idaho. Bishop Barker's boss had previously owned the cottage, which was built in a state park, so he held the deed to the cottage, but land was leased from the state. When his boss decided to purchase a larger cottage in the same area, he approached Bishop Barker about buying the smaller cottage. It was necessary for his boss to sell the smaller cottage quickly in order to purchase the larger one because the stake park allowed a person to hold only one land-lease. Bishop Barker asked his counselors if they wanted to purchase the cottage with him, and they both jumped at the opportunity.

In a July 28, 1954, letter to his father, Tom described the cottage and invited family members to drive up and use it. He wrote:

"We have just completed a real estate transaction that I am sure will create the proper desire for our relatives to make a visit to our part of the country. Last evening I made a down payment or I should say my share of the down payment on a little cottage on Lake Chatcolet. This lake is located in the tall pine Coeur d'Alene Lakes region. Not even Yellowstone Lake has the pines that this area has. The cottage is not an overly fancy affair, but it is very comfortable with two bedrooms (four beds), a kitchen, and two bathrooms. Of course, it has running water, a shower, and a hot water heater. The cottage came complete with the furniture, dishes, pans, etc. It was all ready [for us] to go up and move in. The nice part of it is that it is just a two-hour drive from Lewiston."[9]

Tom did not mention in his letter the cottage's most distinctive feature. It had a live tree growing in the middle of one of its bathrooms.

An important family event occurred while Tom and his family lived in Clarkston. His father remarried on October 22, 1952, approximately twenty months after Nora's death. He had met Eunice Woodruff in April 1952 when he accompanied her to Blackfoot, Idaho, on a business trip. He first became interested in her life story, as a granddaughter of President Wilford Woodruff, and later in her. After they were married, they lived for many years in a home across the street from the Logan Temple.[10]

A New Career Opportunity

Bill Proudfoot had left C. C. Anderson's to become the controller of Weinstock Lubin & Company's Sacramento, California, division. He had stayed in touch with Tom, however, and knew about his success with C. C.'s Lewiston store. Weinstock Lubin was part of the Broadway-Hale department store chain, and when the controller of the Hale's division in the chain was promoted to the corporate offices in San Francisco, Bill recommended that Tom be interviewed to replace him. After the interview, Tom was offered the job at nearly three times his salary at C. C.'s. It was an offer he couldn't refuse.

Tom and Virginia had attached themselves to the Lewiston-Clarkston community. Barbara and Lee hated to leave the close friends they had made in their neighborhood—especially the Carlson children, the daughter and son of the jeweler at C. C.'s Lewiston store, who lived only a street away from them. Clearly the hardest part of leaving Lewiston-Clarkston for Tom was leaving the Lewiston Ward, especially his calling in the bishopric. In the October 1982 general conference, as he taught about the calling of a bishop, Elder Perry spoke about his deep feelings for the other two men in the Lewiston Ward bishopric. He said:

"It was with deep sorrow that I left the association of this bishopric. On our final night in the community in which we were living, they held a party. To avoid saying good-bye, we slipped away from the party before it was over and went to stay at a friend's home. The bishop and the other counselor I had been serving with came over when the party concluded and sat up all night while we rested, awaiting our early departure, so that we would not leave without the proper farewell. With a big lump in my throat, I said good-bye to these two brethren as I went on to other assignments."[11]

CHAPTER 17

SACRAMENTO, CALIFORNIA

Tom and Virginia had a difficult time finding a house to rent in Sacramento. Eventually, they settled in North Sacramento at 1117 Singingwood Road. Tom's chief complaint about the home in a letter to his father, dated January 10, 1955, was that it already had appliances, and so they needed to store their almost-new refrigerator, washer, and dryer in the garage.

In the same letter, he described his new job at the Hale's store in downtown Sacramento:

"The store had as much in sales during December as we had in Lewiston all year. From what I have been able to see of the job, I sit around and let someone else do all the work, and I just make plans and [do] analysis. It is so different, I am completely lost."

In a letter to his sister Gay a few months later, Tom said this about his new job:

"I have been able to keep my head above water on the job so far. It should be the best opportunity for self-development I will ever have. If I can master this job, I should be on top of the world. If I fail, I guess I can always go back to school teaching."[1]

Fortunately, the Sacramento store manager, Bill Ahern, was a great manager and merchandiser. He recognized Tom's potential, and he took him under his wing and mentored him. Bill had an eye for buying merchandise that would sell in the Hale's store, whether it was appliances or women's apparel. He knew how to display merchandise in the store in the most inviting ways. He also knew how to build an organization and motivate people. Most important, he could communicate his insights to others in ways they could quickly understand. He may have been the perfect boss for Tom at this stage of his career, and together Tom and Bill became a powerful team.

While Tom and Virginia had enjoyed their time in the Lewiston, Idaho–Clarkston, Washington, area, they quickly fell in love with Sacramento. The people were friendly. It was a city filled with energy. Everything about Sacramento seemed to move at a faster pace than in Lewiston. The area was growing quickly—like other California cities, it was filled with cars driving on fast highways. The weather was wonderful, although a little too hot in the summertime.[2] The daytime heat, however, was mitigated by what was locally known as the delta breeze, which originated in the evening from the southwest, off the delta of the Sacramento River. Tom loved sitting outside in the evening in Sacramento and feeling the breeze push the hot air out of the valley. Nearly every summer evening in Sacramento was idyllic.

Soon after they had arrived in North Sacramento, Virginia's talents were recognized. She was called as the Primary president of the Arden Ward by Bishop Elwood (Woodie) Stentzel. Tom made an interesting connection between his desire to buy a TV and Virginia's Primary calling in an April 8, 1955, letter to his sister Gay and her family. He wrote:

"I have been trying to talk Virginia into letting me have one [a TV]. She believes that we are together such a few hours each day that with a TV set we would hardly speak to each other. Since they put her in as Primary President, I never see her anyway. As I come in the door, she goes out with her Primary workers."

It was only a few months later, during the fall of 1955, that Bishop Stentzel asked Virginia to leave the Primary to become the president of the YWMIA. In a December 1, 1955, letter to Bishop Stentzel that Virginia never mailed, she described an internal struggle she was experiencing between the demands of her new calling and her role as a mother:

"During the past few days, I have had somewhat of a struggle with myself in trying to determine where my responsibility lies. This [holiday] season is such a busy one for Tom—he is seldom home. In trying to carry on my M.I.A. activities, we have problems concerning the car, baby-sitters, their transportation, etc.—small problems, really. I am certain they must seem very trivial to you when you are carrying such a great responsibility; but lately, to me, they have loomed rather big in trying to sustain a normal home life. I do have the full support and cooperation of my husband, and he encourages and aids me in my church activities. Sometimes, however, when he is so busy, it seems my place in the evenings should be with our children."

Virginia then told Bishop Stentzel how much his initial visit to their home in early 1955 and, subsequently, her brief call in the Primary had meant to her. She had not been well acquainted with Bishop Stentzel prior to his visit, but during the visit he felt "like an old and trusted friend."

Virginia then confided in her bishop how difficult it was for her to be a ward leader and especially how the spirit she had felt during his short visit to their home had sustained her through even the most difficult times. She wrote:

"Only because of this humbling experience have I been able to respond to the calls of service which I have received in this ward. Since then, there has never been any question in my mind as to your position as the Father of the Arden Ward. Sometimes, I am still easily discouraged. The role of leadership is new to me, having always shunned responsibility. My callings here have come as a blow and a shock as I have realized their utter seriousness. However, I am beginning to realize that only by activity and accepting responsibilities do we grow and develop, keep our faith alive and become nearer to our Heavenly Father."

Virginia wrote a closing paragraph—essentially a summary of her gratitude and an expression of Tom's and her support for their bishop. Then, after signing this letter she never sent, she adds a short handwritten postscript: "I thought I had a problem, but somewhere along the line, it seems to have disappeared. V."

When Bishop Stentzel made an urgent appeal to the members of the Arden Ward during sacrament meeting on Christmas Day 1955, Virginia was deeply touched. On the previous day, Virginia's thirty-second birthday, flooding had devastated a community about an hour north of Sacramento—the Yuba City/Marysville area—and the flood victims were in desperate need of any help members of the Church in northern California could provide. Virginia did not say anything at the moment to Tom about her thoughts and feelings, but she remembered something else she had written to Bishop Stentzel in her December 1 letter:

"I felt as though I could do anything you ask me to do. It was as though you were leading me by the hand spiritually. I believe that day, if you had asked me to give up all my material things, I could have done it. Even now, as I think about it, my heart overflows and my eyes flood with tears."

Now that Bishop Stentzel had asked the members of the Arden Ward to sacrifice, what would Virginia do? A few nights later, as Tom arrived home after work, there was a truck and trailer in the driveway, and a man, whom Tom didn't know, was in the trailer tying down several items from their home. Tom rushed into the house to see what was going on, and he was greeted by Virginia, who said, "Oh, didn't I tell you? After sacrament meeting last Sunday, I informed the bishop if anyone needed some of our things for flood relief, they could have them."

In a letter to his father dated January 30, 1956, Tom wrote:

"The damage in the towns around us was terrible. My wife felt so sorry for the people she has about broke me with her donations. She gave away the kids' bed, our refrigerator, washer, and two chairs. I have been almost afraid to go home at night for fear of finding our bed gone. Between the building fund and the flood, more cookies and cakes have gone out of her kitchen than most bakeries in town produce."

Linda Gay Perry

As it turned out, Tom and Virginia needed to buy a new set of appliances quickly. The people who had bought their home in Boise were finally able to get a mortgage, and Tom and Virginia could arrange their finances to purchase a home. They found a three-bedroom house they both loved a few miles to the east of Singingwood Road in a small development called Arden Park. The house at 3915 El Ricon Way became their home for the next six and a half years.

In front of the home at 3915 El Ricon Way was where Barbara, wearing a blue crepe paper hood and a square academic hat made mostly of white cardboard, posed after she had graduated from kindergarten. The large backyard was where Tom planted a garden and played catch with Lee more evenings than either of them could ever count. El Ricon was the street on which Lee chased and caught a banty hen and then coaxed Tom into building a chicken coup in the backyard so he could keep it. In the same backyard, Tom and Lee built a fence together. From the porch at 3915 El Ricon, the Perrys watched two floods turn their street into a river. During one of the floods, rescuers tied a rowboat up to their lamppost; during the other, Tom bravely waded through the water to unplug the freezer in the garage. It was the home they remodeled to turn a patio into a family/TV room. In the kitchen, Virginia cooked plum pudding for Christmas, a turkey for Thanksgiving, as well as Tom's favorites, like rice pudding and pea soup. It was at the home's kitchen sink that Barbara washed the dishes most nights and Lee dried them. Most important, 3915 El Ricon Way was where Tom and Virginia brought home a new baby girl, Linda Gay Perry.

Linda was born March 9, 1958, approximately six weeks premature. Hattie Lee, Virginia's mother, had come early to be with her daughter and help her before and after the birth. Virginia's father, John E. Lee, had died on April 23, 1957, and Hattie arrived two months early partly because she was lonely and wanted her youngest daughter's company. As things turned out, her early arrival was fortunate.

Sunday, March 9, 1958, was the day the North Sacramento Stake held its stake conference at the California State Fair grounds. Tom went with Barbara and Lee to the stake conference, which was presided over by Elder Harold B. Lee. At the Sunday morning session, Tom was sustained as a member of the stake high council and was then invited to sit on the stand. Between the morning and afternoon sessions, Elder Lee set Tom apart in his new calling. Then, about halfway through the afternoon session, Tom, again sitting on the stand, received a note that said: "Your wife, Virginia, has gone to the hospital. No emergency."

Because he knew that Hattie was with Virginia at the hospital, Tom decided it was not necessary to leave the conference session early. He left after the afternoon session, just as soon as he found Barbara and Lee and told them that he was going straight to the hospital and that they needed to find another ride home. As soon as Tom arrived at the hospital, he learned the delivery had gone quicker than expected, and he was the father of a new baby girl.

Because she was so premature, Linda Gay weighed less than five pounds when she was born, and her lungs were not fully developed. As a result, she had to stay at the hospital several weeks after she was born. Hattie assumed household duties and took care of Barbara and Lee while Virginia stayed at the hospital. Filled with gratitude, relief, and joy, Tom and Virginia were finally able to bring Linda Gay home to join her adoring grandmother, older sister, and brother. She was a beautiful and delightful baby. It was Hattie who first realized Linda Gay bore a striking resemblance to Virginia.

Linda gave her family another scare when she was around a year old. She contracted encephalitis and needed to be hospitalized and quarantined for over a week. Virginia and Tom would go to the hospital but could watch Linda only from a distance as she stood in her crib and cried. They felt completely helpless while their darling baby girl suffered. Eventually, their prayers were heard, and Linda recovered from the serious, often fatal, illness. She returned to being her happy, sweet self as soon as she was released from the hospital and brought home.

Tom also had the horrifying experience of receiving a telephone call from the woman who was tending Linda and hearing that his little sweetheart had fallen and injured herself. At the time, Virginia, who was still the YWMIA president of the Arden Ward, was at general conference for training by the YWMIA general presidency. The woman who called Tom was the mother of Linda's best friend and playmate. Linda had been in the front yard when the trash collectors approached the house for their weekly pickup. Seeing them frightened her, and she ran toward the open garage. She tripped on the driveway on an uneven piece of concrete and fell headfirst.

When Tom arrived, he saw blood still streaming from a gash above Linda's eyebrow despite efforts to stop it by applying pressure. He raced Linda to the doctor, and she bravely received thirteen stitches to close the wound. She also had to wear a large bandage around her head, and the injured eye was swollen shut for several days.

Tom called Virginia after returning from the doctor's office, and while he was explaining the injury, she started packing her suitcase. Virginia returned on the first flight to Sacramento, and she held and caressed Linda for hours every day until she got the stitches out. Then, for years afterward, Virginia applied castor oil to Linda's scar in hopes it would fade.

Some of Linda Gay's personality is revealed in the paragraph about her in a Christmas letter to friends and family written by Virginia in December 1961. She wrote:

"Our Linda Gay (four in March) has certainly brought lots of sunshine and joy into our home. She is such a loving, lovable little girl—a real diplomat. We think she is very choice and hope we can keep her this way without spoiling her too much. She rattles on and on at home with a sort of Scandi-Germanic accent. She is not fond of Santa Claus. She went downtown to see him last year and really didn't like the looks of the old fellow very much. So this year, she insisted on dictating a letter for me to write telling him thanks for the gifts last year, but to please not come to our house this Christmas, as he might make too much noise and wake her and Barbara up. She personally made certain the letter was stamped and mailed. So—we are having our first Christmas without Santa Claus."

In an April 19, 1962, letter to his sister Mignon, Tom echoed Virginia in his description of Linda Gay. He wrote:

"Gay is really at a great age. She talks from morning to night. She makes friends with everyone she meets, and gets more attention at the store than any ten customers."

Tom capitalized on Linda Gay's universal appeal and almost launched an international modeling career when he had her pose in her Easter bonnet and dress for a Hale's advertisement in the *Sacramento Bee* just after she turned four.

Building Projects

The Church of Jesus Christ of Latter-day Saints was experiencing unprecedented growth throughout California in the 1950s and early 1960s. Virginia showed her missionary zeal near the end of the 1961 Perry family Christmas letter when she addressed members of other faiths on the family's mailing list. She wrote:

"By the way, for those of you who are non-members—'How much do you know about the Mormons? Would you like to know more?' If so, we will arrange a missionary meeting or send you a Book of Mormon. Investigate this church! With national leaders and captains of industry proclaiming its virtues, this church is enjoying its era of most rapid growth."

As the LDS Church in California grew at a rapid pace, wards and stakes were divided and new meetinghouses were built. At the time, local members of the Church were expected to raise a significant portion of the cost of new meetinghouses.

The fund-raising burden had been lightened by the Church since the time Bishop L. Tom Perry had led the efforts of the members of the Logan Ninth Ward to build a new chapel,[3] but a ward building fund project was still an immense undertaking. As with the Logan Ninth Ward chapel project, members were invited to participate in raising funds, from Primary children giving pennies to wealthier members contributing, in some cases, thousands of dollars.

Given his fond memories of building projects in Logan and on the island of Saipan, Tom embraced his assignment as the chair of the building-fund committee for a new meetinghouse to be built on Hurley Avenue in North Sacramento. He knew the assignment would be extremely demanding, but he was confident that the project, with the Lord's help, would be successful. After all, it felt as if he had been in training his entire life for such an assignment.

Tom made sure he understood everything he could about the Church's policies for ward building-fund drives. He had known since boyhood that there were three ways for members to make contributions to a ward building fund: (1) monetary contributions, (2) participation in fund-raising projects, and (3) donated labor on the building itself. His experiences with the Logan Ninth Ward chapel, built when money was especially tight in the early years of the Great Depression, gave him a special appreciation for the tremendous benefits member participation in fund-raising projects brought to ward unity.

His experiences with the Saipan chapel project had taught him about the strong bonds that are formed when people pound nails together. Tom's vision of the project involved an initial round of asking for monetary contributions, but he placed the primary emphasis on fund-raising projects and donated labor on the meetinghouse. Then, if there was still a shortfall, he would conduct a final drive for monetary contributions.

One of the major funding-raising projects in which ward members participated was providing the concessions for the California State Fair. In the April 1980 general conference, Elder Perry remembered this sweet experience. He said:

"I remember one hot summer evening when we were engaged in a ward building-fund project. We had contracted to supply the food service at a state fair. I was assigned to the dishwashing detail along with Bay Hutchings, another member of our ward. We were working across the counter from the customers who were enjoying our delicious food. There was a call from the cashier's cage: 'Dr. Hutchings, the hospital is calling you.' Suddenly, all the forks were suspended in midair. The customers turned one to another and exclaimed, 'A doctor washing dishes?' We had to immediately explain that this was a Church building-fund project. No one was being paid for his services. The waiters, cooks, dishwashers, and busboys were doctors, lawyers, merchants, chiefs—all having one great time working together for our project."[4]

When Tom worked on the building, providing his donated labor, he usually took Lee with him. In a November 9, 1959, letter to his aunt Emma Holmgren, Tom shared how much Lee enjoyed their routine of going to work on the meetinghouse from 6:00 a.m. to 9:00 a.m. every Saturday. He wrote:

"Lee has been so anxious to work on the church with me that he gets me up and going on Saturday morning. One week we were up later than usual on Friday night. To be sure that he would be ready to go on Saturday, he went to bed with his clothes on. I was sure surprised when I called him, and he jumped out of bed all ready to go."

In the same letter to Aunt Emma, Tom shared that the building was to be dedicated on November 29, 1959, and how he was certain they would raise the final eleven thousand dollars needed to complete the final building-fund drive before the meetinghouse was dedicated. He also mentioned how beautiful the building was and how he knew it would benefit the growth of the Church in Sacramento.

Tom wove together his service chairing the ward building committee with his assignment on the stake high council. Because of the large geographical size of the stake—there were units as far away from Arden Park as Placerville (forty miles) and Auburn (thirty miles)— Tom's service on the high council required a great deal of Sunday travel to fulfill speaking and other assignments. Tom decided that in order to spend more time with Lee,[5] he would take him along on many of his speaking assignments. Because Lee would often sit alone in the congregation, Tom devised an ingenious way to keep him attentive and well behaved. He enlisted Lee's help as he gave his talk. He instructed Lee to use the signs of the three monkeys, representing see no evil, hear no evil, and speak no evil. When his father was not standing straight at the pulpit, Lee would cover his eyes. When his father was speaking too loud, Lee would cover his ears. Finally, when it was time for his father to finish his talk, Lee would cover his mouth. Whether Lee's signals improved Tom's talk or not, they kept him occupied and quiet.

During the 1959–60 school year, Tom also taught early morning seminary. A nonmember girl attended the seminary class with an LDS friend, and every morning of the first month, she thanked Tom as she left class but told him she had decided it would be her last class. At the end of the school year, she was among only a handful of students with perfect attendance, and she had committed to baptism.

Virginia and the children would get up every morning for breakfast with Tom so they could have family prayer together before he left to teach his class every day from 7:00 a.m. to 8:00 a.m. Then Virginia would help Barbara and Lee finish their homework before they left for school at Mariemont Elementary.

In March 1961, Tom was released from the high council and called and sustained as the second counselor in the American River Stake presidency, replacing Bay Hutchings, who was called as first counselor when the previous first counselor, George Leavitt, moved to Hawaii. Elder ElRay L. Christiansen, the former president of the Logan Temple who had also served with Tom's father in the Cache Stake presidency, was the visiting authority at the stake conference at which the changes were made. Later in the day he set apart Tom in his new calling. Both President Hutchings and President Perry served with President Austin G. Hunt, the stake president. During their service together a new six hundred thousand-dollar stake center was completed and dedicated, as were two new meetinghouses. The American River Stake also began to raise money for building the Oakland Temple.

Tom was involved in another building project during this busy period of his life. Hale's completed a store in the new Arden Fair Mall. The store opened in August 1961, and it marked the beginning of a new era of retail shopping in Northern California. Instead of shopping at department stores in congested downtown locations, shoppers increasingly preferred to shop at suburban malls. In the December 1961 Perry family Christmas letter, Virginia remarked that with all his recent building projects, Tom felt that he had missed his calling as an architect.

Expanding His Sphere of Influence

Bill Ahern, Tom's boss, encouraged Tom to become involved in the Sacramento community through the Chamber of Commerce and businessmen clubs.[6] Bill was a member of the Rotary Club of Sacramento, and he encouraged Tom to join the Kiwanis Club so they could spread their influence and develop contacts across both organizations. The Rotarians and

Kiwanians both claimed service-oriented missions, but they were also networking hubs. This meant that before luncheons and dinners, they scheduled social or cocktail hours to provide opportunities for business people to interact and build associations. Initially, Tom attended most of the luncheons and dinners, but he usually timed his arrival to avoid the social hour. When Bill learned about Tom's practice, he discouraged it because Tom would miss valuable time during which he could build networks and associations with other business leaders.

Tom promised his boss he would arrive earlier, but he also explained that when everyone else had a drink in his hand, he felt uncomfortable without one. At the April 1988 general conference, Elder Perry described how he felt at the time. He said: "I kept wondering what to do with my hands. You can always put one hand in your pocket, but you look a little foolish with both of them there. I tried holding a glass of 7-Up, but it had the appearance of an alcoholic beverage."[7]

How did Tom resolve his dilemma? He enlisted the help of someone else, in this case someone he could confide in who knew more about social hours than Tom could ever hope to know. He asked the bartender if there was a nonalcoholic drink that was distinctively different in appearance from an alcoholic drink. The bartender thought for a moment, went back to the kitchen, came out with half a gallon of milk, and poured Tom a glass.

What happened next? According to Elder Perry's general conference talk, the initial response was mixed, but the practice soon caught on and was embraced by others. He said:

"Pouring a glass of milk at a cocktail hour was a unique event. It seemed to attract the attention of everyone, and I became the target of a lot of jesting. It embarrassed me at first, until I discovered that I was meeting more business leaders than I had at any previous gathering. I found that I did not have to violate Church standards to become a viable, contributing member of my chosen profession. It was more the case that success came because I *did* adhere to my values. It soon became a practice at the social hours in that community to always have a carton of milk on the bar. I was amazed, as time passed, by how many of my associates were joining me for a glass of milk during the hour that we spent together."[8]

In time, Tom realized he was again following the example set by his biblical hero, Daniel, when he refused to eat the king's meat and drink his wine.[9] Like Daniel, Tom learned that the Lord blesses those who follow His teachings and adhere closely to the values and principles they have been taught. Moreover, such men naturally stand out among other men.

Bill Ahern also encouraged Tom to join associations like the Retail Merchants Association and the Golden Gate Controllers Association. In the process of becoming more involved professionally, Tom made an hour-long presentation about expense control at the Western States Controllers Convention held in Phoenix, Arizona, in August 1959. Something serendipitous resulted from the trip. Tom had taken Lee along to meet his Arizona cousins, the sons and daughters of his oldest sister, Zada, who had died of a brain tumor two years earlier. Zada's husband, Lou Adams, had recently remarried and joined two families into a large family. They lived on a farm in Mesa, and during the days Tom attended the convention, Lee spent time on the farm.

One evening as Tom was talking to and catching up with Lou, his brother-in-law told him about his system for tracking the production of each of his cows. Tom became fascinated with the way Lou used the information he collected to improve milk production on his farm. Tom went back to Sacramento with an idea forming in his mind. He believed that by tracking the performance of Hale's billing operators, he could experiment with different approaches to improving their performance. He developed a system that led to significant performance improvements, and it came to the attention of a reporter at *Women's Wear Daily,* who wrote a glowing story about Tom and his billing system.

The competitive situation in Sacramento was nearly perfect for Tom, and it brought back the enthusiasm and competitive spirit he had learned on the volleyball court. Hale's major competitor in the area was Weinstock's. Because both store chains were owned by Broadway-Hale, performance information was shared between them to create healthy competition. And Weinstock's was a worthy, head-to-head competitor for Hale's. Historically, the two divisions had run neck and neck in the Sacramento area, but Weinstock's had usually been slightly ahead. Because Tom was also competing against his former boss, Bill Proudfoot, this made the competition especially engrossing and victory especially sweet.

For most of the time Tom worked for Hale's, his focus was the downtown store. He realized that if the downtown store was drawing more traffic than Weinstock's downtown store, Hale's would likely win the friendly but heated competition. Accordingly, Tom was always looking for ways to improve and sustain sales in the downtown store. For example, he would go down to the sales floor and challenge a top salesperson in one of the departments to see who could sell the most in an hour. In Tom's mind, these contests were positive whether he won or lost because they excited the sales staff.

When bats, which had found a dead space between the Hale's store and another building, invaded the store one day and disrupted sales, Tom led the charge of employees, armed with boards on which bolts of fabric had been bound, and batted the flying rodents out of the air. Whatever it took during the workday, Tom was willing to do it to beat Weinstock's.

Partially due to the intense competition between Hale's and Weinstock's, the Hale's downtown store was recognized by *Women's Wear Daily* as the highest producing department store in the United States in both 1958 and 1959.[10] The recognition was not something either Bill Ahern or Tom expected, and it certainly wasn't an honor either of them sought. But suddenly, Tom's work as the controller and second-in-command at the store was receiving national attention, and he started receiving several inquiries from companies interested in hiring him away from Hale's. One of those inquiries came from Associated Merchandising Corporation (AMC), a private company that supplied all the Federated Department Stores.

Associated Merchandising Corporation

AMC had initially contacted Tom in the fall of 1958, and this led to a meeting in Los Angeles with the treasurer of Bullock's, one of the chains of Federated Department Stores. At the time, Tom's mind was focused on the opportunities that were coming to him at Hale's because of the new store to be built in the Arden Fair Mall. He felt strongly that his professional future, at least for the next five to ten years, was with Hale's. After the interview at Bullock's, Tom sent a letter to AMC, telling the company he enjoyed the West Coast and that he wasn't looking for a change at that time. AMC wrote back, thanking him for his letter and informing him that they had been able to fill the position with a good man from New York.

In 1961, however, AMC again contacted Tom, this time wanting to talk to him about becoming a corporate officer. In a letter to his father, dated April 20, 1962, Tom described AMC and its affiliate, Aimcee Wholesale Corporation (AWC). He said:

"The AMC buying office represents some of the best stores in the nation. They are all big stores. Totally, they have a volume of $2 billion. The AWC has a volume of $120 million.

They have foreign divisions in Brussels, Copenhagen, Florence, London, Milan, Munich, Paris, Vienna, Zurich, Athens, Bangkok, Barcelona, Buenos Aires, Bombay, Hong Kong, Nuremberg, Osaka and Yokohama. This is a real big outfit."

AMC's executive placement director flew to San Francisco to interview Tom, and then the company flew him to New York City to meet with the president and vice president-treasurer. As he flew across the country on April 19, 1962, Tom wrote a letter to his sister Mignon about his possible career change.[11] This was how he described the sudden turn of events in his life:

"Last week I received another letter [from AMC] stating that the big job was now opening up and would I talk to them in San Francisco. I agreed and we had our talk. They put me on a jet, and I am now on my way to meet with the President and the Vice President-Treasurer. The Vice President-Treasurer has decided to retire early (within the next three to five years). They are now looking for a replacement to join the staff as Corporate Controller and Corporate Secretary of the wholesale division. I would work directly with the Treasurer until the time of his retirement and then move into his job. If they offer the job to me, I'll have a real fight remaining true to California. Right now the family vote is:

"Virginia—agreeable, if the offer is real good

"Barbara—No

"Lee—Go

"Gay—New York? What's that?"

Tom did not mail the letter until April 22. At the bottom of the letter, he added a postscript:

"I was offered the job. They met my first salary demand. I should have gone $5,000 more. The family voted 5 to 0 to move. Do you want to move back to New York? We will be leaving here in June and taking about a month to go east."

CHAPTER 18

SCARSDALE, NEW YORK

It was the last day of school at Mariemont Elementary for Barbara and Lee—half a day for signing autographs and saying good-byes. When they arrived home, the movers were finishing their work, and the Chevrolet station wagon was in the driveway with their suitcases packed in the luggage rack on top. Tom, Virginia, and Linda Gay were walking through the nearly empty house. Barbara and Lee chose to walk around the backyard. The lawn was green and mowed, and the peas in the garden were about ready to be picked, but someone else would be picking and enjoying them.

Tom intended to pull the station wagon out of the driveway just as the moving van pulled away from 3915 El Ricon Way. As soon as he had checked and signed the final papers with the moving crew foreman, he carried Linda Gay and herded the rest of the family to the station wagon. Seat belts were not standard equipment at the time, and the Perrys' station wagon car did not have them. Tom had folded down the backseat of the wagon for the trip so the children could have maximum space, and he had even installed a foam pad to make the area more comfortable. It was a pleasant way for children to travel across the country, which, in turn, made it more pleasant for the parents.

Because of their late start, the Perrys made it only to Elko, Nevada, by dark, and they spent the night at a motel, arose early, and drove to Salt Lake City. Tom and Virginia both wanted to linger with their children on Temple Square and take pictures with their Polaroid camera. They could not stay very long, however, because they needed to be in Logan by mid-afternoon. The Perry family there had planned a three-day reunion, and Tom wanted to be in Logan in plenty of time for the kickoff event, a 6:00 p.m. dinner at the Bluebird restaurant.[1] The plan was to drive directly to Hyde Park, unpack the car at Hattie's house, visit with Hattie, Jessie, and Vernal for a few hours, and then drive to the Bluebird.

All of Tom's living siblings and their families came to the reunion. Mark Adams, Zada's son, even attended the gathering. It was assumed that with Tom's family moving to the East Coast, this would be the last time for a long time they all would be together. Most of the reunion was spent the same way Tom had spent most of his summer Saturday afternoons as a boy—in Logan Canyon.

Tom and Virginia also wanted to spend as much time as possible with their aging parents. Tom's father, who had recently turned seventy-seven, seemed to be in good health and was energized by the gathering of his children and grandchildren. But Hattie Lee, who was eighty-two, seemed to be failing. Virginia knew that her sister Jessie was becoming concerned about their mother's health.

This special time with family was something Tom, Virginia, and their children would remember and cherish for the rest of their lives. After a few days the time came for them to leave Logan and everything familiar. They said their final good-byes, piled back into their station wagon, and headed south before turning east. They intended to follow Interstate 80. In 1962, however, there were still many uncompleted segments along the coast-to-coast interstate highway. Accordingly, they had ample opportunities to become lost, and occasionally they did. Their schedule was relatively loose, especially by Tom's standards, for this was also a vacation. For example, they took time to drive to Nauvoo and then to Kirtland as they progressed farther east.

Tom and Virginia's house-hunting strategy was to start in Fairfield County, Connecticut, and Middlesex County, New Jersey, where they expected prices to be more reasonable. Before purchasing a home, they wanted to test the commute to the city.

After two weeks of house hunting and living in the Bridgeport Howard Johnson hotel, the Perrys found their dream home on a little, secluded, winding country lane tucked back in the New Canaan, Connecticut, woods. Many years later, Virginia related the following story and lesson learned from the experience that followed. She said:

"We all fell in love with it [the house]. Tom said, 'Well, now the thing to do is to test the commuting time.' So, early the next morning, he caught the New Haven train for New York City.

"He returned later in the afternoon with a disappointed look on his face. It had taken one and a half hours to commute to his office. He told the children: 'Well, I guess you'll have to choose between this home and me. If we live here, it will take all my extra time to commute back and forth.'

"The children dejectedly looked at one another and then, with only a moment's hesitation, one piped up and said, 'We'll take the home, Dad. We probably won't see you, anyway.'

"Even though the statement was made partly in jest, Tom got the message and took it seriously. We moved to Scarsdale, where the commuting time was 35 minutes. Tom made sure he had every Saturday off, and we tried to make this a family day. I think Tom realized the great importance of having a balance in life and not letting his professional work monopolize too much of his time."[2]

The house at 71 Ewart Street in Scarsdale, New York, was purchased from members of the Church who were moving to Los Angeles. In a July 9, 1962, letter to her Grandpa Perry, Barbara described the house: "It's a fairly new house (about 3 years old). It has 4 bedrooms, a family room, a built-in gas stove and oven in the kitchen, 3 bathrooms, a dining room, and it has six levels (counting the basement and attic). This is quite different from the rambler style that mother and dad liked in California. In Scarsdale, the schools are very good. The house is close to the church and to dad's commuter train. So it's very handy."

The offer Tom and Virginia made on the Scarsdale house was accepted on the same day Barbara wrote her letter to Tom's father. The owners, however, did not want to vacate the house until late August. Tom and Virginia decided the best thing to do was remain in Connecticut the rest of the summer, where the family had been attending the Bridgeport Ward. They found a second-floor, four-room apartment at 1 Turkey Hill Road in Westport that was only two miles away from two beautiful beaches. Tom commuted to New York while Virginia and the children spent most weekdays on the beach. But Tom spent several evenings on the beach until sunset and most Saturdays. He was a good sport about spending long days at the office while everyone else played. He was happy because his wife and children were happy. It was a summer none of them wanted to end.

71 Ewart Street

The summer in Westport did end, as all summers do. The previous owners moved out, and the Perrys moved into 71 Ewart Street in late August 1962, just in time for a new school year. The Perrys' new home had a Scarsdale mailing address, but they lived in the Eastchester School District. Barbara started the seventh grade at Eastchester Junior High School, and Lee enrolled in the sixth grade at Greenvale Elementary. The adjustment was particularly difficult for Barbara, who had been the most popular girl in her relatively small sixth-grade class. Now she attended a very large junior high school filled with strangers. A few months later, in a letter to his father dated January 30, 1963, Tom described his children's challenges. He wrote:

"Barbara and Lee are slowly getting themselves adjusted to the new way of life. The change was the most difficult for them. The schools are larger and subject matter more difficult. Our schools here rate the highest in the nation. They even pay the grade-school teachers around $10,000."

The other major difference about New York life that Tom reported to his father in the letter was his mode of transportation to work: "The train ride back and forth to Scarsdale is very pleasant. We surely picked the right place to live. It requires just 30 minutes to make the trip. On the way home at night, I finish what work I had left over at the end of the day, and in the mornings I read. I like it much better than the traffic fight of the California freeways."

Tom did notice, however, a distinct difference between the friendliness of Easterners and Westerners. He found New

Yorkers to be rather cold and distant, and then it occurred to him that he wasn't being very friendly either. He realized that part of the problem was that all the commuters were locked into the same daily routine. The only way to create a friendlier atmosphere was to interrupt the routine. He devised a plan.

Tom chose a man with whom he wanted to become better acquainted, watched his routine for a few mornings, and initiated a counter-routine. He arrived at the Scarsdale train station at about the same time as the other man, watched him buy his *New York Times*, and as soon as the man started to walk toward his favorite spot on the train platform, Tom increased his pace and beat him to it. The man, exercising his perceived right to his regular place on the platform, stood shoulder to shoulder with Tom and tried to nudge him off his spot. Tom stood his ground.

When the train arrived, Tom quickly jumped on before the other man and took his favorite seat. By this time the other man was fuming. By interrupting his routine, Tom had likely ruined his entire day.

On the second day of Tom's initiative, he did exactly the same thing to the other man with the same results. When Tom arrived at his usual time on the third day, however, he found the man already standing at his spot on the train platform. Tom walked over to him and started chuckling. The man initially scowled at him, and then the thought that he was acting very childish brought a sheepish smile to his face. Tom introduced himself as a California transplant who was determined to break up the routine of the commuters at the station. The two men boarded the train and sat together, and they had a delightful conversation until arriving at Grand Central Station.

Once the routine of one man was interrupted, other changes began to occur. Tom and his new friend continued competing each morning to see who could occupy the spot on the platform first. Their little game began to spread. One day another man decided he would race them for the spot—then five men and then ten men. Finally, it almost got out of hand. Onlookers began to make friendly wagers on who would arrive at the spot first. The atmosphere at the Scarsdale station had completely changed because Tom was determined to make a friend by interrupting his routine.

Perhaps Tom's fondest memory of his group of commuting friends was from the 1965 holiday season. A small band from the Salvation Army came to the platform one morning, and Tom and his friends sang Christmas carols with them. Most of the other men on the platform joined them until the train arrived.[3]

Another memorable commuting experience occurred just before that holiday season. It was the Great Northeast Blackout on November 9 and 10. The blackout occurred just as many of New York City's commuters were leaving work, and Tom spent the night on a train parked in Grand Central Station. In a letter to his father dated February 13, 1966, Tom gave a detailed account of the ordeal. He wrote:

"The more profit-minded members of the city were selling food and drinks along the train platforms. The drink lasted longer than the food and soon a few were feeling a little high and the platforms were no longer wide enough for them to walk on. I found myself as part of the team who would assist the heavy drinkers up from the tracks when they would fall from the platform. Some were not in very good condition after making such a fall. About midnight, everyone decided that we were going to be around for some time, and they started to find the best spot to sleep. I found myself on a seat on the train and settled down for the night. I tried one hundred different positions and finally decided that six foot four inches was just too large for the space I was allowed for sleeping. At about 2 a.m. the power in the batteries failed and from then until 5 a.m. it was total blackness. When the lights did come on, everyone had a different idea as to which train would be the first to leave. Between five and nine, we were racing back and forth from train to train trying to select the first one out. We made it into Scarsdale at nine-thirty. I now have a flashlight and a radio in my office. If it happens again, I will sleep on my desk. I am thinking of adding a pillow and a blanket to my emergency supplies."

1440 Broadway

Tom worked on the tenth floor of 1440 Broadway, on the corner of Broadway and 40th Street. His primary strengths, learned in both Lewiston and Sacramento, were in designing and implementing effective accounting systems and controlling costs. Whenever Tom wrote his father, he enjoyed telling him about how much money his ideas had saved AMC and AWC, whether it was fifteen thousand dollars or five hundred thousand dollars.

As corporate controller, Tom was responsible for making budget presentations to AMC's board of directors. He was warned by William (Bill) T. French, AMC's president and CEO, that the board could be rather demanding of the person presenting the budget. AMC was a private company owned by the twenty-seven Federated Department Store chains, and its raison d'etre was to concentrate purchasing power to lower costs and then to return a large percentage of the savings to the owners. From the perspective of the board members, AMC performed an important service, but they wanted the service for the lowest possible cost.

Given Bill French's warning, Tom fretted about his first board presentation. The next day he visited the boardroom to look around and figure out a way he could make the presentation more effective. He noticed that a large part of the walls of the boardroom was covered with flannel for its acoustical qualities. At the April 1999 general conference, Elder Perry told the rest of the story. He said:

"As I looked at the large piece of flannel, I thought of my Primary teacher and the use of the flannel board. I sent to Salt Lake for some flannel-backed paper. When it arrived, I prepared three different projections of the budget on that paper. As the budget presentation was made and the discussion followed, I could pull off one budget projection and replace it with another as appropriate. The members of the board were fascinated with my presentation using the flannel board technique. Each time I would present one of our second options and tell the board the consequences, they would immediately go back to the first budget projection, the one we really wanted to have approved. The presentation seemed to be very effective, and when it was over, I was complimented, thanks to my Primary teacher."[4]

Again, Tom had seen his training in the Church positively affect his career. Bill French approached Tom after the board meeting and said, "If a church mission taught you how to preach like that, then I want to go on one." Soon afterward, Tom received a promotion to treasurer of AWC. On Virginia's birthday, December 24, 1964, Tom received another promotion—this time to vice president and secretary-treasurer at AWC.

Tom's position with a wholesaler that did two billion dollars a year in business brought Virginia some special privileges and benefits. In a letter to his father dated March 7, 1963, Tom told the following story about one of Virginia's recent shopping experiences:

"I have had Virginia on a shopping trip on Seventh Avenue. I have been letting her go directly to the clothing manufacturers to select her dresses. This way I can get them at cost. She thinks she is real smart going around in $125 suits which we buy at about half the retail price. The only problem was when I had her go to a hat manufacturer. They had so many hats she couldn't make up her mind as to which one she wanted. They probably had over 1,000 hats, and I thought that she was going to try all of them. She finally gave up and went over to Lord & Taylor [a popular New York department store] to select a hat. After she found one that she liked I wrote down the style number and color and ordered it for her. She did much better when she had only 50 or so to select from."

Working for a major New York firm also gave Tom a unique educational opportunity at a time when computers were just beginning to reshape how business was conducted. Tom attended IBM's executive computer concepts course in July 1965. He briefly described the course in a letter to his father dated July 10, 1965:

"The purpose of the course is to teach the executive to understand the computer. I started last Friday and will be in school until next Friday. We start at 8:30 each morning, Saturdays and Sundays included, and finish up each day at about 10:00 p.m. That is why they have us stay in a hotel—to give us some rest each day without the trip home. They have five in the class, and we have three instructors. We even have all of our meals together. The instructors stay in the same hotel as we are in."

Several years later, Tom's early training in computers proved invaluable to him in his service as a General Authority in the Church. Even now in his 90s, he remains an early adopter of new computer technology,[5] and he was a major driving force behind many of the Church's major initiatives in the use of computers and information technology over the past four decades.[6]

The New York World's Fair

Bill French said the following about Tom:

"I would say that the principal difference between Tom Perry and anyone else with whom we were associated was his enthusiastic and continual demonstration of his Christian faith. He always knew that today's problems were relatively unimportant in the total scheme of things as he went about vigorously and joyously solving them."[7]

Another way to say what Bill French said about Tom is that he was a wonderful representative of the LDS faith.

G. Stanley McAllister, president of the New York Stake, met Tom at a New York Stake Pioneer Day picnic. He had already heard a great deal about Tom from Bishop Roy Fugal, the bishop of the Bridgeport Ward, who had grown close to the Perry family during their summer in Westport. Earlier, Bishop Fugal had hoped the Perrys would buy the home they liked in New Canaan and become permanent members of his ward. Perhaps President McAllister had done additional intelligence gathering and called President Austin Hunt of the American River Stake to ask him about his former counselor. Still, he wanted to meet Tom face-to-face and take his own measurements of the man.

The New York Stake was soon to be given a unique opportunity to change the face of the Church in New York City and surrounding areas—the LDS Church intended to sponsor a pavilion at the 1964–65 New York World's Fair. President McAllister wanted to determine whether Tom was the right person to represent the New York Stake and work directly with Elder Bernard P. Brockbank, an Assistant to the Twelve charged with overseeing the pavilion project, and with Wilburn C. West, president of the Eastern States Mission.

President McAllister chose an interesting, unobtrusive way to have a long conversation with Tom. He had noticed that

Lee carried his baseball glove around with him at the picnic. President McAllister mentioned that he enjoyed baseball, and he invited Lee to play catch with him. He stood next to Tom and conversed about a wide range of subjects while playing catch with Lee. Lee, of course, was more than willing to let the conversation continue as long as somebody was throwing a baseball with him.

A few months later at a stake conference held in January 1964, Tom was sustained as a member of the stake high council, stake mission president, and special assistant to the Eastern States Mission president. It is likely that at the time, Tom did not understand the significance of his new calling and the demands it would make on him. In a letter dated January 30, 1963, Tom told his father about his new calling. He said: "This has been one of the slow areas in growth in the Church. Anything I do should be an improvement."

A few months later the scope of his responsibilities was becoming clearer to Tom. In a letter to his father dated March 7, 1963, Tom wrote:

"My latest project in the Church is serving on the World's Fair Committee for our exhibit. It is really going to be something. The Church was able to get an excellent location right on the main street of the fair. They are expecting between 2,000 and 3,000 people to pass the exhibit each hour. They are organizing a special World's Fair Mission, which will run for only the two summers the fair is open. The plan calls for bringing here to this mission the best missionaries from all the Church to spend their last six or seven months on the World's Fair Mission. They will have some 100 missionaries there for each summer."

In addition to their other responsibilities, Tom and Virginia were called as World's Fair missionaries and asked to spend two nights a week and some Saturdays at the pavilion, both proselyting and supervising the missionaries. Tom and Virginia loved their assignment, but often they would be at the pavilion until nearly 11:00 p.m., after which they still faced a long drive or train ride home. Tom admitted to his father in a July 4, 1964, letter that it was difficult for him to keep up with everything else while spending two evenings a week at the pavilion. He admitted that he hoped to cut back a little. When Virginia was called to be Relief Society president in the Westchester Ward in August 1964, she immediately cut back to one night a week and to fewer Saturdays.

The Church learned a great deal about public relations from hosting a pavilion at the New York World's Fair. In a March 28, 1965, letter to his father, Tom wrote about spending a full day with Elders Harold B. Lee and Bernard P. Brockbank at the Mormon Pavilion working on improvements for the summer of 1965. In an earlier letter to his father dated January 5, 1965, Tom wrote:

"We have had a wonderful year in 1964. We should have made a written record of the events that happened to us this summer. We have baptized over 500 in the New York Stake alone as a result of the fair. We really didn't find out how to use the fair until about the time it closed. We are presently getting about 100 [baptisms] per month."

Then Tom disclosed to his father an unintended consequence to him of the fair's success:

"We had so much growth that it has caused my release as stake mission president. I am still High Council adviser to the mission, but now have the job of heading the building program in the stake. Seven of the nine units will need new building programs next year."

Tom and Virginia were called again to serve as World's Fair missionaries during the summer of 1965, but given their other

Church responsibilities, they were expected to spend only one night at the pavilion each week.

President McAllister also assigned Tom, in his role as a high councilor, to work closely with the Rego Park Branch in Queens. Roughly 75 percent of the branch's membership was a direct result of the Mormon Pavilion.[8] When Tom's niece Laraine moved to the New York area, where her husband, Paul Ferguson, was transferred by the U.S. Army, Tom admitted to Laraine's mother (his sister Gay) that he was torn over where he should encourage them to live. Part of him wanted them to live close to Scarsdale, but another part of him wanted them to live in the Rego Park area, where they could help strengthen a branch of the Church in need of seasoned Church leaders.

Tom learned a great deal from his high council assignment to the Rego Park Branch. The branch required constant attention, and some of its problems were quite challenging. A few years later, when he was president of the Boston Stake, Tom said on many occasions that it was President G. Stanley McAllister who taught him how to use a stake high council more effectively. This was mostly a tribute to President McAllister's leadership, but it was also an expression of gratitude to the leaders and members of the Rego Park Branch, who taught Tom how to lend support as a high councilor.

The Home Front

Virginia's mother, Hattie Lee, died on May 7, 1963. Her death was unexpected. Virginia's sister Jessie had alerted her that their mother was not feeling well. Virginia had sent Jessie some money to help pay doctor bills. In a letter to her mother dated April 15, Virginia mentioned the illness and her concern but also her hope that the illness was temporary. In the family's 1963 Christmas letter, Virginia paid the following tribute to her mother:

"Ginny's mother passed away in May. This saddened us a great deal, but we felt her life was greatly blessed even in her passing, without prolonged illness or suffering. We are grateful for the life she lived and for the example she has left with us."

Tom and Virginia flew to Utah for the funeral. In addition to attending the funeral, Tom spoke.

If anyone was busier than Tom during the period the Perrys lived in Scarsdale, it was Virginia. As if being a wife, mother, ward Relief Society president, and World's Fair missionary was not enough, Virginia somehow found time to add performances at the World's Fair with the Singing Mothers. Important roles with the Inter-Church Council, Mothers of Boy Scouts, American Mothers, and the National Women's Council added to her busy schedule. In a January 9, 1965, letter to Jessie, Virginia admitted that sometimes it was almost more than she could handle.

Virginia's service as Relief Society president was deeply appreciated by both of the bishops of the Westchester Ward with whom she served. The bishop who called Virginia was John Q. Cannon, who was later replaced by John E. Griffith. In a note to Virginia dated May 23, 1966, Bishop Griffith wrote:

"What a comforting feeling it is to know that our 'Westchester well' will never run dry, that our Relief Society ladies will never thirst, so long as they are blessed with such dedicated leadership.

"The beautiful example of your life, the warmth of your sweet spirit and the strength of your testimony set you apart as one of God's truly elect. How fortunate we are in Westchester Ward to have such a capable, devoted and loving Relief Society President."

While extremely busy, both Tom and Virginia tried to be attentive parents. Before Virginia was called to serve as Relief Society president, she served as a counselor in the ward

YWMIA presidency to Sister Elma Stoddard. Because Lee and Barbara also attended MIA, this left Tom alone with Linda Gay on Tuesday evenings. In his January 30, 1963, letter to his father, Tom described this precious time with his four-year-old daughter. He wrote:

"She really takes over and runs the house when just the two of us are there. She cleans off the table, helps me with the dishes, and won't let me turn on the TV until the house is in order. Then she gets me a pillow, blanket and something to eat while we watch our one TV show before it is time to put her to bed."

Barbara recalled a special memory of her father during a challenging time in her life. She said:

"I remember that when we first moved to New York I had a hard time in school. One night I was finally able to get all my homework done except for English. By that time it was bedtime, and I was hoping I could get it done quickly. I read the assignment, and my heart dropped to my feet: 'Make an outline of the story *The Legend of Sleepy Hollow.*' I had no idea how to make an outline.

"My father came up to say goodnight and found me crying. He told me not to worry and said he would help me in the morning.

"When I got up the next morning I found a sample outline on my desk. My father had left for work early, but he'd written a sample outline before he had left. I always had been taught to put things into my own words, so, using his model, I was able to finish my assignment.

"The next evening I had to do another outline, and I was able to do most of it myself. My father proofread it and told me how to improve it. This is just like him—always helping."[9]

The Perry family enjoyed their vacations together during these years. In a July 4, 1964, letter to his father, written during a family vacation, Tom said:

"I remember when the family would spend almost every 4th of July at Bear Lake. This year finds us at Candlewood Lake doing about the same things we were doing back in those days when we would travel to Bear Lake.

"We are on vacation. We rented a little cottage at the Lake for two weeks. This is a beautiful spot only about two hours from Scarsdale. The telephone and TV are far enough away to give us a nice rest. The swimming is very good and the nights cool for sleeping. If the beds were better, we could spend all of our time either swimming or sleeping."

One of the most delightful aspects of living close to a world's fair was the visitors it brought to the Perry home, including several family members. Tom's sister Gay and brother Ted and their families traveled to New York for the fair and stayed with their brother's family. Tom's father also came for a visit during the summer of 1965. Virginia took special care of Grandpa Perry, not just taking him to the fair but also into New York City to see the Empire State Building, the Statue of Liberty, and several museums. Grandpa Perry, an avid learner throughout his life, was so energized by all there was to see on his first trip to New York City that he nearly wore out Virginia.

Tom's father's visit to New York became an even more cherished memory when he passed away less than a year later, on May 5, 1966. Now, both Tom and Virginia had lost both of their parents. While there was a deep sadness associated with the loss, there was also joy in the thought that once again their parents were together.

The life history of Tom's father provides ample evidence that he never felt very far away from Nora. When Tom received his copy of his father's life history as a Christmas present in

1964, it was his father's references to these feelings of closeness to Nora that affected him most. In a January 5, 1965, letter to his father, Tom wrote:

"Our family is pleased and delighted with our best of all Christmas gifts. When we received your package, I dropped everything and spent a very wonderful hour reading your history. I was especially interested in your feeling of communication with Mother after her passing on. The love she had for her family is stronger than the walls that now separate us from her. I, too, have felt her presence. . . . Before I was called to the Stake Presidency in California, I felt her presence so strong as I was working at home one evening. She let me know I was to be called to the Stake Presidency. . . . She is a wonderful mother."

Elder L. Tom Perry spoke about the responsibilities of fathers at the October 1977 general conference. About his father, he said: "I will be eternally grateful to a father who thought enough of me to give me his name. It was a name of honor and respect in the community in which I grew up. It carried before it the title of bishop from the time I was six months old until just a few months before I left to go on my mission. How proud I was of his service."[10]

Another Move

On the day before his father died, May 4, 1966, Tom wrote him a letter that his father never read. In the letter, Tom mentioned an employment offer he had received from a small store chain in the Boston area. He wrote: "I was in Boston Friday afternoon receiving a very attractive offer to join a hard goods department store that does $40,000,000 as financial director of the company. I will probably stay with AMC, but I am considering the Boston opportunity."

The timing of his father's death likely influenced Tom's decision to leave AMC and join Lechmere Sales Corporation, the hard goods department store headquartered in Cambridge, Massachusetts. Events such as the death of a parent or loved one have a way of reordering the priorities in our lives. Perhaps Tom had told the story enough times about buying the house in Scarsdale instead of New Canaan that he was finally learning his own lesson.[11] Life adjustments, such as throttling back to spend more time with family, are far easier said than done. And no matter how genuine a person's intent, it's difficult to break out of existing patterns. Relapses and lag effects are more common than not in most cases of significant change. This is not hypocrisy; it is an integral part of being human while striving to better oneself.

The death of Tom's father and the earlier death of Virginia's mother helped both of them take still another inventory of their lives. They realized that while living in New York had been exhilarating, it had also become a little too frenetic to accommodate the balance they both wanted to achieve in their lives. They could look back and feel a satisfying sense of accomplishment, especially regarding their service to the Church at the New York World's Fair, but a slight course correction was warranted.

Of course, there were other, mostly professional reasons for Tom to change employment. Bill French was planning a major reorganization of the company that would greatly expand Tom's responsibilities as well as his workload. AMC had become so large and dominant in some market sectors that it was receiving a great deal of scrutiny from the Federal Trade Commission. Tom found that new government regulations were making it far more difficult to reach performance targets and effectively grow the company. Accordingly, the thought of working for a smaller, less-encumbered company was very enticing. Also, the fact that AMC was owned by twenty-seven department store chains meant the company had many key stakeholders to please. And Tom missed being directly involved with stores—both improving the performance of existing stores and expanding a retail chain by building new stores. Finally, Lechmere was an interesting company with an ingenious merchandising model. It was brimming with potential, and the offer was attractive enough to turn Tom's head.

Tom really didn't know which of those factors weighed in more heavily than the others, but he considered all of them in the process of making a decision.[12] What he did know with complete certainty, however, is that he, Virginia, and their three children had prayed about the decision, and all of them received the impression that they should move again. While they didn't know for certain, it might have been the simple case that now that the World's Fair was over and the Mormon Pavilion had closed down, the Lord had another work for them to do in Boston.

CHAPTER 19

WESTON, MASSACHUSETTS

In early June 1966, Tom and Virginia engaged a real estate agent, and they traveled to the Boston area with Lee and Linda Gay on several weekends to look at houses.[1] Their search for a new home focused on the suburbs directly to the west of Boston—Wayland, Wellesley, Needham, Lincoln, and Weston. They decided to buy an unfinished home in Weston and turn it into their dream home. They had been impressed with the builder's work on other homes in the area, and they loved the floor plan of the home he had started at 46 Bradyll Road in a relatively newly developed area one and a half miles north of Weston's town square.

The unfinished house was larger than the house in New Canaan, Connecticut, with which the Perrys had fallen in love during the summer of 1962, but it evoked similar feelings. The house was situated on an acre of land, and most of the property was wooded. Moreover, there was no other building behind the new house for approximately a mile. It felt private and peaceful, and yet Tom's commute to the Lechmere store in Cambridge was less than thirty minutes.

The property was also distinctive because of several rock outcroppings. In the backyard, for example, there was an enormous rock just beyond the beginning of the wooded area—as large as a subway car. Tom worried about the implications for yard work—New England had a reputation for rocky soil. For Virginia, it evoked a special place. She decided their new home needed a name, such as the North Lie estate in Denmark to which her grandfather Christen Christensen Lee renounced his claim in exchange for enough money to immigrate with his wife to America. Because Virginia had been taking Spanish classes in New York, she chose a Spanish name. A few months later, in a December 1966 Christmas letter, she described the house, the property, and its new name:

"We have a new Gambrel Cape home which we feel is perfectly suited to the needs of our family. It has been built upon a firm foundation—in fact, the contractor nearly despaired in trying to blast out enough rock to pour a level basement. The huge, picturesque boulders jutting through the earth in our yard are a source of beauty to us, and we call our home 'La Roca' because it was built upon a rock."

Another purpose of their weekend visits during June 1966 was to attend church at the Weston Ward. The Weston Ward congregation met in a building that had once been the Unitarian Church in Wellesley, a community just south of Weston. It was a small congregation that covered a large geographical area. Tom and Virginia realized their children were going to have fewer Church friends in the Boston area than they had in the Westchester Ward. In fact, there were no boys in the ward who were Lee's age, and the situation was only slightly better for Barbara and Linda Gay. At the time, the

Church in the Boston area was far less established than it was in New York. The hopeful news, however, was that the groundbreaking for a new six hundred thousand–dollar chapel and stake center to be built on the south side of Weston was only a few months away.

Tom began work at Lechmere Sales Corporation on Friday, July 1. Their home in Weston would not be finished for more than a month, so he needed to find a place to live. Paul Thompson, a doctoral student at Harvard Business School who was in Utah with his family for the summer, subleased their apartment to Tom until the house was ready. Virginia and the children remained in New York for most of the summer. Virginia busied herself with selling their New York home, arranging the move, and making all the decisions about paint, flooring, and fixtures for their new home while Tom focused on his new job.

The Weston Ward Building Project

Soon after the Perrys moved into their new home in Weston, they had an unexpected visitor. Wilbur Cox, president of the Boston Stake, accompanied by his wife, Nora, knocked on their door and welcomed them to the area. It was not until President Cox asked to see Tom privately that the Perrys realized this was more than a social visit.

The next Sunday, President Cox intended to sustain Dean Bagley as the new bishop of the Weston Ward, and he wanted Tom to serve as his first counselor. Tom had met Dean Bagley only once, but Tom had impressed him. It occurred to Tom, who was excited to serve as his counselor, that he would likely become deeply involved in the Weston Ward building project, and that was exactly what Bishop Bagley had in mind. In their first meeting, Bishop Bagley asked his new first counselor to chair the ward building committee. Tom embraced the assignment with his trademark enthusiasm.

Tom's new calling and assignments in the Weston Ward and his involvement at work helped him warm up to the Boston area immediately. Virginia and the Perry children were a little slower to shift allegiances. In a letter to her Aunt Gay and Uncle Albert, Barbara said, "I really miss the Westchester Ward, though—the ward here is so small, and we meet in an old Unitarian church."[2] In the family's 1966 Christmas letter, Virginia implied she still missed New York. She wrote:

"It was difficult to leave our beloved Westchester Ward with all the gracious, friendly people there. But we have carried with us fond memories of cherished experiences. . . . Through day-by-day, week-by-week associations, to be partakers of the special spirit and love which characterize Westchester, was indeed to us a rich blessing and a treasured experience. Also, New York is truly a fascinating place to live!"

By the time Virginia wrote a November 29, 1967, letter to her sister Jessie, however, her tone had changed. She wrote:

"Tom and the children, too, are very fond of Weston. Gay is the only one who coaxes for New York visits. Tom took me to New York in October to attend a National Council of Women conference. The weather in the City was awful—the air so muggy and heavy. I had forgotten that it could be that way in New York City. I got sick while we were there, too, so I was really glad to return home."

Virginia became a full-fledged New Englander, and, when she wrote her November 1967 letter to Jessie, even Linda Gay had already shifted her loyalties considerably. What led Linda to embrace her new home, and also captured her heart, was a major league baseball team—the 1967 Boston Red Sox. The Red Sox had been expected to be cellar dwellers in the American League—given 100-to-1 odds to win the pennant.

But during the miraculous baseball season of 1967, not only did the Red Sox win the American League Championship, but they also took the World Series to seven games against the St. Louis Cardinals before losing to them and their dominant starting pitcher, Bob Gibson. Tom and Lee also renounced all previous allegiances to other major league baseball teams and became avid Sox fans.[3]

Also in Virginia's November 1967 letter to Jessie, she reported that the Weston Ward was already meeting in their new meetinghouse. The building was still not ready to be dedicated, but it was getting closer.

The summer of 1967 was a very busy summer for the Perry family and the other families of the Weston Ward. As part of their building fund contribution, the ward assumed responsibility for the interior painting and landscaping. Lee learned so much from painting alongside his father during the summer that he confidently launched a small painting business that operated during the summers of 1969 and 1970, and he used the money he saved to partially fund his mission. For her part, Linda Gay planted a tree that still shades the Weston Stake Center property. Perhaps the most heroic contributor, however, was the Boston Stake patriarch, Ira Terry, who single-handedly did most of the landscaping around the meetinghouse.

Again, Tom witnessed a ward become unified as members worked together with the common goal of building a place to be dedicated for their worship of the Lord Jesus Christ. The experience, while physically and emotionally draining, was another highlight in his life. Virginia expressed her hopes that the new building would fuel missionary work in the area. In her November 1967 letter to Jessie, she wrote, "Weston is a small town (11,000), but it seems that most of the residents know about the new church, so we expect the missionary program to move forward with great zeal."

Virginia's comment to Jessie proved to be prescient. In May 2004, Harvard Business School professor Clayton Christensen interviewed Elder Perry for a book about the history of the Boston Stake.[4] To enlist a response from Elder Perry, Clayton said: "It looks like in the decade between 1967 and 1977, there were nineteen complete families that joined the Church in the Weston Ward—well over 200 people. It just seemed like it was a magical period."

Elder Perry responded:

"It was a great period. This building meant so much in that day. . . . Suddenly we had our own building—a substantial building—a very differently constructed building than the old churches in the community. This building had a great life and spirit.

"I remember when the Lightwood Tennis Club started over here. They wanted to hold their organizational meetings. I invited them over to our building, and they couldn't believe it. We held it in the cultural hall and set up chairs for them. Many attendees remarked about how wonderful it was to have basketball standards and a place where the young people could come."[5]

The open house and dedication of the Weston Ward chapel and Weston Stake Center took place in March 1968. Five thousand invitations were mailed to members of other faiths in the Weston-Wellesley area, and the open house was held over the first three weekends in March. Finally, the meetinghouse was dedicated on March 17, 1968.

Gradually, the LDS meetinghouse at 150 Brown Street in Weston became an integral part of the Weston community. When Weston High School had a big dance, the Weston Ward held a dance on the same night. Member youth were encouraged to invite their nonmember friends to Church dances. The popularity of the dances grew because the different atmosphere of the LDS meetinghouse drew youth who were uncomfortable with the standards and atmosphere at the high school dances.

Lechmere Sales Corporation

Tom's employer during this period of his life, Lechmere Sales Corporation, traced its origin to 1913, when Abraham "Pop" Cohen, a Russian immigrant, purchased a harness-making shop located in what became Cambridge's Lechmere Square. The Metropolitan Boston Transit Authority's (MBTA) Lechmere station was eventually built across the street from the original store location. As demand for harnesses declined and the use of automobiles increased, Pop Cohen decided to add tire sales to his business. In 1945, Pop brought his three sons—Maurice, Norman, and Philip—into the business, and it was incorporated as Lechmere Tire & Sales Company in 1948. In 1956 the Cohens purchased an old bus garage at 88 First Street in Cambridge, and they converted it into their main retail store. This allowed them to expand the range of their product line—from large appliances like refrigerators to vinyl records. Later the company built a new one-hundred-thousand-square-foot facility that further broadened the store's diverse product line.

Lechmere's address led to a distinctive pricing strategy. To help customers remember the Cambridge store's address, all its prices were a dollar amount plus eighty-eight cents. The most distinctive feature of Lechmere's stores, however, was that most of the products on the sales floor were display models. A customer shopping for a small appliance, for example, would select it, take a ticket number to a sales clerk, and pay for the appliance. Then the item would be found by a warehouse worker and rolled down a conveyer belt for the customer to pick up. Larger items, such as large appliances, could either be delivered or picked up at a loading dock in the back of the warehouse. While this low-cost merchandising model was later adopted and adapted by other retailers, particularly by warehouse stores, in 1966 it was unique, and Lechmere experienced explosive growth. Lechmere had added the second store in Dedham just before Tom joined the company.

When Tom joined Lechmere in 1966, Pop Cohen was a very old man, and his eldest son, Maurice, was the company's president and CEO. Pop Cohen still came to work almost every day, sat in a chair by the pickup counter, greeted customers, and slept. His three sons ran the business, but Maurice was clearly the one in charge and the driving force behind company growth. Maurice hired Tom primarily because Lechmere had outgrown its outdated financial and control systems. There were accounting problems, of course, but the larger problem was that Lechmere did not have trustworthy financial information with which to make both day-to-day pricing decisions and decisions about how fast to grow the business profitably. In a July 3, 1966, letter to family members after only one day at his new job, Tom wrote: "They [Lechmere] have plans for two more stores, and I have the job of working out the financing and the systems for the expansion. This should keep me out of trouble for the next five years."

Tom and Maurice quickly developed a close working relationship as well as a deep friendship. For example, when Tom mentioned that he enjoyed taking a short nap at lunchtime, Maurice arranged for a room at the Charter House Hotel across the street from the Cambridge store so Tom could walk over and take a nap when his schedule allowed it.[6] Tom had an arrangement with a friend in New York, Preston Nibley, who had a brother who worked for Chrysler. Through his brother's connections, Preston was able to buy a new car every year at a deeply discounted price. Tom would buy the year-old car from

Preston each year for five hundred dollars less than he paid for it. One day when Tom mentioned to Maurice that he had just bought a different car and needed to sell his old one, Maurice offered to buy it. Because Tom didn't want to drive a car that was newer than what his boss drove, he offered to sell Maurice the year-old car he had just purchased. Maurice, who knew a good deal when he was offered one, quickly accepted.

Explaining to Tom that Lechmere was a family and family-oriented business, Maurice encouraged him to hire his children to work part time for Lechmere. Barbara, for example, worked for Lechmere on Saturdays and assisted Tom in different clerical functions, such as adding rows and columns on a spreadsheet. Lee worked for Lechmere during the summers of 1967 and 1968, at first doing much the same work Barbara had done and later working in the accounts payable department. The experience gave Barbara and Lee early exposure to the retail business and, more important, quality time with their father on the commute to and from work.

After only a few months of working with Tom, Maurice Cohen became certain he was the missing piece to Lechmere's senior management team. He still confided in his brothers, but he increasingly confided in Tom and sided with him. When Tom explained that the company would likely overleverage itself with the aggressive expansion plan that had been developed by the Cohen brothers before his arrival, Maurice listened. Tom recommended that the company seek a partner to fund an even more aggressive growth strategy. With the right deal, Lechmere could continue to operate semi-autonomously and expand the number of stores even more quickly. After several weeks of considering the idea with his brothers, Maurice gave Tom the green light to seek a partner.

Tom's search for a partner led him to one of the Federated Department Store chains—Dayton Corporation. In a November 12, 1968, letter to his sister Gay, Tom wrote:

"This was a big day for us at Lechmere Sales. I have been working with the President of our firm for about one year now on a proposed merger with Dayton, Inc. We announced today that we had agreed to the merger. Now if the FTC approves, we will be Lechmere Sales Company, a division of Dayton, Inc. This merger will bring Dayton's volume to about $400,000,000. I am back in the big time again. . . .

"I have been very lucky to be in the right place at the right time since becoming involved in retailing. With the grades I had in high school it is rather surprising to me. I have to give all the credit to the organizational training the Church has given me."

By the time the sale was completed, on February 28, 1969, Dayton had merged with J. L. Hudson Company, another Federated store chain, and become Dayton Hudson Corporation. Lechmere became a subsidiary of the newly merged company.

The Boston Stake Presidency

Tom loved serving in the Weston Ward bishopric with Bishop Bagley. Thcy had such a delightful association together that they did not want it to end. When President Cox was called to be the president of the California Central Mission, Elder Boyd K. Packer, an Assistant to the Twelve and the president of the New England States Mission, was assigned to preside over a Boston Stake conference held on April 13-14, 1968, and also reorganize the stake presidency. During his May 2004 interview with Clayton Christensen about the history of the Boston Stake, Elder Perry recalled his experience in being interviewed by Elder Packer. He said:

"I'll never forget when we interviewed with Elder Packer, who was our assigned visitor, for a new stake president to replace President Cox. Dean Bagley went in, and they asked about me. Bishop Bagley told them some nice things about me, but then he said: 'You know when he gets excited, he goes out behind the barn and smokes a cigar.' I went in after him, and they did the same with me that they had done with Dean Bagley. I said, 'He's all right, except that when he gets under a lot of pressure, he beats his wife.'"[7]

Neither Tom nor Dean Bagley was chosen by the Lord through Elder Packer to replace President Cox. Instead, Bill Fresh, who was serving as the bishop of the Lynnfield Ward, was called and sustained as the new president of the Boston Stake.

Bill Fresh had served as the Lynnfield Ward bishop for only six months before his call to be the stake president. He and his family, however, had been members of the Lynnfield Ward before Mobil Oil Company, his employer, had transferred him to New Jersey. During the summer of 1967, Bill received an impression that he would be returning to Massachusetts and would become bishop of the Lynnfield Ward. A few days later, Bill was not surprised when he was asked by his superiors to return to the Boston area as the head of Mobil's New England division.

Just like most of us, however, Bill had a little bit of Jonah in him. Ignoring the rest of his earlier impression, he and his wife began looking for homes in the Lexington, Wellesley, and Weston areas so he could have a shorter commute to Boston than he would from Lynnfield. Then Bill received an unexpected call from Wilbur Cox. President Cox told Bill that he was delighted to hear that he and his family were returning to the Boston area. He asked Bill if they had decided to live in Lynnfield again. Bill admitted he had thought about it but that they were looking for a home in areas closer to Boston. President Cox intimated that the Lynnfield Ward could use Bill's leadership, but he also told Bill that he couldn't make the decision for him about where he and his family should live. Bill and his family chose to purchase a house in Lynnfield, and they moved there in September 1967. Bill was called as bishop of the Lynnfield Ward at the beginning of October.[8]

It was Bill Fresh, not Elder Packer, who broke up the Weston Ward bishopric. Although he had never met Tom, Bill selected him to serve as his second counselor in the stake presidency. Once he was called to serve as the stake president, Bill was given a list of names and two hours to choose his counselors. He immediately felt impressed to ask Don Parker, a member of the current stake presidency, to serve as his first counselor. As Bill continued to look at the names and pray, a name on the page seemed to rise above the others, as if it were on stilts. The name was L. Tom Perry, and Bill concluded that the Lord wanted Tom to serve as his second counselor.

When Elder Packer checked to see if Bill had selected his counselors, he reported that he had. But he confessed, "I haven't the foggiest idea who L. Tom Perry is!" Elder Packer said, "That's no problem. We'll just ask him to offer the closing prayer in the Saturday night session." When Tom stood to offer the prayer, Bill saw for the first time the man who would become his counselor and lifelong friend.[9]

Tom loved serving with President Fresh. In Tom's mind, President Fresh was a noble and great soul and a wonderful leader. President Don Parker moved after a brief period of time, and another future lifelong friend joined the presidency of the Boston Stake—Gene Dalton.

Despite their closeness and mutual love and respect, President Fresh and his counselors faced a tall order leading the Boston Stake. Tom described their challenge in an October 13, 1968, letter to his sister Gay. He wrote:

"The Boston Stake covers half of Massachusetts and all of Rhode Island. We are usually on the road to one of 15 wards or branches at 7 a.m. and return about 10 p.m. It is a stake that has everything from full-program wards down to a little branch of only 90 members. We even have two University wards. It is almost an impossible stake to administer. If we can get 300 or 400 more members, I believe they will divide it."

Tom also told his sister that he had started taking a day off each week to enjoy his family and their home in Weston.

A Trip to Hawaii

By the fall of 1968, Barbara had graduated from Weston High and left to attend Brigham Young University. Tom and Virginia had purchased airline tickets to Salt Lake City to attend October general conference, and they intended to take Linda Gay with them so she could see Barbara. The plan changed, however, as Virginia reported in an October 1, 1968, letter to her sister Jessie. She wrote:

"I just have time for a note to let you know about our sudden change of plans. We won't be coming to conference after all. We have good hotel reservations in Salt Lake and everything, but we will have to cancel them. We have been offered an expense-free trip to Hawaii at the same time and we can't pass that up. Tom's boss usually takes the trip each year, but this time he wants Tom and me to go."[10]

Tom and Virginia loved their trip to Hawaii. They both wrote letters to family members giving detailed accounts of their vacation. During their week at Waikiki, Tom's day began at 5:30 a.m. with a run along the beach, followed by a swim, and then breakfast with Virginia. After breakfast they spent the morning sightseeing and then returned to the beach for the afternoon. In the evening they would attend a Hawaiian show and luau. They rented a car one day to drive to Laie to attend the Hawaii Temple and the show at the Polynesian Cultural Center. It was truly a week in paradise for them.[11]

The trip also proved eventful and nearly tragic. In a December 15 letter to her sister Jessie, Virginia reported:

"Although I didn't know it at the time, I was *pregnant* when I made the trip. A funny thing happened while we were in Hawaii. One day a fellow looked at me and said: 'I don't know whether you realize it or not, but you are wearing fertility beads' (some lovely beads I had just purchased). We laughed at him, but it wasn't long until I began to wonder at what he had said. The pregnancy turned out to be ectopic (tubular) so I am now recuperating from a major operation. . . . I had developed acute anemia because of bleeding—had to have 5 pints of blood. The tube had ruptured, and I was in a rather dangerous situation. I'm glad it's over and grateful to be among the living!"

Virginia was so grateful for the exceptional care she received at the Boston Hospital for Women that she decided to become a volunteer there. In a January 1969 letter to her sister Jessie, Virginia wrote:

"I am now working each Wednesday as a volunteer at the Boston Hospital for Women. I work in the recovery room with the patients and am beginning to enjoy it very much. I wear a white uniform and sometimes a mask. I am learning to do all sorts of things, like changing a bed with the patient in it, temperature, pulse, bed pan, etc."

Virginia and her close friend, Eugenia Herlin, even considered enrolling in a two-year nursing program in the fall of 1969, but they were too late submitting their applications.

The Old Folks Home

In the fall of 1969, Lee also left home, joining Barbara at BYU. Linda Gay missed her older sister and brother. When she wrote letters to her siblings, the return address on the envelope was:

"Old Folks Home
"46 Bradyll Road
"Weston, Massachusetts 02193"

At the same time, the Weston Ward was becoming considerably younger. Virginia reported in a September 15, 1969, letter to Jessie that eighteen of the ward's most active families, including Bishop Bagley and his family, had moved away. Virginia added:

"We've had lots of new young couples move in. We [she and Tom] are beginning to feel that we are among the older members of the ward."

Tom became the landlord to one of the new young families who moved into the Weston Ward. In the same September 1969 letter to Jessie, Virginia reported that Tom had purchased, as an investment property, the former Ashland, Massachusetts, home of the stake patriarch, Ira Terry. Brother Terry had sold his home to Tom because he was called to serve as the mission president in the Northern California Mission. The young family who rented the house had struggled to find a place to live that they could afford. According to Virginia, Tom came to their rescue. She wrote:

"They couldn't afford the rent Tom was going to ask, but he felt sorry for them and cut it down; so we are barely coming out even on the loan payments."

The rental home was on nearly six acres of land that Brother Terry, who loved to garden, had tended with great care. Tom kept for himself most of the responsibility for the yard, and the renters didn't seem to mind having a free, part-time gardener. During the summer of 1970, Tom discussed his garden in a letter to Gay. He wrote:

"I am trying to grow a garden on our Ashland property. It is a problem when it is 16 miles away. I have enough equipment to take care of ten times as much garden."[12] Virginia believed that Tom would probably want to move to Ashland to be closer to his gardens, except he knew she was very attached to La Roca—the old folks home at 46 Bradyll Road in Weston.

CHAPTER 20

President of the Boston Stake

In the late fall of 1969, President Bill Fresh decided to leave Mobil and move to New Hampshire[1] to lead a start-up company. Elder Gordon B. Hinckley was assigned to attend the Boston Stake conference held on January 24–25, 1970, to reorganize the stake presidency. Elder Hinckley called Tom to replace President Fresh, and Tom selected Gene Dalton and Clifford Clive to serve as his counselors.

Tom had served in bishoprics and stake presidencies since he was thirty years old, but this was his first experience holding the keys of presidency since he was an Aaronic Priesthood quorum president. Tom, now forty-seven, realized quickly that there was a significant difference between serving as a counselor in the stake presidency and being the stake president.

Tom was humbled by his new calling. He believed there were other men far more qualified than he was to serve as stake president, but he also realized that the Lord had called him through one of his special witnesses. If the Lord had called him, there must be a reason, and he sought the inspiration he needed to understand the Lord's mind and will for the members of the Boston Stake.

As Tom pondered his role as a stake president, he began to see the Boston Stake in a new, more promising light. Given all the wonderful universities in the Boston area, the Boston Stake was able to attract an amazing number of talented young people. Tom asked himself why, given all of this talent, did the stake struggle? Why was it falling short of its potential? He decided that one of the major reasons the stake struggled was that it had not learned how to use the talents of the young people who moved into the area to study at Boston's elite universities. Moreover, because the Church was not particularly strong in the Boston area, the Boston Stake was a fueling station for these talented young people but not a destination point. Tom concluded that nothing would change unless he planted the idea in the members' minds that the Boston Stake was one of the great stakes of the Church. It was a place to study but also a place to stay, succeed in a career, raise a family, and, of course, build the Church.

Tom began to share a new vision of the Boston Stake with priesthood leaders. He called it the best stake in the Church east of the Mississippi, with the line moving farther west all the time.[2] Perhaps leaders and members were initially skeptical, but none of them could dispute the Boston Stake's tremendous pool of talent. Whether it really was the best stake in the Church east of the Mississippi, people began to believe it could be, and Tom's vision became a self-fulfilling prophecy.

A Divine Organization and Order

As the president of the Boston Stake, Tom became the Lord's executive. He believed he had received inspiration—a vision of what the stake could become. The next thing to do was to break down the transformation of the Boston Stake into simple, orderly steps.

Seeking inspiration about how to proceed, Tom began to study and ponder the order by which God created the universe and, in turn, all forms of life on earth. Tom gleaned from his study an understanding of God's divine system of organization and order that has helped him break down, order, and organize complex assignments ever since.[3]

Using the second chapter of Moses as his guide, Tom began to share his insights about how God brought His organization and order to the chaos that existed before the creation of the universe. God started with a purpose—to bring to pass the immortality and eternal life of man.[4]

Tom's counsel to every Church leader in the Boston Stake was to approach every assignment with God's purpose in mind—to bring to pass the eternal life of man. He taught:

"See, you don't have to worry about immortality, the Savior has provided that for us. But every church leader—I guess you could say the same as the Lord did, 'For this is my work and glory to bring to pass the eternal life of man. . . . Now that's what your work is. The rest of it is just frosting on the cake, road maps to help you get there. But the real objective is to get man to the point where his family unit has the opportunity of growing forever."[5]

As stake president, Tom believed his primary role was helping the ward and stake leaders help the members receive eternal life, and this belief gave purpose and focus to everything he did.

To accomplish His purposes, God's first step in the Creation was to introduce the light of His word and power.[6] The light, therefore, encompassed both divine law and divine power. It both illuminated and fueled God's creation. In God's case, the light was His, and in man's case, it was borrowed light—the light of personal inspiration as well as the inspired doctrines, principles, and policies of the Church. The power was also God's—delegated to men when they are ordained to the Aaronic and Melchizedek Priesthoods and contingent on their personal righteousness.

Tom knew his doctrinal understanding needed to increase, and he became even more motivated to study the scriptures consistently. He also wanted to increase in priesthood power, and he resolved to work to strengthen his faith and increase his personal worthiness. These two resolves help him receive the light of inspiration.

There was another source of light—the information disseminated to stake presidents by the Church's leaders—and, in this case, the principal challenge for Tom was dealing with too much, not too little information. Tom soon found it was difficult to keep up with all the mail he received from the Church offices in Salt Lake City. There was so much mail from Salt Lake that it often would not fit in their mailbox, and Virginia had to convince the mailman to drive up the driveway and throw the mail in the garage. Taking delivery of all the mail, however, was only the beginning. All of it needed to be read and distributed.

Virginia came to Tom's rescue by volunteering to read his nonconfidential mail and different handbooks for an hour each day into a tape recorder so he could listen to them while he commuted to Cambridge. This was so helpful to Tom that he considered copying Virginia's tapes to share with the other members of the stake presidency. The idea proved impractical, however, because Virginia occasionally interjected clever commentary as she read. Tom worried that someone less familiar with Virginia's keen wit might get into an accident while listening and driving.

The second step in the Creation—what God accomplished during the second creative period—was to bring organization and order to the earth by dividing the waters from the land. This was something that played to Tom's strengths and his extensive experience in organizing wards and stakes. Perhaps the greatest benefit of serving in several bishoprics and stake presidencies was that Tom was able to observe and learn organizational skills from several skilled Church leaders—Bishops Barker and Bagley and Presidents Hunt, McAllister, and Fresh. Moreover, he had watched his father lead the Logan Ninth Ward and later serve as the president of the Cache Valley Stake. Gradually, Tom had internalized the best administrative practices of all these great men and leaders. The Lord had prepared him through these experiences, and Tom had blended them with his special strengths to create a unique mix of organizational skills.

Tom firmly believed what he had heard President Harold B. Lee teach—that the Church was like scaffolding to support individuals and families.[7] When thinking about how to organize the Church, he would always reflect on God's eternal purpose—individual salvation and exaltation. This was the basis for his training in the Boston Stake about the necessity of local adaptation of Church programs to the unique needs and circumstances of the members of the stake.

One of the Boston Stake's innovations, a home-study seminary program, resulted from adapting a Church program to local needs. The process started with a few of the stronger wards in the Boston Stake sponsoring an early-morning seminary program. During Tom's tenure as stake president, a few of the youth were involved in serious automobile accidents while driving on icy winter roads to early-morning seminary. As the leaders of the Boston Stake discussed the problem in different stake councils, someone proposed the idea of developing a home-study program. The Boston Stake adapted the existing early-morning seminary curriculum to support the youth studying the gospel at home. The stake also began sponsoring Super Saturdays at the stake center once a month so the youth of the stake could gather and strengthen each other. As the program evolved, it came to the attention of some of the leaders in Salt Lake City, and they visited the Boston Stake to learn more about the program. Eventually, the program was adopted across many stakes of the Church where it fit local needs better than the early-morning seminary program.

An added benefit of local adaptation was that the leaders and members of the Boston Stake felt a strong sense of ownership for Church programs they fit to local circumstances. Occasionally, leaders had to reign in members who strayed outside the lines of established doctrine and policy, but these incidents were usually treated as useful learning opportunities. The energy and excitement generated by local adaptation was palpable. Leaders and members felt empowered by Tom's leadership.

Helen Claire Sievers, for example, called Tom, in his role as president of the Boston Stake, "the most empowering person [she] ever worked for." There are several reasons that Tom's leadership style empowered others, but what separated Tom from other leaders was the level of enthusiasm he brought to a project or program. Sister Sievers also said about President Perry: "He had a twinkle in his eye that was infectious, and you'd find yourself smiling at him, and at the world. It made you want to work your heart out for him."[8]

Tom taught the leaders of the Boston Stake that during the third creative period, God established a supply line—the beginning of a food chain for all living creatures, including man, who would eventually inhabit the earth.[9] Tom believed in supporting the leaders and members of the Boston Stake as much as possible to help them become successful. He realized that not all members would be successful, but if they weren't, the reason should never be inadequate support.

Tom recognized that much of the talent in the Boston Stake was concentrated in only a few wards. For the stake to reach its potential, the rich talent of a few wards needed to be spread across a fifteen-unit stake in which many of the units suffered from a lack of talent. Fortunately, President G. Stanley McAllister had taught Tom how to do exactly that using the stake high council.

High councilors became lifelines to the weaker units of the Boston Stake. Just as Tom had done as a high councilor assigned to the Rego Park Branch in New York, the high councilors in the Boston Stake stood shoulder to shoulder and helped guide bishops and branch presidents throughout the stake. In both his role as a stake president and a General Authority, Elder Perry has often said:

"The good stakes are the ones that the high councils are just as devoted and put in the same amount of time as the stake presidency. And when you do that, the burden comes right off your [a stake presidency's] shoulders because a supply line has been established that runs through a high councilor."[10]

Most of the work done to support the fifteen units of the Boston Stake was done in the Aaronic and Melchizedek Priesthood committee meetings conducted by one of the counselors in the stake presidency. Reporting lines were cleaned up so each high councilor reported about his unit and his other assignments through one member of the stake presidency. Tom rarely attended either the Aaronic or Melchizedek Priesthood committee meetings. He respected the stewardship and agency of his counselors and their respective committees. He knew that anything that needed his attention would be brought to the stake presidency meetings. In other words, he respected the channels established by the Boston Stake's supply line.

During the fourth creative period, God created the sun, moon, and stars "for signs, and for seasons, and for days, and for years."[11] God gave to mankind another critical piece in the establishment of organization and order—a way to keep and schedule time. As a stake president, Tom believed that time was a sacred resource that needed to be managed carefully. He ran disciplined meetings and scheduled them as precisely as the commuter trains he rode in New York. His counselors quickly learned about Tom's strong preference for short high council meetings and his intolerance of long ones.[12]

Tom also expected reports to be submitted in a timely manner. He purposely scheduled stake leadership meetings during the first week of the month, and the bishops were expected to submit their correlated reports prior to the meeting. Tom described the process in the following way:

"We used to have a clerk who would sit and take all of the correlated reports as they [the bishops and branch presidents] would come in. He would send me a little slip that would say—such and such a ward didn't turn in a report. If we let that go on forever, the poor stake clerk was calling down there 10 or 11 times a month trying to get a report in and the reporting cycle was thrown completely off schedule. We just decided we wouldn't tolerate that. They would bring in their correlated report on the night of stake leadership meeting or stay with me until it was done."[13]

Early in Tom's tenure as stake president, one of the bishops did not bring his ward's correlated report with him to the meeting. Tom stayed with the bishop until he finally finished his report—at 3:00 a.m. It was the last time the bishop had a problem submitting his correlated report on time.

Again, Tom expected most of the work of the high council to be done in smaller Aaronic and Melchizedek Priesthood committee meetings. During the time his counselors met with their respective committees, Tom met with the stake clerk and executive secretary. Their meetings focused on assessing the stake's progress, and they incorporated the final lesson Tom learned from the Creation story: at different times in each creative period, God looked upon his work and judged it good.[14] Even God employed a quality-control system.

Tom's system of quality control in the Boston Stake relied on the stake clerk to gather the necessary performance information and on the executive secretary to analyze it.[15] Tom's Church and business experience taught him to look at both upward and downward trends in each of the units of the Boston Stake and the stake overall. If there was a strong upward trend, he wanted to know enough about the reasons for it so he could share them with other units. If there were downward trends, he wanted to identify their causes and address them quickly so that small problems did not grow into large problems. The results of Tom's work with the clerk and executive secretary were shared first with his counselors in stake presidency meetings. Then the counselors issued the appropriate assignments to the high councilors and their respective committees. It was a highly efficient system for driving continuous improvements in the Boston Stake.

The Fall of 1970

The fall of 1970 proved to be eventful for the Perry family. Lee and Barbara had returned home to Weston for the summer after eight months at BYU, and Lee had submitted his papers to serve a mission. He was called to enter the Salt Lake Mission Home on September 6, 1970, and was assigned to serve in the Japan West Mission under President Kan Watanabe. Tom was able to set Lee apart before he left on his mission because of a recent change in Church policy authorizing stake presidents to assume this responsibility. Lee's setting apart would have been special by any measure, but it was particularly so because he was one of the first missionaries Tom set apart. About the experience, Lee later said:

"My father is not one to show a lot of emotion, but he was in tears during the blessing. And then he followed it up by writing a letter and putting it into my suitcase without my knowledge. When I got to the mission home and opened my bag, there was the letter. In it, he told me he was proud to be my father. Since I've always idolized him, that was pretty significant. It stayed with me as a source of strength and comfort throughout my mission."[16]

On Thanksgiving Day 1970, a near tragedy struck the presidency of the Boston Stake. Gene Dalton, Tom's first counselor, suffered a major heart attack. In a Christmas Day letter to his sister Gay, Tom described what happened:

"My first counselor went to Cape Cod with his family for Thanksgiving and had a heart attack while they were there. He is still in the hospital at Cape Cod. We almost lost him. He is a young man, only 43. He has a family of five girls. The oldest is just one year younger than Gay. We have been making several trips between the Cape and here to take his wife down for visits. The older girl usually spends weekends with us while her mother is down at the hospital. His illness has had all of us examining the type of lives we have been living. He is a professor at the Harvard Business School. The shock that he almost lost the opportunity of rearing his family has caused him to do a great deal of self-evaluation."

Fortunately, by the time Virginia wrote her sister Jessie a letter dated February 19, 1971, she could report that Gene's doctors had told his wife, Bonnie, that he was making a "very good" recovery.

Tom's employer, Dayton Hudson, the company that had acquired Lechmere, began to make some unusual requests for information from Tom during the fall of 1970. These were not the normal requests for financial performance information that a subsidiary would be expected to share with its parent company. They were mostly requests for more personal information about one of the Cohen brothers. Tom did not feel he could respond to their requests and remain loyal to the Cohen family. He dug in his heels, refusing to comply, and after a short time his relationship with Dayton Hudson's senior management began to deteriorate. By Christmas, the situation had reached an impasse. In the same Christmas Day letter to Gay, Tom wrote:

"I am having a very lazy Christmas season for the first time in nineteen years this year. I am still at war with my employers and taking every day of my vacation this year for, I believe, the first time. I will be on vacation during the entire time that Barbara is home.

"Working conditions are slowly becoming impossible with our new owners. I am certain that we will agree to separate before long. It can't go on much longer like this."

Tom formally left Lechmere on March 1, 1971, but he never returned to work there on a regular basis after New Year's.[17] He did not mention it in his Christmas letter to Gay, but Tom was also contemplating another piece of grim news as winter approached. He did not mention it to Gay because Virginia had sworn him to secrecy. She had been diagnosed with an extremely aggressive cancer and given only six months to live.

Upon receiving her oncologist's diagnosis, Virginia turned immediately to Tom and said, "Don't tell anyone about this. I don't want it to change our way of life or have anyone treat us differently." Outside her team of doctors, nobody in the Boston area, except Tom, knew about her condition. In a February 19, 1971, letter to her sister Jessie, who had been like a second mother in raising her, Virginia only reported: "I had an operation the middle of January. Because Tom was home to take care of me, I was only in the hospital 5 days. He did a great job."

Virginia's Secret

It was relatively easy for Virginia to keep her illness a secret from two of her children—Barbara was in Utah, and Lee was in Japan. She also chose not to tell Linda Gay, who was nevertheless old enough to know something was wrong. There were a few times, for example, when Linda answered telephone calls from doctors' offices, and she was given a message to pass on to her mother about her white blood count. On several occasions, Virginia, sensing Linda's worries, reassured her daughter by telling her that the doctors were pleased with the progress she was making. Virginia didn't volunteer additional information, and Linda trusted her mother enough not to ask probing questions.[18]

Tom did tell Chase Peterson—a member of the Boston Stake, vice president at Harvard University, and a medical doctor—about Virginia's illness, and Chase volunteered to coordinate her treatment. This proved to be a great blessing to Virginia and clearly helped extend her life. Dr. Peterson knew the best cancer specialists in the Boston medical community, and he used his considerable influence to arrange for Virginia to see them quickly.[19]

Beginning in January 1971, Virginia was operated on three times by Dr. Charles Easterday, a skilled surgeon at the Boston Hospital for Women. Dr. Easterday had his surgical routines, and so did Virginia. Elder Perry described her routine at the April 1975 general conference:

"Her pattern of life in the hospital was always the same. With her careful planning, she would attend church on Sunday, the operation would be performed early Monday morning. By Tuesday, she was trying to get out of bed. By Wednesday she would be up moving around, trying to regain her physical strength. Thursday would find her helping the nurses assist others who were in the hospital. Friday she would spend trying to convince the doctor that she was ready to go home. By Saturday morning the doctor would give up in despair and discharge her. Sunday she would be back in church looking radiant. No one would ever suspect that she had just gone through major surgery. After the meeting I would rush down to take her home to get her some needed rest. And as I would come close to her I would hear her say to someone else in need, 'Now don't worry about a thing. I'll have dinner ready for you and at your home on Thursday night.'"[20]

Each of Virginia's surgeries was followed by the most aggressive chemotherapy treatments available at the time. The side effects of the chemo treatments made Virginia's life extremely unpleasant, but she refused to feel sorry for herself through the ordeal. She desperately wanted to live, but she also knew her life was entirely in the hands of the Lord. After a difficult night—and she endured many of them—Tom would plead with her to remain in bed. Her answer was always the same as she arose to cook him breakfast: "No, I am not going to start that."[21] Virginia must have whispered to herself hundreds of times the same words she wrote to her son, Lee, in the mission field in a May 18, 1971, letter: "We know if we put our trust in our Heavenly Father and rely on Him, He will not forsake us. He will hear our petitions, and we will be able to see and know His hand is over us."

After leaving Lechmere, Tom was unable to resolve his work situation for approximately a year. Given Virginia's health issues, Tom actually considered it a blessing not to be heavily involved at work. He worked at various small ventures, mostly at a small start-up, Flowtron, that produced a small but powerful space heater, and at a small variety store in Mansfield, Massachusetts. Virginia told Lee about his father's employment situation in an April 30, 1971, letter, primarily to reassure him. She wrote:

"I hope you are not overly concerned about things at home. Don't be. Your Dad is not discouraged in that regard. He has a couple of things going. We are confident things will work out. So don't add any unnecessary worries to your mind."

It was during this period that Tom and Virginia began to visit Walden Pond frequently. Elder Perry relived those cherished times with Virginia in his address at the October 2008 general conference. He said:

"We drove to a place just a few miles from our home to get away for a few moments of relief from our troubles, talk, and give emotional comfort to each other. Our place was Walden Pond. It was a beautiful little pond surrounded by forests of trees. When my wife was feeling strong enough, we'd go for a walk around the pond. Other days, when she did not feel up to the exertion of walking, we'd just sit in the car and talk. Walden Pond was our special place to pause, reflect, and heal. Perhaps it was partly due to its history—its connection to the efforts of Henry David Thoreau to separate himself from worldliness for a period of years—that Walden Pond offered us so much hope for simplicity and provided such a renewing escape from our overly complex lives."[22]

Following Barbara's Wedding

Tom and Virginia's daughter Barbara married Terry Haws on January 26, 1972, in the Salt Lake Temple. They were delighted by Barbara's choice for an eternal companion. In an

April 26, 1971, letter to her brother, Lee, Barbara described her future husband:

"It's funny, but to look at him you wouldn't think he was my type. He's short, dark, and wears glasses, but he's a tremendous person, and that's what I'm looking for. He's strong in the Church and has a strong, but subtle influence on me. I think I could talk forever about him, but I'll spare you."

Tom and Virginia quickly bonded with Terry and his delightful family. On their way home from the wedding, Tom was interviewed in the Salt Lake Airport by the president of the Church College of Hawaii (now BYU–Hawaii) about a finance position affiliated with the college. In a letter to Jessie, Virginia mentioned the interview but did not expect it would lead to a move to Hawaii. Virginia's health, especially the exceptional treatment she was receiving in Boston, was the primary reason Tom was hesitant to pursue an opportunity to live in paradise.

Soon, different executive placement firms became aware of Tom's situation, and the job market began to open up for him. There were two firms that wanted to interview him—American Factors (Amfac), headquartered in San Francisco, and R. H. Stearns in Boston. First, Tom flew to San Francisco to interview with Amfac, a large conglomerate with several holdings that included the Joseph Magnin and Liberty House department store chains. There were many reasons Tom and Virginia were reluctant to leave Boston, so Tom decided to make salary and profit-sharing demands he was certain the company would not meet. Then, to his surprise, they met all of his terms. Tom, however, decided to decline the attractive offer. About the experience, Virginia said:

"When Tom returned home he said to me: 'Ginny, I didn't know why, but all during my flight to San Francisco, I had the uneasy feeling that something wasn't right about this position. I was welcomed with cordial enthusiasm and all my requirements were met. Then I was told that board meeting was held each Saturday morning. You know I've had experience with board meetings before, and sometimes they last all day.'"[23]

The offer was so attractive, however, that Tom struggled with his resolve when it came time to call Amfac's president and turn it down. He went upstairs to their bedroom, sat at his desk, and pondered what he was going to say. He took his scriptures out of the drawer to read them for a few minutes as he sought inspiration. Quite randomly, he opened his scriptures to section 111 of the Doctrine and Covenants, and he started to read the introduction. What immediately caught his attention was that the revelation was given to Joseph Smith in Salem, Massachusetts. This led him to read with greater interest because he knew this was the only revelation in the Doctrine and Covenants received in the state where he lived. Nothing in section 111 particularly stuck out in Tom's mind until he came to verse 7. It said, "Tarry in this place, and in the regions round about." The remainder of the section provided further assurances to the Prophet Joseph that if he tarried longer in Massachusetts, the reasons would be revealed to him at a later time.

Tom had received his own assurance. He picked up the telephone, called Amfac's president, and turned down the offer. The president was surprised, and he did not understand how Tom could turn down the offer when it contained everything he had requested. Of course, Tom was unable to explain all the reasons. He hadn't learned them yet.

Assuming he should accept the only offer that would allow him to "tarry" in Massachusetts, Tom quickly accepted the position of treasurer for R. H. Stearns Company. He began his employment at Stearns, a small but successful department store chain, in April 1972.

Tom was still in the first month of his new job when the Boston Stake hosted a young single adult conference for nine hundred members from as far south as Washington, D.C., and as far north as Canada's Maritime Provinces.

The May 1972 Young Single Adult Conference

Glade Howell, the coordinator of LDS seminaries and institutes for the Boston area and also a member of the Boston Stake high council, recommended to Tom that the stake host a multistake and district young single adult conference. Tom sought permission from Church leaders in Salt Lake City for nearly two years until it was finally granted. The plan was for a three-day conference, during which attendees would be housed in the homes of local Church members.

After permission was granted, two important Church leaders asked to attend the conference—Elder Marion D. Hanks and Neal A. Maxwell, who at the time was Church Commissioner of Education. Sister Elaine Cannon[24] also asked to come so she could report on the conference for the *New Era*. A greater surprise for Tom came one day while he was at work. His secretary said, "There is a man by the name of Lee from Salt Lake who wants to talk to you." Tom was not sure who was calling, but it sounded like a phone call he should take. The person calling Tom was President Harold B. Lee, who at the time was serving as First Counselor to President Joseph Fielding Smith. President Lee asked if he could also attend the May 1972 conference.

Tom and Virginia hosted President Lee at the three-day conference. Later, Tom described the experience of having President Lee there: "We had a glorious time with him. During that last meeting, he talked for about 45 minutes, as only President Lee could talk, to the young people. He bore such a strong witness. When it was over, no one moved. The Spirit was so strong that nobody wanted to get up and leave. It was such a spiritual feeling."[25]

Only two months later, on July 2, 1972, President Joseph Fielding Smith passed away, and President Harold B. Lee became the eleventh president of The Church of Jesus Christ of Latter-day Saints.

CHAPTER 21

The October 1972 General Conference

Lee was scheduled to arrive home from his mission to Japan, and Tom, Virginia, and Linda Gay waited patiently for him to step off the plane at Boston Logan International Airport. The Perrys were not particularly concerned when Lee did not initially appear. He had a flair for the dramatic, and they figured he was waiting to be the last person off the plane. When the flight attendants entered the concourse, Tom asked one of them how many more passengers were still on the plane. "No passengers—just the captain and co-captain," she responded. Suddenly, the Perrys were worried. Lee had called them from New York City after his flight from Tokyo had landed, and he had assured them he had plenty of time to make his connecting flight to Boston.

Unfortunately, the Perrys did not have time to figure out what had happened to Lee after his phone call and why he wasn't on the plane. Tom, still the president of the Boston

Stake, had scheduled a prospective missionary interview at their home for that evening. He had been nervous about it, but the young man was eager to have his interview, and Tom figured he could squeeze it in while Virginia and Linda prepared something for Lee to eat.

Lee had made two mistakes at John F. Kennedy International Airport. First, in his excitement he had called home too quickly—before he realized he had to ride a shuttle to another terminal to catch his flight to Boston. Second, he had miscalculated the time change between Tokyo and New York. A connection he believed he had plenty of time to make was actually very tight. Accordingly, while he was having a leisurely conversation with his parents on a pay phone at JFK, he was missing his connecting flight. After arriving at the other terminal, he called home to explain what had happened and to share his new flight information, but his family had already left for the airport.[1]

When Lee finally arrived at Logan Airport in Boston, his family was driving back to Weston for Tom's interview. Lee called home, but there was no answer, and there was nothing he could do but wait and keep calling on a pay phone. Finally, Virginia answered the telephone at the Perry home. Lee explained what had happened to him at JFK, and Virginia was relieved her son was safe. The young man who had been waiting for his missionary interview when the Perrys arrived at their house was understanding when Tom explained to him what had happened. The young man suggested that they reschedule their appointment. Tom, Virginia, and Linda then jumped back into the car and headed back to the airport. In forty-five minutes they found Lee waiting for them with a very large suitcase and duffel bag in front of Logan Airport. The reunion was just as joyous as the previous hour had been frantic.

Lee was home for only a few weeks before he left to attend the fall semester at BYU. The sadness of having to separate again so quickly, however, was partially mitigated by Tom, Virginia, and Linda's plans to attend the October 1972 general conference. The plan was for them to fly to Arizona, where Barbara and Terry were living, spend a few days, and then rent a car and drive to Provo. They figured they would arrive in Provo very late, stay in a motel, pick up Lee at his dormitory room in Deseret Towers at 8:00 a.m. on Thursday, October 5, and eat breakfast together at the Morris Center cafeteria.

Once again, however, everything did not go according to plan. The Perrys left Barbara and Terry's apartment as planned on Wednesday, but as they approached Beaver, Utah, on I-15, Virginia realized that Delta, Utah, was only 100 miles from Beaver[2] and they could spend the night with her sister Mary and her husband, Orlin Hunsaker.[3] They tried to call Lee that night from the Hunsakers' home, but they were unable to reach him.

When nobody knocked on his door at 8:00 a.m. Thursday, Lee was disappointed but not overly concerned. He waited as long as he could, left a note on his door explaining where he had gone, and ran to his 10:00 a.m. basketball class. He figured he would return to his room after class and, he hoped, connect with his family for lunch. All he really knew was that his parents and Linda were probably driving somewhere between Tempe, Arizona, and Provo.

About midway through Lee's basketball class, a BYU Security officer walked onto the basketball court and talked briefly with the class instructor. He asked if a Tom Perry was in the class. The instructor did not know that the Lee Perry on his class roll was Lee Tom Perry, and he told the officer he must be mistaken.

When the officer returned during the final minutes of class, he asked the instructor to check again. Fortunately, Lee overheard them talking, and he volunteered his full name. The officer then escorted him to a nearby office. As they walked, he said to Lee, "I don't know what this is all about, but the First Presidency is looking for your father."

The officer picked up a telephone, dialed a number, and handed the phone to Lee. The man on the line identified himself as D. Arthur Haycock, personal secretary to President Harold B. Lee. He told Lee that President Lee had a matter of some urgency to discuss with his father, and he asked him how he could contact Tom. Because Lee knew only that Tom was somewhere between Tempe and Provo, he was not particularly helpful. Brother Haycock thanked Lee, and he asked to speak again to the officer. He instructed the officer to drive Lee back to Deseret Towers and stay with him until his father arrived.

When the officer and Lee pulled up to Ballard Hall at Deseret Towers, Lee saw his father walking out the front door with a confused look on his face. When Tom looked in Lee's direction and saw him get out of a BYU Security car, his face became more confused. Lee had been home from his mission only a month and a half. What kind of trouble could he have gotten into already? Lee ran toward his father, and before Tom could ask for an explanation, his son announced, "President Lee is trying to reach you, Dad!"

Suddenly, the blood drained from Tom's face. He remembered there was a pending matter he had intended to discuss with the Office of the First Presidency during his conference visit. He had not figured the matter urgent enough to warrant a phone call from President Lee, but what else could it be? Tom asked Lee to take him up to his dorm room, and he called Brother Haycock. Brother Haycock did not explain the reason, but he arranged an appointment for Tom to meet with President Lee in the late afternoon.

THE OFFICE OF THE FIRST PRESIDENCY

Tom drove to Salt Lake City with Virginia, Lee, and Linda Gay. They parked at the Hotel Utah, and Virginia decided she and the children would wait in the hotel lobby while Tom went to see President Lee.

Tom walked into the Church Administration Building through the front door and entered the Office of the First Presidency on the main floor. Everything around him looked much as he remembered it when his father, then the bishop of the Logan Ninth Ward, had taken the deacons, teachers, and priests to meet President Heber J. Grant and President David O. McKay in the First Presidency boardroom. Tom introduced himself to Brother Haycock, and he was told President Lee was expecting him.

As Tom opened the door to President Lee's office, he was overwhelmed when his eyes met President Lee's eyes as he looked up from behind his desk. Tom had spent significant time with President Lee in Boston only five months earlier, but much had changed since then. President Lee was now the President of The Church of Jesus Christ of Latter-day Saints. He had been chosen by the Lord as the only person on earth authorized to exercise all the keys of the priesthood. It was impossible for Tom to comprehend standing, again, in the presence of the prophet. President Lee stood up and came around from his desk. He took Tom's arm and invited him to sit down in a chair next to him.

The next few moments changed Tom's life as President Lee asked him two questions. The first question President Lee asked was, "Would you accept the call to serve as an Assistant to the Twelve?" Before Tom could answer, President Lee asked: "How soon can you move west?"

About his time with President Lee, Tom later said:

"It was an overwhelming, and a very spiritual experience. There is nothing like sitting face-to-face with President Lee and receiving a call like that. It seemed like several minutes before I could say anything."[4]

After Tom had accepted the call, and he indicated he could probably wrap up his affairs in Boston and move west by the end of the year, President Lee instructed Tom to be considerate of his employers and to make sure he left under good terms. He also explained to Tom that he would be sustained the next morning at the opening session of general conference, which was also a solemn assembly. President Lee gave Tom permission to tell Virginia and his children about his new call, but he was instructed not to tell anyone else until he was sustained. Finally, President Lee asked Tom if he had any questions. When Tom could not think of anything to ask, he simply thanked President Lee. He left the Office of the First Presidency and walked directly to the lobby of the Hotel Utah, still a bit dazed by what had just happened to him. He needed to see Virginia to steady himself.

As Tom entered through the South Temple Street doors of the hotel, he saw Virginia across the lobby talking to his cousin Richard Sonne and his wife, Norma. Richard, a regional representative, was in town for general conference. Richard was the son of Elder Alma Sonne, who at the time was the longest serving Assistant to the Twelve. Tom now knew that the next day he would join his uncle Alma as a newly sustained Assistant to the Twelve, but it was news he could not share with his cousin.

Tom tried to act as if nothing had just happened to him, and while he knew he should act more excited to see the Sonnes, all he could think about was finding a quiet place to share his news with Virginia and the children. Virginia, seeing Tom's ashen face, suggested the family walk over to Temple Square and find a quiet corner in which to talk in what is known today as the North Visitor's Center. On the way, Tom whispered to Virginia, "I think we're in trouble."

Upon finding a private spot in the Visitors' Center, Tom shared the news. Virginia teared up and said, "Oh, I've expected it." Linda asked, "Does this mean no more trips to Fenway just when the Red Sox are starting to get good?" When Tom nodded, she started to cry. Lee said, "Do you know what this means? You're going to be giving talks all the time, and you've never been very good at that sort of thing."[5]

Tom and Virginia had decided in planning their trip to general conference that to be close to Lee for the weekend, they would make motel reservations in Provo, not in Salt Lake City.[6] Their reservations were at the Royal Inn, near the northwest entrance to the BYU campus. In the rush for Tom to meet with President Lee, however, they had forgotten to check into their motel room. So they drove back to Provo and checked into their room. Once they had carried their luggage into their motel room, they realized they also had forgotten to eat lunch. They decided to join Lee for dinner at the Morris Center cafeteria. After dinner, they went to the Ballard Hall lobby and spent the rest of the evening talking. A few minutes after 9:00 p.m., Tom suddenly realized that only he had a ticket to the Tabernacle for the solemn assembly in the morning. Virginia and the children would get into the Tabernacle to see him sustained only if they left Provo very early in the morning. They decided to call it a night.

Tom had a difficult time sleeping that night. The family arose early, picked up Lee at Deseret Towers when it was still dark outside, and drove to Salt Lake. They noticed an unusual amount of traffic on I-15 for so early on a Friday morning, and by the time they arrived in Salt Lake, the reason became clear to them. They had miscalculated how many people wanted to attend the solemn assembly in the Tabernacle. Temple Square was overflowing with people, and as soon as Virginia saw the long lines outside the Tabernacle, she decided that Lee, Linda, and she should go to the nearby Salt Palace arena[7] to watch the conference. With his stake president's ticket, Virginia assumed Tom would have no trouble getting inside.

Tom went to one of the Tabernacle doors indicated on his ticket and found his place at the back of the line. As the usher at the head of the line began to seat people and the line progressed, Tom began to worry that he also might not get into the Tabernacle. When the usher informed everyone left standing in line that the Tabernacle was full and that they should probably go to the Salt Palace, Tom momentarily panicked. He decided he needed to approach the usher and plead for a seat. Tom told the man, "I can't explain why, but I really need to be inside the Tabernacle." Recognizing the desperation in Tom's voice, the usher found him half a seat at the end of one of the pews. Tom sheepishly sat down and introduced himself to the man he was crowding next to him on the pew. They had plenty of time to get to know each other while waiting for the solemn assembly to begin.

A few minutes after 10:00 a.m., the men's chorus of the Mormon Tabernacle Choir sang the sacred hymn "Give Ear, Oh Lord."[8] When the chorus had finished, President N. Eldon Tanner stepped to the pulpit to conduct what is officially known as the "procedure for sustaining President Harold B. Lee, for the reorganization of the First Presidency, and the sustaining of all the other General Authorities and general officers of The Church of Jesus Christ of Latter-day Saints." This unique sustaining procedure, followed only when a new President of the Church is sustained at the beginning of his administration, dates back to the sustaining of President John Taylor as the Church's third President. It involved two parts—the first part for sustaining the President, his counselors, the Quorum of the Twelve Apostles, and—at the time—the patriarch of the Church; and the second part for sustaining the remainder of the General Authorities and general officers of the Church.[9]

During the first part of the sustaining, Elder Bruce R. McConkie was sustained as the newest member of the Quorum of the Twelve Apostles. At the beginning of the second part, three men were sustained as new Assistants to the Quorum of the Twelve: Elders O. Leslie Stone, James E. Faust, and L. Tom Perry. When Tom was sustained, the man sitting next to him recognized his name, excitedly turned to congratulate him, and accidently pushed Tom off the end of the pew. Tom offered his sustaining vote while seated on the floor of the Tabernacle. Fortunately, it was not very long before Tom was invited to take his place on the stand with the other General Authorities.

As Tom sat on the stand in the Tabernacle, he looked around and observed the other brethren—men he had revered all of his life. He watched some of their mannerisms, but what struck him most powerfully was the incredible spirit of brotherly love he felt as he sat among them. He still wondered if he belonged, but he immediately felt their acceptance.

The Perrys returned to Provo following the Friday afternoon session. After another fitful night's sleep in their motel room, Tom arose at 5:00 a.m. and walked to the Provo Temple. He described the experience later in an interview with a reporter:

"As I meditated on why I had been called, I thought of all the training I had received in the Church; I thought of the great leaders who had guided and instructed me throughout my life; I thought of the years of training I had gained in stake and regional organizations; and then I thought that perhaps I had been called because of this training. Perhaps it might allow me to be of some assistance to the General Authorities."[10]

Tom was the next-to-last speaker in the Sunday afternoon session—just before President Lee closed the conference. He was brief in offering three pledges. He said:

"Elder Loren Dunn, as I left for lunch, whispered in my ear and said, 'They grade General Authorities on how little time they take in their first address.' I am trying for a straight A today.

"I would like to make three pledges: First of all, to my dear wife, whom I love, sustain, and support. If she continues to support me the way she has in the last twenty-five years, I know I cannot fail any assignment.

"Second, to my three lovely children, Barbara, Lee, and Gay. I will try to live worthy of the inspiration of the Lord to be a priesthood leader in the home.

"And finally, to President Lee, his great counselors, the Council of the Twelve, I sustain and support you. Let me help you carry the great burden which is yours.

"This is the church of Jesus Christ as it has been established in the latter days. I am grateful for that testimony, for the strength it gives me. I say this humbly, in the name of Jesus Christ. Amen."

The Monday after general conference, Barbara and Terry Haws received the surprise of their lives. Tom, Virginia, and Linda, without even a clue about Tom's new calling, had just left Barbara and Terry's apartment on the previous Thursday morning. Barbara and Terry were still waiting for a telephone to be installed in their apartment, so there was no way for Tom to contact them after he had met with President Lee. In addition, only the Saturday and Sunday morning sessions were broadcast in Arizona. The Haws family had no idea Barbara's father was sitting on the stand as they watched the two sessions of general conference.

On Monday evening their elders quorum president, with whom Terry served as a counselor, stopped by to congratulate them on Elder Perry's new calling. In an October 27, 1972, letter to her Aunt Gay and Uncle Albert, Barbara described Terry's and her reaction. She wrote: "We stood there with our mouths opened. I called home and found out it was true. We are honored and proud of Dad!"

I'll Go Where You Want Me to Go

Tom had turned fifty years old exactly two months before President Lee issued the call that changed his life. Perhaps in a church in which hundreds of men have responded to the call to be General Authorities, and thousands of men have responded to the call to be mission presidents, it does not seem extraordinary that a man doesn't ask a single question when he is asked to give up a life he has spent fifty years building and start a new one, but it is.

After general conference, Tom, Virginia, and Linda Gay flew back to Boston. Several months earlier, Tom had felt that the Lord wanted him to "tarry" in Massachusetts, and now the Lord was asking him to leave and return to Utah. For Tom, the message was clear—he had finished what the Lord wanted him to do in Massachusetts, and it was now the right time, according to the Lord's timetable, to go, and the right thing, according to the Lord's plans, to go to. All that was important was to focus on wrapping up his affairs as soon as possible. If this was his focus, everything would work out the way the Lord intended it.

This meant that Tom needed to tell his employer, R. H. Stearns Company, that he was leaving after working there for only six months. It meant he had to be released as the president of the Boston Stake. Elder Howard W. Hunter went to Boston and presided over the stake reorganization held on October 28-29, 1972, and he called one of Tom's counselors, Richard Bushman, to replace him. It also meant he had to sell Virginia's dream home and his beloved Ashland property, pack up, and move.

By the fall of 1972, Virginia had been teaching the Cultural Refinement lessons in the Weston Ward Relief Society for three years. One of the lessons she gave had been about obedience, and she had shared with the women of the Weston Ward an article from the September 1970 *Improvement Era* magazine by Albert L. Zobell Jr. titled "I'll Go Where You Want Me to Go."[11] The article was about Elder Melvin J. Ballard's life and his connection to hymn 270 in the 1985 LDS hymnbook. The words of the hymn come from a little book by Mary Brown titled *Make His Praise Glorious.* Later, music was added by Carry E. Rounsefell, and it was published in a somewhat modified form by a friend. Elder Ballard liked to sing the hymn at stake conferences and other special church meetings, and he was instrumental in adding the hymn to the LDS hymnbook.

The reason Mary Brown's words carried so much meaning for Elder Ballard was that he discovered them at a critical time in his life. It had been his dream to attend Harvard University, and as soon as he had saved enough money to go, President Wilford Woodruff called him to serve a special mission. When Elder Ballard's two companions, B. H. Roberts and George D. Pyper were released, he was reassigned and his mission extended. This was a blow to him, and it was just after he had submitted his letter of acceptance that he found Mary Brown's poem.

The message Virginia taught the women of the Weston Ward was that Elder Ballard's life reflected the words of the hymn—he went, said, and became everything the Lord wanted him to be. In her lesson she invited the sisters in the ward to do the same, and she promised that their lives would be blessed if they did.

It was always Virginia's way to expect herself and her family to do everything she invited others to do, and so she, Tom, and their children were going where the Lord wanted them to go. She would leave her friends, her home, and the New England lifestyle she had come to love. She would also leave the doctors and nurses who had prolonged her life, although they continued to consult with Virginia's new doctors in Utah about her treatments.

To leave on good terms with R. H. Stearns, as President Lee had instructed him to do, Tom decided to continue working through most of the Christmas holiday season. Despite having to leave Stearns unexpectedly after working there only seven and a half months, Tom left a positive, lasting impression. The company president, William M. Sanderson, said about Tom:

"His extreme dedication to everything he did was respected in his work, as well as in his Church activities. The warmth of his personality enabled him to fit in quickly . . . and he was very well liked by all. . . . He left here an impression of devotion to his religion and his family, for which we all greatly admired him."[12]

It was the afternoon of December 18 when the moving van left the house at 46 Bradyll Road in Weston. Tom, Virginia, and Linda Gay jumped into a tightly packed Chevrolet Vega sedan[13] and drove west. They were sad to leave, but they never looked back. They knew they were going where the Lord wanted them to go.

CHAPTER 22

Bountiful, Utah

Elder Perry, Virginia, and Linda arrived in Salt Lake City just two days before Christmas 1972.[1] After trying to drive their Chevrolet Vega through a couple of minor Midwestern snowstorms, they decided to wait out a major storm that hit the Rockies at exactly the wrong time. It proved difficult enough, even with chains, to drive the Vega over the higher mountain passes.

The Perrys' real estate agent found them an apartment off 300 South in Salt Lake City until they could find a house to buy. Given their circumstances, they had decided to downplay their celebration of Christmas. It did not make a lot of sense even to buy a Christmas tree when all their Christmas decorations were still in transit from Weston. Joined by Lee, they felt blessed that the four of them could be together for Christmas for the first time in three years.

Elder Perry knew that his new assignment with the Church would be as an associate director of the newly formed Melchizedek Priesthood Mutual Interest Association (MPMIA) for single adults. Another newly called Assistant to the Twelve, Elder James E. Faust, was appointed as the managing director, and Elder Marion D. Hanks, like Elder Perry, received the assignment to serve as an associate director. Elder Perry had also received in the mail a list of the stake conferences he was assigned to attend during the first half of 1973. The first stake conference he was scheduled to visit was the Marin California Stake, which was presided over by President Weston L. Roe.[2]

Elder Perry had decided that he was arriving so close to Christmas that he would not even try to go to his new office at the Church Administration Building (CAB) until after New Year's. As far as he knew, none of the other General Authorities even knew his family had arrived in town. Accordingly, it was a big surprise when Elder Marion D. Hanks and his wife, Maxine, knocked on the door of their apartment with a welcome basket and invited the Perrys to join their family in their Christmas Eve celebration the next evening.

Elder Perry and Virginia felt a little uncomfortable accepting the invitation. They had always considered the celebration of Christmas Eve to be a special time for family, especially since it was also Virginia's birthday. They did not want to intrude on the Hanks' family's Christmas Eve traditions. Elder Perry and Virginia quickly discovered, however, that Elder and Sister Hanks would not be dissuaded. Finally, their kind invitation was accepted.

The Perry and the Hanks families shared a delightful Christmas Eve together. They sang carols, read scriptures, exchanged experiences from their previous Christmases, and enjoyed delicious food. As the Perry family left the home at the end of a memorable evening, Elder and Sister Hanks presented them with a small, decorated Christmas tree. They had both noticed when they visited the Perrys at their small apartment that they had no Christmas tree.

Elder Perry, Virginia, Lee, and Linda returned to their temporary home that Christmas Eve deeply touched by the thoughtfulness and generosity of the Hanks family. They realized they had been taught a timeless lesson about being a gracious receiver at Christmastime.[3]

889 South Davis Boulevard

On the same day Elder Perry began work at the Church Administration Building, January 2, 1973, he and Virginia also became grandparents. Following a tradition established by her father for proclaiming the birth of a firstborn son, Barbara Perry Haws's baby announcements predicted future athletic glory. She wrote:

"This is the HAWS radio station in Tempe, Arizona, with Barbara and Terry Haws announcing the arrival of that great center for the Haws family basketball team:

Terry Delmar Haws, Jr.
at 2:38 AM
on this beautiful, sunny day of
January 2, 1973.
He is 21 inches tall and
weighed in at 8 lbs. 1 oz. and
he's a cutie!!!"

Elder Perry and Virginia were ecstatic about the birth of Little Terry (LT), and Elder Perry made it widely known to the senior Brethren that he was always ready and willing to take a stake conference assignment in the Phoenix-Tempe-Mesa, Arizona area.

Elder Perry could not completely immerse himself in his new assignment with the MPMIA until his family had found a permanent place to live. Whenever he could, he left work a little early to look at houses with Virginia. They quickly decided to concentrate their search in the Bountiful area, just north of Salt Lake City.

By this time in their marriage, Elder Perry and Virginia's house-hunting ritual had become highly predictable. Elder Perry consistently wanted less of a house than Virginia, but he always deferred to her wishes. Ultimately, this narrowed their search to two unfinished homes in Bountiful. They were both being built by the same builder and were of similar quality, but one was larger than the other. The larger home, located on the northeast corner of South Davis Boulevard and Bountiful Hills Drive, had a mansard roof, and Virginia fell in love with it. Elder Perry recognized the gleam in her eye when she walked through the home, and all of his practicality melted away. Virginia would be happier if they purchased the house at 889 South Davis Boulevard, and her happiness mattered far more to him than any other consideration.

The house Elder Perry and Virginia purchased, however, was not as far along as the other one they had considered. This meant they would need to continue living in their apartment in Salt Lake until the end of February. Linda Gay enrolled in Bountiful High School, which was located just below their new home, and Elder Perry drove her to school before work each day.

Moving to Utah required a much greater adjustment for Linda than for her siblings. Barbara continued her life in Arizona, mostly unaffected except for the brief stir her father's new call caused in her ward. Lee was already in Utah at BYU, and while his father's call brought him some increased attention, it was not necessarily a bad thing for someone who was naturally a little shy. Linda, however, had to adjust to a new place, attend a new school, and find new friends.

The biggest change for Linda was the mixing of school and Church. She was used to having Church friends, with whom she was extremely close, and school friends, with whom she was less close. Now the cultures of school and Church were mixed, and the lines between them were not as clearly marked. It was neither good nor bad, but it was definitely an adjustment for her.

Fortunately, Linda found some new friends who were very kind and accepting of her. Perhaps, more than anyone else, her history teacher, Phil Olsen, made Linda feel welcome at Bountiful High School, and he helped her find her place. In addition to being a history and health teacher, Mr. Olsen was also Bountiful High School's new baseball coach. Baseball became the basis of his unique bond with Linda. One day Linda started talking in class about the Red Sox. This caught Mr. Olsen's attention immediately. He started testing Linda's knowledge of the Red Sox and baseball, and he soon discovered it was encyclopedic. His biggest surprise came when he learned that Linda knew how to keep score using a baseball scorecard, which gave him an idea. Linda became the official scorekeeper for the Bountiful High baseball team. This was something she loved to do during her years at Bountiful High.

Virginia focused mostly on selecting fixtures and decorating their new home. She also arranged for a new team of doctors to treat her cancer. Her doctors in Boston had recommended an oncologist in Bountiful to supervise her chemotherapy. Virginia decided to receive her treatments at McKay-Dee Hospital in Ogden instead of at LDS Hospital in Salt Lake to lower the risk of being recognized by someone she knew while she was at the hospital. Elder Perry had informed President Lee about Virginia's illness at the time of his call as a General Authority, but he did not give reports to the prophet concerning Virginia's health, except when President Lee asked about her, which was frequently. President Lee also showed special kindness and compassion to Virginia whenever he saw her. It was as if he sensed her spiritual depth and goodness. He would also often remind her that he and the other Brethren were praying for her in the temple.

The person with whom Elder Perry confided most about Virginia's health was Elder James E. Faust. The Fausts had invited the Perry family to dinner soon after they arrived in Salt Lake. Elder Perry and Elder Faust were already forming a natural bond at work, but the dinner helped Virginia feel closer to Elder Faust's wife, Ruth. Ruth Faust assumed the role of introducing Virginia to the other General Authorities' wives. Ruth also volunteered to help Virginia shop for items for her new home, and as the two women spent time together, Virginia decided to share with Ruth that she had cancer. About their relationship, Elder Perry said:

"Ruth was one of the few people who knew that she [Virginia] was having this difficulty. . . . Ruth became Virginia's confidant, encouraging her to keep her spirits up during that period."[4]

Elder Perry deeply appreciated Elder Faust's support and encouragement and his occasional prodding when he worked too late. Elder Perry said, "He would always get after me if I wasn't paying enough attention to Virginia. He was a very thoughtful man that way."

Beyond this inner circle, only a few others knew about Virginia's cancer. Another person to whom Elder Perry and Virginia soon confided that information was Dr. Dewey McKay, who was a member of their ward[5] and who became Virginia's internist. He was a very caring man, with whom Virginia was comfortable sharing her challenges and concerns. He was especially helpful when she was conflicted about which course of treatment to pursue. Dr. McKay was not a cancer specialist, but he made it his personal mission to assist in prolonging her life. For this reason, he read extensively to learn about the latest progress in the treatment of Virginia's particular cancer.

Virginia also decided to tell Lee and Barbara, but still not Linda, about her cancer. She carefully chose a time when she was doing well so she could be upbeat with them about her prospects.

The Perrys moved into their new home at 889 South Davis Boulevard in Bountiful on March 1, 1973. Workmen were still coming every day to apply the final touches, but it was mostly finished. A feature in their home inspired Elder Perry's address at the April 1973 general conference. He said:

"The home we have just purchased since moving west has one unique feature. The small study provided has an adjoining large closet about one-fourth the size of the entire study. We thought when we were considering the purchase of the home that this closet was an error in design. Since occupying the home, it has become one of my favorite places. Here is where I can shut myself off from the world and communicate with my Father in heaven. 'But thou, when thou prayest, enter into thy closet, and when thou hast shut thy door, pray to thy Father which is in secret; and thy Father which seeth in secret shall reward thee openly'" (Matthew 6:6).[6]

The Melchizedek Priesthood MIA

The Melchizedek Priesthood MIA was the start of a strong single adult program in the Church. The light of inspired direction was provided by President Harold B. Lee, who likely had added to his understanding of the single adult members of the Church when he attended the conference hosted by the Boston Stake in May 1972. The MPMIA was a high priority for President Lee. He wanted a priesthood umbrella over the unmarried members of the Church who were eighteen years old and older. He already had great empathy for the single adult members of the Church. His first wife, Fern, died on September 24, 1962, and though he remarried in less than a year, he knew firsthand the loneliness of losing a spouse and being a widower. Moreover, President Lee's second wife, Joan, whom he married on June 17, 1963, had been single until she married him when she was sixty-five years old.

President Lee and the four members of the Quorum of the Twelve—Elders Thomas S. Monson, Boyd K. Packer, Marvin J. Ashton, and Bruce R. McConkie—appointed as advisers to the MPMIA also provided most of the organizational structure of the program. Elders James E. Faust, Marion D. Hanks, and L. Tom Perry gave direction about organizing the program at regional, stake, and ward levels. For example, there were two groups of single adult members—young single adults (ages eighteen to twenty-five) and special interests (twenty-six and older)[7]—and the relationship between the MPMIA and the Latter-day Saint Student Association (LDSSA) was clarified.[8]

Elders Faust, Hanks, and Perry were assigned by their advisers from the Quorum of the Twelve to complete the organization at the general Church level by hiring an executive secretary. Elder Hanks suggested a young man who had recently received his doctorate in American studies from Yale University and had joined the faculty at the LDS institute of religion at the University of Utah—Jeffrey R. Holland. Elder Hanks had been Jeffrey Holland's mission president in England. Elder Perry also knew Brother Holland. He had served as a counselor in the presidency of the Hartford Connecticut Stake when Elder Perry served in the stake presidency in Boston. They lived in the same region, and several times they had attended regional meetings together. Elder Faust did not know Brother Holland, but given the strong recommendations of his two associates, he wanted to interview him. At the conclusion of their interview, Elder Faust asked Brother Holland to fill the executive secretary role, and he accepted.

The four brethren appointed to direct the MPMIA program were also expected to work within the general guidelines they had been given to develop a specific program at the regional, stake, and ward levels that would better meet the needs of the single adult members of the Church. All of them wanted to design the new program, which would serve as a supply line for the single adults, from an informed perspective. They interviewed many single adults and their local Church leaders to gain insights about their circumstances and needs. About Elder Faust, who led the many interviews they held, Elder Perry observed that he had a way of "making the individual feel warm and comfortable and relaxed. And when they would leave, through his influence, I think they viewed the world as a better place than when they came in. In fact, . . . I've never seen him in a situation where he didn't have the individual he has been interviewing feel comfortable in his presence and inspired after leaving. He possesses a most unique talent that very few men on this earth have."[9]

About Elder Perry's contribution to the design of the MPMIA program, Elder Faust said: "President Harold B. Lee, in his charge to the Managing Directors (Elder Marion D. Hanks, Elder L. Tom Perry, and myself), told us to add the flesh to the bones of inspiration which he had received and be 'innovative, bold, and creative.' Elder Perry is an original thinker. This great gift, along with his wealth of experience, in business and in the Church, makes him particularly effective. He is courageous and persevering. His experience with modern business techniques makes him invaluable in helping the Church leaders provide the most modern business techniques to the administration of the work of the Lord. His greatest skills, however, are his people skills. His warmth, his understanding, his friendliness, his courtesy, his kindness, and his graciousness make him a very welcome member of any group or meeting in which he is involved."[10]

Once the initial design for the program was determined, the four Brethren began to implement it. As time passed, they continued to learn by doing, and they made the necessary adjustments to ensure that the program was meeting the needs it was designed to meet. In other words, they established a feedback system of accountability and quality control.[11]

Down Under

Elder and Sister Perry traveled together on his first assignment outside North America in May 1973. He had a stake conference assignment in Honolulu on May 6 and 7, and then they traveled to Australia and New Zealand to participate in area conferences.

It was chilly in New Zealand, and during one of the meetings, Virginia became very cold and could not seem to get warm.[12] Elder Perry whispered to one of the leaders about the problem, and a blanket was quickly brought to her. Later the Maori woman who supplied the blanket insisted that Virginia keep it. It became a blanket Virginia kept in a little room on the main floor of their Bountiful home, and she used it during the day to warm herself whenever she needed to take a short rest.

Virginia was asked to speak at many meetings during their time in Australia and New Zealand. Before their first series of meetings in Sydney, Australia, they stayed at the Travelodge in Parramatta, New South Wales. Virginia wrote out a talk she would give several times on the trip on three sheets of hotel stationery, front and back. Her address was about adjusting to the joys and sorrows of mortal life. She said:

"Several years ago when we were living in the state of New York, I remember attending a Relief Society Conference. President Belle S. Spafford was there.[13] Also President Harold B. Lee—he was then Elder Lee.

"Sister Spafford asked for a definition of education from the audience. Several were given. I recalled a definition given by Plato. Many centuries ago, someone asked him: 'What is a good education?' And he replied: 'A good education is that which gives to the body and to the soul all the beauty and all the perfection of which they are capable.'

"I was rather pleased with myself because I was able to remember the quotation, but my elation was short-lived because when President Lee arose and addressed the group, he said: 'Well, so much for Plato.'

"Then President Lee said he had his own definition of education, and he liked it better. He said: 'The best education is that which gives to the individual the strength and ability to adjust.' I remembered his words and during the ensuing years I have had many occasions to ponder his words and recognize the great wisdom they contain.

"Life is filled with adjustments—joys and sorrows, trials and temptations. That's what life is all about—this is the time of our schooling. We are gaining an education from the time we enter this mortal existence until we leave it. There are always adjustments to be made, and how we make them is all important. Our actions and reactions here will determine in large measure how we spend the rest of eternity. . . .

"President Lee has also said: 'The all-important thing in life isn't what happens to you. The important thing is how you take it.'

"As we consider the adjustments necessary in life, it may be well to remember the biblical story of Joseph who was betrayed by his brothers and sold into Egypt. . . . Always, Joseph stayed close to God and kept his values in proper perspective. He had the strength and courage to do right. He was able to make the best out of whatever happened to him. . . .

"May we prepare ourselves so that we, like Joseph of old, will be armed with an inner strength—even the power and inspiration of God—so that no matter what happens to us in this life during our mortal school, we will cling to the iron rod of the gospel and stand firm in our testimony of truth and right."

As Virginia spoke to the members of the Church in these two great "down under" nations, the Spirit testified to everyone present that she was a person who had in-depth, real-life experience with her subject matter. Virginia always had a very personal way of connecting with people when she stood and spoke from behind a pulpit. Her talent to communicate was further magnified during this trip with her husband. It was as if the Spirit was testifying to the members of the different congregations in which Virginia spoke that this was a noble woman of enormous substance. The attendees were being instructed by the Spirit to savor her words of wisdom, for they were unlikely to hear from her again.

Chairman of the Church's Bicentennial Committee

On Monday, September 17, 1973, Elder Perry received an additional assignment. He was appointed by the First Presidency to serve as the general chairman of the Church's Bicentennial Committee. The announcement of his appointment coincided with the 186th anniversary of the signing of the Constitution of the United States. The assignment was massive in scope, involving the correlation of all Church activities and observances in connection with the United States Bicentennial in 1976. In making their statement about the appointment of Elder Perry, the First Presidency said:

"We urge members of the church and all Americans to begin now to reflect more intently on the meaning and importance of the Constitution, and of adherence to its principles, in giving strength not only to this country, but to the entire family of nations.

"In these challenging days, when there are so many influences which would divert us, there is a need to rededicate ourselves to the lofty principles and practices of our founding fathers. While we must never permit an erosion of the freedoms the Constitution guarantees, we cannot let permissiveness replace responsibility."[14]

Elder Perry reviewed this statement many times to ensure that his decisions and actions were consistent with the direction he had been given by the First Presidency. He was excited about his new assignment, and he embraced it with his characteristic enthusiasm. He even modified his October 1973 general conference address to incorporate a patriotic theme. He started the talk with a connection to his time in Boston. He said:

"There is a section in old Boston town where the gas lanterns still adorn the streets to remind us of a bygone era of 'the old lamplighter'—a profession that has become obsolete with the modern age. But the service of bringing light to a troubled world must never end."

He concluded his address with a challenge to the members of the Church to be sharers of light, like the old lamplighters. He said: "Let us sound the call today to revive the old profession of lamplighters. Let us each pick up our torch and illuminate the sacred histories, the eternal truths that divine providence has bestowed on us. Let us have the faith and courage of Nephi, roll up our sleeves like Ben Franklin, and '*go* and *do* the things which the Lord hath commanded.' May we be prepared and ready to celebrate with pride and thanksgiving our 200th anniversary with the comforting knowledge that we have made a worthy contribution to safeguard and protect those divinely inspired principles upon which this nation was established."[15]

This was the first of many speeches Elder Perry gave over the next three years that focused on love of country, the blessings and responsibilities of citizenship, and the United States Bicentennial.

CHAPTER 23

CHRISTMAS TO CHRISTMAS 1973–74

On December 25, 1973, Elder Perry, Virginia, Lee, and Linda celebrated their first Christmas in their Bountiful, Utah, home. It was a wonderful, traditional Perry family Christmas and a stark contrast to the makeshift Christmas celebration of 1972. All their decorations were taken out of boxes and displayed throughout their home. These were decorations acquired in Idaho, California, New York, and Massachusetts, and each of them added beauty and memories of people and places. Virginia read the Clement Moore poem *'Twas the Night Before Christmas,* opened her birthday presents, and served plum pudding on Christmas Eve. Then the family turned to the second chapter of Luke in the New Testament and read the Christmas story.

In the morning there were stockings hung on the fireplace stuffed with treats, presents under the tree, and an abundance of delicious food and desserts throughout the day. It was a gloriously normal Christmas that ended a bit earlier than usual because they had a long trip ahead of them the next day.

On the morning of December 26, 1973, the Perrys arose early, lifted their suitcases into the trunk of their car, and drove to Arizona to spend a few days with Barbara and Terry Haws and, of course, LT. It was a long drive, and Elder Perry and Lee split most of the driving. They did not arrive at the Haws home until well past LT's bedtime.

They greeted Barbara and Terry, unpacked the car, and sat down at the kitchen table. Out of the corner of his eye, Lee saw the image of President Harold B. Lee on the television. The television was turned to the evening news, but the volume was turned nearly all the way down. Lee quickly got up to turn up the volume. The part of the report they heard indicated that an LDS Church leader had died, but they had missed hearing who it was. Lee quickly turned the channel, and they soon heard from another news report that President Harold B. Lee had passed away earlier in the day.

The news came as such a shock that nobody knew what to say. Elder Perry had been in meetings a few days earlier with President Lee, and he had seemed vigorous and healthy. Like most of the members of the Church, Elder Perry expected President Lee, who was only seventy-four years old, to serve as the prophet for many years. Moreover, President Lee was a man of incredible vision. What would the Church do now that he was gone?

Elder Perry still had not said very much when he asked Barbara if he could use their phone. He called the Church operator and spoke briefly with Brother D. Arthur Haycock, who instructed him to return to Salt Lake as soon as possible.

By the time LT woke up on the morning of December 27, the Perrys' car was repacked and the family had eaten breakfast together. There was time only for Elder Perry and Virginia to piece together a few Legos with LT and give him a parting hug before they were in the car and on the road back to Utah. The conversation had been lively on the way to Arizona, but the trip back to Bountiful was quiet and introspective.

The Saturday, April 6, 1974, Solemn Assembly

A solemn assembly was held on April 6, 1974, the 144th anniversary of the organization of The Church of Jesus Christ of Latter-day Saints, to sustain Spencer W. Kimball as the Church's new President. A morning and afternoon session of general conference had been held the previous day, but President Kimball had decided to wait until Saturday morning to hold the solemn assembly on the Church's anniversary.

President Kimball asked President N. Eldon Tanner to conduct the sustaining of Church authorities at the solemn assembly. The assignment was similar to President Tanner's assignment at the solemn assembly held Friday, October 6, 1972, at which President Harold B. Lee was sustained as the Church's President and Elder L. Tom Perry was sustained as a new Assistant to the Twelve.

President Tanner had already followed the process for sustaining the First Presidency and the patriarch of the Church, Eldred G. Smith, when he turned his attention to sustaining the Brethren in the Quorum of the Twelve. First, he asked the First Presidency to stand. Then he said:

"It is proposed that we sustain Ezra Taft Benson as president of the Quorum of the Twelve Apostles of The Church of Jesus Christ of Latter-day Saints.

"Those in favor will raise their right hands; those opposed will manifest it by the same sign.

"It is proposed that we sustain as members of the Quorum of the Twelve Apostles of The Church of Jesus Christ of Latter-day

Saints: Ezra Taft Benson, Mark E. Petersen, Delbert L. Stapley, LeGrand Richards, Hugh B. Brown, Howard W. Hunter, Gordon B. Hinckley, Thomas S. Monson, Boyd K. Packer, Marvin J. Ashton, Bruce R. McConkie, and *L. Tom Perry*."[1]

Elder Perry had learned the previous Thursday evening, April 4, that he would be sustained to fill the vacancy in the Quorum of the Twelve created when President Kimball became the President of the Church following the death of President Harold B. Lee. Elder Perry had been involved all day Thursday with the training of regional representatives. Near the close of the training, Elder Faust, Elder Hanks, and he had made a presentation about the Melchizedek Priesthood MIA. He was "dead tired" when he arrived home in Bountiful at about 6:30 p.m. Only a few minutes after he had walked through the door and greeted Virginia, the telephone rang. He almost hesitated answering it, but he thought it might be Elder Faust calling him for his observations about the training they had just given. Instead, it was Brother D. Arthur Haycock. He asked Elder Perry to return to the Church Administration Building to meet briefly with President Kimball.

By the time Elder Perry entered the Office of the First Presidency, everyone in the outer office had gone home, except Brother Haycock. Brother Haycock smiled at Elder Perry, directed him to open the door to President Kimball's office, and then excused himself and left for the evening.

When Elder Perry entered President Kimball's office, the prophet arose, walked up to him, and threw his arms around him. He pointed Elder Perry to a chair in the middle of his office, and soon Elder Perry realized he was participating in a thorough worthiness interview. After completing the interview, President Kimball issued the call to Elder Perry to fill the vacancy in the Quorum of the Twelve. Then President Kimball arose, hugged Elder Perry again, and invited him to return home to tell his family about his new call.

Elder Perry returned home, where Virginia, Lee, and Linda Gay were waiting to eat dinner as soon as he returned. Elder Perry asked them all to sit down at the kitchen table. After he shared the news about his call with them, nobody knew what to say. They ate dinner in near silence, although none of them was particularly hungry.

After dinner, Elder Perry telephoned Barbara, told her about his new calling, and arranged for her, Terry, and LT to fly up for the solemn assembly on Saturday morning. After the phone call, Elder Perry went to bed, but he tossed and turned most of the night.

The Sunday Morning Session

Elder Perry was the fourth speaker for the Sunday morning session of general conference. This gave him a little time to gather himself, control his emotions, and revise his talk. What he said at both the beginning and the end of his address described how he felt at the moment. He said:

"This is a general conference in which I find my emotions very close to the surface. I have just been sustained by a vote of the membership of the Church to a position which is overwhelming. I hope under the circumstances it is permissible to be a little personal as I speak this morning.

"I was reared in a home in which the children were taught great love and respect for the General Authorities of the Church. I remember as I was learning the names of the members of the Council of the Twelve as a Primary graduation requirement, my father spent time and patience to teach me about the lives of each, as well as the required memory work.

"To this day, I think you can ask me at any time to recite the names of those great men from Rudger Clawson to Charles A.

Callis; and I can repeat them rapidly and remember events in their lives.

"As I was thinking about this assignment, I thought, what if there is some father in the Church who would like to spend some time in family home evening telling about the current members of the Council of the Twelve? This thought startled me. What could he ever tell about me?

"As I thought and searched, I realized there is a theme to my life which is worthy of being repeated and I think would be of value to those young children in your homes. It is this: He was reared in a home in which his parents loved and appreciated the gospel of Jesus Christ. They understood the admonition of Paul to the Ephesian saints when he wrote, 'Finally, my brethren, be strong in the Lord, and in the power of his might.'. . .[2]

"President Kimball, I publicly accept the call that you have conveyed to me to serve the Lord. I know of your divine call. I know within you there is the same attribute which distinguished Joseph of old to the Pharaoh of Egypt who declared to his servants that Joseph was 'a man in whom the Spirit of God is' (Genesis 41:38).

"I hope and pray that in some way I may be capable of helping you lift the great burden that you carry by my service in this quorum.

"President Benson, I love and appreciate you and your great leadership. I am devoted to service in our Father in Heaven's kingdom. Use me in any way that I am capable.

"And to my two great colleagues whom I have worked so closely with, Elder Hanks and Elder Faust, there has been a special brotherhood that has developed between us. How patient they have been in helping to train me in the things that I should do in these great callings. I express to you my gratitude and thanks."[3]

Summer and Fall 1974

There was an immediate settling down following Elder Perry's call to be an Apostle as he reengaged in the daily and weekly routines that characterize the lives of all General Authorities. There were some new assignments and a different set of meetings to attend. Elder Perry kept approximately the same travel schedule for the rest of 1974, however, beginning with a stake conference in Enterprise, Utah, on April 13 and 14 and ending with a stake conference in Kalispell, Montana, on December 7 and 8. Elder Perry filled eighteen different stake conference assignments during those eight months. Given that there were no assignments from late June to the second week of August, and his traveling ended for the year in early December, he had few free weekends except during those few summer weeks.

Elder Perry and Virginia were excused from an assignment to an area conference in Sweden in August 1974. In a May 22, 1974, letter to her sister Jessie, Virginia wrote:

"We have been assigned to attend the Area Conference in Sweden in August, but Lee is graduating from BYU at the same time. So, I guess Tom will speak to President Kimball to see if we can be excused. It's really hard to give up the trip, but of course we would want to be at Lee's graduation."

What Virginia did not tell Jessie was that even if Lee had not been graduating, as much as she wanted to go to Sweden, the international trip might have been too much for her. She was beginning to lose her four-year battle with cancer. During the summer of 1974, the tide dramatically turned against her.

After Lee graduated from BYU, he decided to take a year off before graduate school and work in Salt Lake. There were two reasons for his decision. First, Elder Perry had been assigned during the final two weeks of October to go to Japan, and part of the assignment involved a mission tour of Lee's former mission in southwestern Japan and Okinawa. The mission also included Nagasaki and Sasebo, where Elder Perry had been stationed as a marine after the Japanese surrender that marked the end of World War II. It was decided that Lee should accompany his father on this assignment to a place so meaningful to both of them. The second reason was Virginia's rapidly declining health. Her chemotherapy treatments at McKay-Dee Hospital in Ogden were becoming more intense and frequent. Because of the scheduled trip with his father, Lee did not begin work until November 1. Until then, he served as Virginia's helper and chauffeur.[4] And Virginia began to need more and more help. Both her cancer and the treatments to combat it were beginning to take a heavy toll.

The trip to Japan was a highlight for both Elder Perry and Lee. In just ten days they were able to see much of Japan and meet with many of the members Lee had known on Kyushu and Okinawa. In addition to touring the Japan Fukuoka Mission, accompanied by President and Sister Arthur Nishimoto, they also toured the Japan Sapporo Mission with President and Sister Kotaro Koizumi.

Elder Perry shared some of his allotted time with Lee at nearly every meeting they attended. Elder Perry even asked Lee to interpret for him a few times at the beginning of the trip. Although his father did not realize it, Lee quickly did—his Japanese had deteriorated enough over the previous two years that his acting as an interpreter was probably not a good idea. In telling stories about their trip together, Elder Perry has often described how he would say just a few words over the pulpit, and Lee would interpret for several minutes. The truth of the matter was that Lee's interpretations were needlessly wordy. Lee did not remember many of the Japanese words for the English words used by his father, and instead of using the appropriate

Japanese words, he had to explain what the words meant using the Japanese he did remember.

Near the end of the trip, Elder Perry reorganized the Tokyo Stake, and he called Yoshihiko Kikuchi to be the new stake president. It was the beginning of a lifelong friendship and brotherhood between the two men, both chosen servants of the Lord.

December 14, 1974

December 14, 1974, was an unusual day—it was a Saturday and Elder Perry was home. It began like most other days. Elder Perry arose early and began to get ready for the day. As he left the bedroom to go downstairs to his study, he heard Virginia speaking to him. She seemed sleepy, and Elder Perry assumed she had endured another difficult night. He encouraged her to stay in bed and rest. Virginia sat up and told her husband she might rest later, but she needed to prepare his breakfast. Elder Perry waited so he could help her walk down the stairs. On the way she insisted that she wanted to make him breakfast because she wasn't sure how much longer she would be able to do it.

At the April 1975 general conference, Elder Perry described what happened to Virginia next:

"Her last acts were so typical of her. She was up preparing breakfast for her family. I heard her drop a dish and give a little moan. As I rushed from my study, thinking she had injured herself, I found that she was suffering from a stroke that was causing her to lose the use of her right arm. I quickly picked her up and carried her in to a little couch I had just recently convinced her that she should have near her kitchen so she could rest during the day.

"There was terror in her eyes as the paralysis started to spread down her side. I told her I was going to rush a call to the doctor. She said, 'First, give me a blessing.' As I laid my hands on her head that morning, the Lord in his great mercy let me know that her time had come. As I left the room to call the doctor after that blessing, she was literally fighting to move her right arm and her right leg. And the last words I heard her utter were, 'I will not live as a half a person.'"[5]

By this time, Lee, who was upstairs preparing to go to work, heard the commotion downstairs. He hurried downstairs and saw his mother lying on the couch moaning and unable to move. Noticing Lee, Elder Perry quickly took him by the arm and told him Dr. Dewey McKay and an ambulance were on their way. He convinced Lee there was nothing he could do for his mother and that he should go upstairs, finish getting ready, and go to work.

Lee did leave for work just as the paramedics were taking his mother on a stretcher to the hospital. Dr. McKay was standing by the front door, watching the paramedics and looking deeply concerned.

Elder Perry, Dr. McKay, and his wife, Lorraine, drove to the hospital behind the ambulance. Sister McKay, who was the Bountiful 29th Ward Relief Society president, had arranged for a neighbor to stay with Linda Gay. Elder Perry and the McKays waited together at the hospital until the doctors attending Virginia came to tell them she had died.

At the April 1975 general conference, Elder Perry described the final hours of Virginia's life. He said:

"Her next two hours, her last in mortality, were the only two I know of in her life that she was not carrying her full load and a little extra for someone else. The Lord in his mercy has let her pass through the veil and relieved her from her anxiety and pain. Now she is whole again, and I am certain paradise is a much more joyful place because she is there."[6]

Around 1:00 p.m., Elder Perry left the hospital and returned home to tell Linda Gay the grim news. After holding her as she sobbed for several minutes, he suggested they drive to the store where Lee was working and pick him up.

At about 2:00 p.m., when Lee came back from a storage room at the store with a requested item of clothing for a customer, he saw his father with his arm around Linda, talking to his manager near the sales counter. Elder Perry's back was toward Lee, so he could not see his father's face. Lee, however, did notice that his father had a tight hold on Linda, almost as if he was holding her up. Lee quickened his pace, anxious to learn about his mother's condition. When he saw his father's face and Linda's face, he did not need to ask. His father looked pale and solemn, and Linda was crying.

Elder Perry told Lee to get his coat, Lee's manager took the item of clothing from him, and he assured Lee that he would take care of his customer. Lee went back to the storage room, put on his coat, and returned to the sales counter. Elder Perry put his other arm around Lee, and the three of them began to walk out of the store. They had walked only a few steps when Elder Perry said to Lee, "Your mother didn't make it." Now, Elder Perry was keeping two children from collapsing by holding them tight.

Christmas 1974

During the next few days, the Perrys' living room was used more times than it had been used since their home was built. A constant stream of visitors to 889 South Davis Boulevard in Bountiful included all the members of the First Presidency and their wives, all the members of the Quorum of the Twelve who were physically able to visit and their wives, Elder and Sister Faust, and Elder and Sister Hanks. Hundreds of others expressed their sympathies through visits, food, and letters.

Virginia's funeral was held in the Bountiful 29th Ward chapel at noon on Wednesday, December 18. Bishop Otis E.

Winn conducted the memorial service. There were only two speakers—Elder Perry's brother Ted and President Ezra Taft Benson. Elder Faust gave the invocation, and Elder Hanks pronounced the benediction. A cortege traveled to Cache Valley, where Virginia was buried in the Hyde Park Cemetery, just up the street from the Lee family home and the home of her sister Jessie Seamons. Jessie's husband, Vernal, dedicated the grave.

Christmas 1974 must have been celebrated in some way by Elder Perry, Lee, and Linda Gay, but none of them recalls clearly the presents they exchanged or what they did. As empty as Christmas Day felt, Christmas Eve felt even emptier. There was no reading of *'Twas the Night Before Christmas* and no plum pudding. They would have gladly forgone all of their Christmas Eve traditions to have had their wife and mother there with them to celebrate her fifty-first birthday.

CHAPTER 24

A Tribute to a Noble Soul

Elder Perry returned to his office in the Church Administration Building soon after New Year's. Lee continued to live at home and work in Salt Lake, and Linda, who did not feel ready to return to school, would often go with her father to his office.

On January 18, 1975, Elder Perry received a call from Brother D. Arthur Haycock requesting that he come downstairs to the Office of the First Presidency. When Elder Perry arrived, Brother Haycock motioned him into President Kimball's office. President Kimball was holding his telephone up to his ear, and as soon as Elder Perry appeared, President Kimball said to the person on the other end of the line, "He just walked into my office." President Kimball handed Elder Perry the telephone, and he was instructed to wait on the line to be connected to John Warner.[1] Elder Perry did not know who John Warner was, but he quickly learned he was the administrator of the American Revolution Bicentennial Administration.

After Mr. Warner had introduced himself, he invited Elder Perry to serve as a member of the American Revolution Bicentennial Advisory Council. Elder Perry was one of only two religious leaders asked to serve on the council, the other being the Most Reverend Joseph Bernardin, the archbishop of Cincinnati, Ohio. In a press release on January 20, 1975, the White House announced to the national press the creation of the twenty-five-member council.

The *Ensign* magazine announced Elder Perry's appointment to the council in its March 1975 issue. It reported:

"United States President Gerald R. Ford has named Elder L. Tom Perry of the Council of the Twelve to the 25-member American Revolution Bicentennial Advisory Council.

"Others on the council include former First Lady Mrs. Lyndon B. Johnson, writer James A. Michener, and Hobart D. Lewis, editor-in-chief of *Reader's Digest.*

"The council was created to advise the Bicentennial Administration, a group that coordinates bicentennial organizations of the 50 states, the District of Columbia, and Puerto Rico. Some foreign countries are also planning celebrations in observance of the bicentennial.

"'For a whole year we will devote time to contemplating and thinking about the things we can do for our government,'" said Elder Perry. 'I think the great message that we have to carry is that of local, individual, family, and community interest in government.'

"Elder Perry is also chairman of the Church's Bicentennial Committee."[2]

Elder Perry did not travel during January 1975. His first stake conference assignment was over the weekend of February 1 and 2 to Scottsdale, Arizona. He and Linda Gay drove to

Arizona together, both to attend the stake conference and to visit the Haws family. Linda, who was close to turning seventeen, was learning how to drive, but the winter weather in Utah had slowed her progress. Elder Perry decided to have her practice her highway driving as soon as they reached warm weather. He planned Linda's first turn at the wheel to be short—less than fifteen minutes. It was never Elder Perry's intention to fall asleep while Linda drove, but he did. He woke up two hours later, and Linda was still driving. Clearly, the past month and a half had taken its toll on the junior Apostle.

Linda became her father's traveling companion for most of his nearby stake conference assignments during 1975, including visits to St. Anthony, Idaho; Richfield, Utah; Morgan, Utah; Blackfoot, Idaho; and Syracuse, Utah. A few times Lee joined them as well. Linda was also able to accompany her father on an assignment to England and Scotland in April 1975—a once-in-a-lifetime experience she still remembers fondly. She also attended many public dinners and other occasions with her father. Linda was a constant in her father's life during this period, and she faithfully stayed at his side as they attended both the ecclesiastical and public functions required of him as a General Authority.

Elder Perry was deeply moved by how his children, particularly Linda, supported him. In early 1976, after one of the most challenging years of his life, Elder Perry acknowledged the helping role his children had performed. He said:

"This last year has caused me a greater appreciation for my children than I've ever had before. They've been sensitive to my needs in a very, very special way. They knew that I'd suffered a great loss, and their loss was great, too. But they've never allowed it to be shown in our family life. Their whole concern has not been for themselves, but what they could do to make my life more fulfilling. There's great safety and great blessing in a family that has learned how to grow together and love together and appreciate each other and lose themselves in making the other members of the family happy."[3]

In a 1975 Christmas letter to Lee, Elder Perry wrote:

"This has been a very difficult year for our family. It has been most rewarding to see the growth of two of my children. . . . I am certain you have found out this year how much faith I have in you and how much I rely on you. I don't know what I would have done without you during the last year. For this I express to you my sincere, deep appreciation."

The April 1975 General Conference

Elder Perry usually asked Lee to help edit his general conference addresses. He did not, however, share his April 1975 general conference address with his son. Elder Perry was the final speaker in the afternoon session on Friday, April 4. The tribute he gave to Virginia was perhaps his best-remembered address up to that point by members of the Church. His message deeply touched everyone who heard it. He began:

"As difficult as it may be, I would like to pay tribute today to a very noble soul who found the joy in living a life of service."[4]

Elder Perry spoke about Virginia's near-constant service to others:

"We had only been married a few days before I found out I had married a woman with great empathy in her heart for her fellowmen. All of those wonderful aromas which came from the air around her kitchen were not all intended for me, for when she would find someone in need, she could not rest until she had made an effort to supply a relief.

"I frequently found myself returning home from a busy day's work, still under great pressures to complete an assignment before the following morning, only to find I had been committed to an act of compassionate service that night. As we would drive to our place of service, I would be mumbling under my breath, 'Why me tonight? How will I ever get that job done before morning?' Then we would arrive at the place of service, and I would see the light in her eyes as she would perform her acts of mercy. I would see children dance with joy and parents weep with gratitude for her concern. On the way home I was mumbling a different tune. I was thanking the Lord for the privilege of being there that particular night."[5]

Elder Perry shared a sampling of the messages of sympathy his family had received following the announcement of Virginia's death, and he expressed gratitude to those who sent them:

"For the hundreds of messages of sympathy we have received, we express our appreciation. If we had taken time to classify them, I think we would have found that we could have sorted them in two piles that typified and characterized her in her life here on earth. The first pile that we would have sorted—as we heard from the eastern part of the United States—would be something like this: 'She gave us our first Book of Mormon and was an inspiration to us. How grateful we are to have known her. We will always remember her gracious hospitality to our family on the day of our baptism. It was such a happy occasion to have dinner in your home on that particular day.' . . .

"The second group of letters would read in part this way: 'Your wife and mother was my stake leader in Spiritual Living. For one year I met with her for forty-five minutes each month and she had a profound influence on my life. She will always be one of the truly unforgettable people I have known. To me she exemplified spiritual living. She understood the needs of others and sought diligently to supply those needs.'"[6]

Elder Perry described Virginia's love for the Church and her deep appreciation and testimony of the Book of Mormon:

"She was deeply grateful for her membership in the church of Jesus Christ. It was the foundation on which her life had been built. It was her sustaining power, her hope for the eternities. She was anxious to share her witness of the mission of our Lord and Savior with others. A fundamental part of her storage program, which included, of course, the basics of wheat, canned goods, and other inventories, was a supply of a dozen copies of the Book of Mormon.[7] She would count those just as religiously as she would count her other supplies and replenish them in the same order. She used to comment about her inventories: 'When we use the food, the inventory is gone. When I make a gift of the Book of Mormon, I never stop receiving the benefit and enjoyment of that gift.'"[8]

Finally, Elder Perry summarized an important lesson he had learned from what had been for him a painful but also sweet life experience. He also extended a challenge to the members of the Church to learn from Virginia's example and emulate it. He said:

"The Lord has said to us, 'Thou shalt live together in love, insomuch that thou shalt weep for the loss of them that die, and more especially for those that have not hope of a glorious resurrection. And it shall come to pass that those that die in me shall not taste of death, for it shall be sweet unto them' (D&C 42:45–46).

"I understand this scripture now as never before. Even though there is great loneliness without her, her passing was sweet because of the way she had lived.

"In tribute to her today, I recommend to you her way of life. I watched service consume pain. I witnessed faith destroy discouragement. I have seen courage magnify her beyond her natural abilities. I have observed love change the course of lives."[9]

"One Nation under God"

There were many changes in Elder Perry's life between the April and October 1975 general conferences. He sold the family home in Bountiful, and he and Linda briefly lived in an apartment in Salt Lake City until builders finished a two-bedroom condominium he had purchased. Elder Perry became a grandparent for the second time—a granddaughter, Esther Haws, was born July 15, 1975.

Lee moved himself and nearly all his belongings to Provo because there was definitely no room for him in the apartment, and there was only a pullout bed in the condominium. His departure was expected, but circumstances did hasten it. The plan had always been for him to begin graduate school at Brigham Young University in the fall. In addition, there was a month or two during the summer when it appeared Lee would be getting married, but the relationship faded.

A surprise came when Linda decided to bypass her senior year of high school and join Lee at BYU. So by September 1975, Elder Perry was living alone in a new condominium in Salt Lake City, mostly without neighbors because he had moved in before most of the other units in the building were completed.

The remaining constant in Elder Perry's life was his work as a General Authority. All outward signs indicated that he was doing well. Of course, because of Elder Perry's enthusiastic nature, it would have been impossible to detect if something was wrong. Appearing beaten or downtrodden was not part of his nature. At the time, even those who knew him best would likely have echoed what Elder Jeffrey R. Holland said in 2012 about his friend and colleague of more than forty years: "I've never seen L. Tom Perry down."[10] Yet, it was a difficult time for him and a period during which his principal coping mechanism was hard work. Lee and Linda were worried that he might be working too hard.

One of the tasks in which Elder Perry immersed himself was his assignment to assist in planning the United States Bicentennial celebration. At the October 1975 general conference, he said about this assignment: "I have never had an assignment which has given me a clearer vision of history and an opportunity to observe the operations of government."[11] In his talk, Elder Perry shared an experience he had had in his role as a member of the American Revolution Bicentennial Advisory Council.

"Some months ago I was asked to assist in inviting many of the religious leaders of America to a special meeting for the purpose of increasing the participation of religious congregations in our nation's bicentennial celebration. About 400 of us assembled in Washington, D.C., and spent two days together discussing ways in which we could make a contribution to this exciting celebration. . . .

"Part of the program covering this two-day period was to divide ourselves into small discussion groups of about twenty in number to examine the role the churches would play during this celebration.

"As we concluded the first day I discussed the possibility with a bright, young colleague[12] I had invited to attend this assembly with me of preparing a declaration for the churches of this land to jointly proclaim to our countrymen, a reaffirmation of our need for divine guidance, an expression of gratitude for the Lord's hand in directing the formation of the government of the United States of America. I don't know how late this young man stayed up that night but when I met him for breakfast the following morning he had an excellent draft of the proposed declaration.

"I was excited with the possibility of presenting it to our small discussion group as we assembled together that morning. However, my enthusiasm rapidly dissipated. We soon discovered it was the consensus of this small group of religious leaders that any declaration referring to the Lord our God would not be acceptable."[13]

After recounting this experience, Elder Perry expressed both concern and hope. He was concerned that a highly vocal minority was able to hijack the committee and block the official declaration from being shared in the conference's general session. Elder Perry was hopeful because the majority of the religious leaders at the conference impressed him with their deep, unshakable commitment to God, family, and country.

The experience, however, taught Elder Perry that Americans who believed they were citizens of "one nation under God" could not be passive about their declarations of belief. He vowed to the members of the Church that he would continue to declare his belief that God inspired the early leaders of the United States in the formation of a great nation. He said:

"I have resolved to do all that is within my power to keep alive the same faith which existed in the hearts and souls of our early founding fathers.

"It was George Washington who declared, 'The people know it is impossible to rightly govern without God and the Bible.' . . .

"I reaffirm before you here today of my faith that the Lord God continues to govern the affairs of his children. His law must be the foundation on which all law is based. We must be willing to support, defend, and live in harmony with his divine law. . . .

"May God grant that we may have the courage to stand up and be counted for that which we know to be right, I humbly pray in the name of Jesus Christ. Amen."[14]

Perhaps Elder Perry was working too hard on the United States Bicentennial celebration, but like trying to detect if something was wrong following Virginia's death, it was difficult to tell whether he was working too hard, because he always worked hard.

When Elder Perry served in the marines, he always enjoyed being out front setting the pace. He believed he could turn something hard into something exciting and fun by being the pacesetter. It is a philosophy that has served him well through both the peaks and valleys of life. It is a philosophy that helped transform someone who still considers himself common into an extraordinary leader. It is one of the principal secrets to his uncommon life of success and accomplishment.

More than anything else, Elder Perry's life reveals how much God can make of a man who always acknowledges, honors, loves, and follows Him. While never granting Elder Perry special exemption from life's hardest tests, God has always blessed him by supporting, fortifying, and empowering him. Elder Perry's consistent message during the Bicentennial celebration directed to a nation and its citizens was the same message he used to sum up his life at the April 1974 general conference after accepting his call to the holy apostleship. It was the admonition of the Apostle Paul to the Ephesian Saints: "Finally, my brethren [and sisters], be strong in the Lord, and in the power of his might."[15]

A List

In mid-January 1976, President Kimball summoned Elder Perry to his office to discuss a delicate issue. He explained to Elder Perry that it was difficult for someone with his calling to function without a wife, and he should begin to entertain the possibility of remarrying. He explained that there was no reason to hurry but that Elder Perry should start to look for someone to whom he could be sealed in the temple. President Kimball suggested several criteria for Elder Perry to consider as he looked for another eternal companion, and then he recommended that Elder Perry make it a matter of prayer.

The interview with President Kimball was brief, but it left a profound impression on Elder Perry. As soon as he returned to his office, he faithfully listed the criteria that President Kimball had shared with him. While Elder Perry was tentative about whether he was ready to look for a new wife, he immediately made the issue a matter of prayer. He still missed Virginia and had not finished mourning her loss, but he also recognized the wisdom in what he had just been told by a prophet of God. The concept of remarriage was initially difficult for Elder Perry to grasp, but it occurred to him that the Lord was preparing someone for him who fit all the criteria on his list and with whom he could fall in love and share the rest of his life.

Notes

Foreword

1. See "Introduction," 3.
2. See chapter 11, "The Marine Corps."
3. See "Introduction," 5.
4. L. Tom Perry, "Build Your Shield of Faith," *Ensign,* May 1974, 98.

Preface

1. See 1 Nephi 4:6.
2. John 3:30.

Introduction

1. Leslie Thomas Perry, *Life Story of Leslie Thomas Perry* (privately published, 1964), 7.
2. See Matthew 25:15.
3. John Steinbeck, "The Leader of the People," in *The Long Valley* (New York: Bantam, 1964), 213.

Chapter 2: Perry, Utah

1. The Perry family history and other historical information in this chapter come from two primary sources: the unpublished autobiography of Leslie Thomas Perry (1964), which he wrote for his children and grandchildren; and the book written by Albert Perry,

my grandfather's younger brother, and published for the Rigby-Ririe-Rudy, Idaho, branch of the Perry family in 1955. I am greatly indebted to both my grandfather and great-uncle. I am also indebted to David Ririe, a grandson of Henry Morgan Perry, who summarized histories of the lives of Henry Morgan and Fannie Young Perry and made them available on the Internet at the following URLs: ririe.org/history/documents/david_ririe_2_henry.asp and ririe.org/history/documents/david_ririe_2_fannie.asp.

2. This document can be accessed at josephsmithpapers.org/paperSummary/letter-from-alvah-tippets-20-october-1834#3
3. When Leslie left home at age fifteen and a half to attend the Church school in Rexburg, it was called the Fremont Stake Academy, but by the time he graduated, the name of the school had been changed to Ricks Academy.

Chapter 3: Birthplace

I am deeply indebted to Conway Sonne and his biography of his father, *A Man Named Alma: The World of Alma Sonne* (Bountiful, Utah: Horizon Publishers, 1988) for the family history and other historical information in this chapter.

1. Depending on American or Danish custom, her name was either Eliza Petersen or Lise Christensen. This issue will be addressed in the text later. See also chapter 8, n. 8.

Chapter 4: The Perry Family Home

1. L. Tom Perry, "The Joy of Honest Labor," *Ensign*, November 1986, 62–64.
2. During those lengthy hearings, Senator Boise Penrose of Pennsylvania famously said in support of Senator Smoot: "As for me, I would rather have seated beside me in this chamber a polygamist who doesn't polyg than a monogamist who doesn't monog."
3. Mignon Perry, my father's older sister, suggests that Leslie Thomas Perry and Elsie Nora Sonne may have met each other in passing on the debate trip to Denver, Colorado, but there is no record of such a meeting.
4. The name Agricultural College of Utah was changed to Utah State Agricultural College in 1929 and to Utah State University in 1957.
5. Leslie Thomas Perry, *Life Story of Leslie Thomas Perry* (privately published, 1964), 2–3.
6. An inaccurate attribution because he had not officially completed his law degree. Also, while I have no record of it, the dedication appears

to suggest that, in addition to his duties as Rexburg city attorney, he was teaching law classes at Ricks Academy.

7. Said by Mark Twain after his obituary was published in the *New York Journal.*
8. The blessing was given in Rexburg, Idaho, on April 1, 1917, under the hands of patriarch Andrew J. Hansen.

Chapter 5: The Garden and Pasture

1. Loren C. Dunn, "Elder L. Tom Perry: Serving with Enthusiasm," *Ensign,* August 1986, 18.
2. L. Tom Perry, "Discipleship," *Ensign,* November 2000, 60.
3. Doctrine and Covenants 82:3.
4. Sam Price was Tom's age, and Elizabeth Price was the same age as Mignon.

Chapter 6: Logan Ninth Ward Chapel

1. Leslie Thomas Perry, *Life Story of Leslie Thomas Perry* (privately published, 1964), 36.
2. This wagon was my father's second. It held a much larger cargo than did his first wagon, which can be seen in a photo of him as a young boy.
3. Comment by Leslie Thomas Perry, *Leslie Thomas Perry: Father of an Apostle,* edited by Ted Perry (privately published, 2004), 49–50.
4. L. Tom Perry, "'Serve God Acceptably with Reverence and Godly Fear,'" *Ensign,* November 1990, 72.

Chapter 7: Logan High School

1. My father was instrumental in raising the funds to restore the Memorial Bridge, which he rededicated in November 2002. Before he offered the dedicatory prayer, however, he said: "In today's world, we need the next generation to come forward with the same determination, the same belief and the same courage possessed by the generation of those we honor today. They have a great heritage to preserve. We need a generation that will bring forth an understanding of peace and what it means to belong to the land of the free."
2. The "Tom has surprised us" entry in Leslie Thomas Perry's personal history is the principal exception to the rule, and Ted Perry believes the cause of his father's faint praise of Tom was more favoritism than incredulity.
3. Or one of his mother's giant cinnamon rolls. Infrequently, Tom did

eat lunch at school, and he soon discovered that if he packed one of his mother's cinnamon rolls, his classmates would line up for the opportunity to trade lunches with him.

4. Nora Perry used to pay Tom to go to the library to read books.
5. See L. Tom Perry, "The Scriptures and the Restoration," CES Fireside for Young Adults, November 2, 2003, 5. Available online at lds.org/media-library/video/ces-firesides?lang=eng&query=ces+fireside+1.+tom+perry#2003-11-05-the-scriptures-and-the-restoration
6. The name was a tribute to Ab Jenkins, who drove the Duesenberg "Mormon Meteor" to a twenty-four-hour average land speed record of 135 miles per hour (217 km/h) in 1935.
7. The overall intramural championship was based on the total number of points earned by a team over the entire academic year. The Mormon Meteors won the Logan High School intramural touch football and volleyball championships; individuals on the team also won and placed in several track and field events. That is how the team accumulated the overall highest point total for the year.
8. The Logan High School colors were crimson and white. The Crimson Trail ran northeast of Logan up Logan Canyon along the side of the mountain between Guinavah Park and the Third Dam.
9. Most of the young men in Logan High School were involved in ROTC during the late 1930s for at least two reasons. First and foremost, they felt a patriotic duty because of the war in Europe and the aggressive nature of the primary Axis Powers—Germany, Italy, and Japan. A second and more practical reason was that everyone who enrolled in ROTC received a uniform. Essentially, this doubled the school wardrobe for these young men during the final years of the Great Depression.
10. Technically, the game was vanball, a modified form of volleyball.

Chapter 8: First National Bank of Logan

1. Recorded in Conway Sonne, *A Man Named Alma: The World of Alma Sonne* (Bountiful, Utah: Horizon Publishers, 1988), 104.
2. Sonne, *Man Named Alma,* 105.
3. My grandfather's investment philosophy was passed along to my father's generation. Perhaps my father was less affected than his siblings Mignon and Ted, who both accumulated a large number of shares of bank stock—initially First National Bank of Logan stock and, following its acquisition, Zions Bank stock. Their investment strategy defies the conventional wisdom of building a diversified

portfolio of investments, and they both benefited and suffered from their unbalanced portfolios.

I can also speak about my generation and my personal holdings of Zions Bank stock. The number of shares I own is relatively modest, and they were all inherited from my father. The problem is I can't ever bring myself to sell my Zions stock. I don't regard those shares with the same detachment as I have toward the other investments I own. Although I really know better, in the back of my mind I feel that I'd be betraying my father and grandfather if I ever sold my Zions shares.

4. Alma Sonne was a cashier for the First National Bank of Logan for eighteen years before he was elected executive vice president and manager on January 11, 1938. Later he served as both president and chairman of the board at the bank.
5. My father is also fond of the statement about interest by President J. Reuben Clark made during the April 1938 general conference, and he has quoted it many times. President Clark said: "Interest never sleeps nor sickens nor dies; it never goes to the hospital; it works on Sundays and holidays; it never takes a vacation; it never visits nor travels; it takes no pleasure; it is never laid off work nor discharged from employment; it never works on reduced hours; it never has short crops nor droughts; it never pays taxes; it buys no food; it wears no clothes; it is unhoused and without home and so has no repairs, no replacements, no shingling, plumbing, painting, or whitewashing; it has neither wife, children, father, mother, nor kinfolk to watch over and care for; it has no expense of living; it has neither weddings nor births nor deaths; it has no love, no sympathy; it is as hard and soulless as a granite cliff. Once in debt, interest is your companion every minute of the day and night; you cannot shun it or slip away from it; you cannot dismiss it; it yields neither to entreaties, demands, or orders; and whenever you get in its way or cross its course or fail to meet its demands, it crushes you" (in Conference Report, 103).
6. Sonne, *Man Named Alma,* 113–14.
7. And unlike his son, who after all is a university professor.
8. Technically, Søren was a half-brother to Eliza. Eliza's biological father was Christian Pedersen, a Danish army officer who was betrothed to her mother, Elsie Marie Larsen. Christian and Elsie lived together, as was customary at the time in Denmark, without the formality of marriage. They had a falling out several months after Eliza was conceived and never spoke again. Although not her biological father, Søren Christensen Petersen was a good father and the only father Eliza knew.

NOTES

Chapter 9: The Logan Tabernacle

1. Isaiah 54:2.
2. See Leslie Thomas Perry, *Life Story of Leslie Thomas Perry* (privately published, 1964), 50.
3. Leslie Thomas Perry, *Life Story of Leslie Thomas Perry* (privately published, 1964), 45–46.
4. At seventeen, Ted had already graduated from high school because he had skipped a grade.
5. In a brief life history of Nora Perry, Ted Perry described the events surrounding Tom's mission call: "Nora's great test came when World War II erupted. Her oldest son [Tom] had received his mission call in November 1941 and, of course, was exempted from the draft even though Japan had attacked Pearl Harbor. But with her husband in the stake presidency there was a little back biting about her oldest son going on a mission while others in the stake were risking their lives. Nora's prayers for her son were long and fervent that the conditions of war would not interfere with his mission. . . . Her biggest shock came when her seventeen-year-old son [Ted] was determined to enter the service."

   I consider what Ted did an act of amazing courage. Moreover, I can see myself interpreting the situation much the same way he did, although I'm not entirely sure I would show the same bravery. I am much like Ted, in the sense that my natural tendency is to overthink things. My father, while not completely immune from this tendency, is far less likely to second-guess himself once a decision is made.
6. I make this assertion with near-absolute certainty.
7. See Doctrine and Covenants 4:2.
8. My father has always been able to fall asleep quickly. With a smile and a wink, he relates it to having a clean conscience.

Chapter 10: Northern States Mission

1. Sister Muir was ill, so President Muir sent his assistants to the train station to pick up the new missionaries.
2. Doctrine and Covenants 38:30.
3. The events of this story occurred much as described, but there are certainly alternative explanations for the mouse's behavior and unfortunate demise.
4. After inviting his twelve-year-old grandson, Terry Haws, to stand next to him during the priesthood session of the October 1985 general conference, Elder Perry told the story of Daniel. He closed his counsel to Terry, a new deacon in the Aaronic Priesthood, with these

words: "These stories in the scriptures will never grow old. They will be just as exciting for you when you are reading them as a deacon, a teacher, a priest, a missionary, a home teacher, an elders quorum president, or whatever the Lord calls on you to do. They will teach you to have faith, courage, love for your fellowmen, confidence, and trust in the Lord." L. Tom Perry, "I Confer the Priesthood of Aaron," *Ensign*, November 1985, 48.

At the April 1988 general conference, Elder Perry again spoke about the example of his biblical hero, Daniel. He said: "Sometimes I think we fear participation because of the opposition we may face. We find again in the example of Daniel someone who met the opposition of being 'in the world' head-on and was able to influence those around him for good." "In the World," *Ensign*, May 1988, 15.

5. Matthew 19:26.
6. Genesis 41:38.
7. In a moment of self-disclosure, my father admitted actually praying for shorter companions for this reason. Given that he is six-foot-four, he found that his prayers were usually answered in the affirmative.
8. See L. Tom Perry, "The Returned Missionary," *Ensign*, November 2001, 76. At general conference, Elder Perry described the baptism as having taken place on a cool fall day. After conferring about it, we decided that it had to have been on a cool early spring day.
9. A position equivalent to that of a zone leader in today's mission structure.
10. Both Tom and Elder Kidd were serving in the military at the time, and they could not attend.
11. Lee Perry, "Elder L. Tom Perry of the Council of the Twelve," *Ensign*, February 1975, 12.
12. While in Cedar Rapids, Elders Perry and Wilkinson participated on the Cedar Rapids YMCA volleyball team with approval of their mission president. In the fall of 1943, this team went to the national finals. Tom was selected as the outstanding player of that tournament.
13. In the life history of his mother, Ted Perry continued the story of Tom's mission call by connecting his first mission in the Northern States Mission to his second mission in the Marine Corps: "Her oldest son [Tom] proved that the mission was the best service he could give for his country, as after his mission he joined the Marines and following a tour of duty on Saipan Island, was with the occupation forces in Japan. His knowledge of the gospel endeared him to the Japanese people and helped make the post war transition peaceful."

NOTES

Chapter 11: The Marine Corps

1. Tom gave a slightly different twist to the story when he wrote a post card addressed to his mother on the night before leaving for San Diego. Somewhat apologetically, he wrote:

   "Dear Mom:

   "You just gave me too healthy of a body. They took the seven top men in the physical examination and put them into the Marine Corps. I was the number one man. So I am now Pvt. Perry of the U.S. Marines. I leave tomorrow morning for San Diego, California.

   "I have tonight off so Ray and I are going to the dance. Write when I have time when I arrive.

   "Love, Tom"

   I wonder how long it took Tom to admit to his mother that he had actually volunteered to serve in the Marine Corps, mostly because he didn't think he would look good in a navy uniform.
2. General Yoshitsugu Saito, the commander of the Japanese forces on Saipan, even convinced the surviving civilians to join the banzai attack. He said, "There is no longer any distinction between civilians and troops. It would be better for them to join in the attack with bamboo spears than to be captured."
3. See L. Tom Perry, "The Returned Missionary," *Ensign*, November 2001, 75–76.
4. Red Beach was the landing beach of the 2nd Marine Division. Like Purple Heart Ridge and Death Valley, it was a nickname given to a place where brave men lost their lives serving their country.
5. The 2nd Marine Division was also a floating reserve for the troops assigned as the landing force in the Battle of Okinawa. If the attack did not go well, division troops were available as reinforcements.
6. My father still has in his possession a copy of the program from the dedicatory service.

Chapter 12: Utah State Agricultural College

1. The GI Bill provided Tom $105 a month in support payments, and it paid for tuition, fees, and books. My father still smiles when he thinks about the packet of school supplies he received through the GI Bill when he registered for classes at Utah State. He claims he still has some of the erasers from the packet.
2. Accordingly, my mother had two half-brothers, Ernest and Victor.
3. I do not want to get too far ahead in the story, but in my mind's eye there is a vision I want to share. My mother died prematurely, in

everyone's mind except God's. She passed away ten days before her fifty-first birthday. I firmly believe, however, that as she looked down from heaven and watched as my father was sealed to his second wife, Barbara Dayton, from that moment on she embraced Barbara as a sister. After all, she herself was the daughter of a second wife, and she was named after her father's first wife, who was her mother's sister. Interestingly, the name my mother and father had selected for their first child, a daughter, was Barbara.

4. In 1963, the South Cache and North Cache High Schools were consolidated and renamed Sky View High School.
5. Maurine Jensen Ward, "General Authorities' Wives: Sister Virginia Lee Perry," *New Era,* January 1975, 46.
6. Ward, "General Authorities' Wives," 46.
7. The senior L. Tom Perry had the mumps just before Tom returned home from Japan.

Chapter 13: The Logan Temple

1. Linda Gay, who was born in 1958, was either not born yet or not old enough to participate in our contest.
2. See Maurine Jensen Ward, "General Authorities' Wives: Sister Virginia, Lee Perry," *New Era,* January 1975, 45.
3. It was common at the time to quote weights in hundreds of pounds: 47.17 pounds is 4,717 pounds, or nearly two and a half tons.
4. All the information in this section comes from Chris's life history, a document created from his journals titled "The History of Christen Christensen (Lee)."
5. Brother Tahon was believed to be more deserving because he had served as the branch president for the past few years. Likely, the brethren reasoned it was now his turn to go to Utah, and Chris and Kristen should wait their turn.
6. By this time, Kristen's parents had adopted the surname Steenbroen, for the place in Denmark from which they came.
7. Tomine is the English version of her name that Chris used in his life history. She was christened Anne Temine Pedersen. Chris Lee spelled her name Thomina in his life history, but Tomine is the spelling used on her headstone in Hyde Park Cemetery.
8. This is a memory of John Lee's grandson Lynn Seamons, who grew up next door to his grandparents.
9. See "Hyde Park, Utah History," compiled by Scott Jeppeson and edited by Jim Belliston (1999), at http://hydepark.utahlinks.org/history.pdf.

10. Hattie Reeder Lee also had noble pioneer ancestors. Her father, Robert Reeder, emigrated from England in May 1856 when he was nineteen years old. He was part of the James Willie handcart company. Robert's father, David Reeder, his younger sister, Caroline, and other family members died along the way, but Robert survived the ordeal. Like Chris Lee, Robert settled in Hyde Park, and Hattie was one of nine children born to him and his second wife, Ellen Flatt.
11. As a young boy, I recall watching my Grandmother Lee (Hattie) comb and braid her hair in the morning. Unbraided, her hair fell all the way to her ankles.
12. This was when John returned from his mission to the Central States.
13. Ward, "General Authorities' Wives," 45.
14. "Life History of Jessie Lee Seamons," unpublished manuscript.
15. Memory of Kay Seamons Erickson, a granddaughter of John Lee.
16. Ward, "General Authorities' Wives," 45.

Chapter 14: The Aggie Ice Cream Store

1. See "'Born of Goodly Parents,'" *Ensign,* May 1985, 21–23; "'A Meaningful Celebration,'" *Ensign,* November 1987, 70–73; "Family Traditions," *Ensign,* May 1990, 19–20.
2. Matthew 6:20.
3. As mentioned in chapter 8, Tom's aunt Emma Sonne Holmgren received the rent from the home at 472 North 100 West for most of her life. The only exception was during the years Tom and Virginia lived in the home.
4. My mother liked to be called Virginia, but my father and many of her closest friends often used her nickname, Ginny.
5. At the time, Gay lived in the old Perry family home at 466 North 100 West.

Chapter 15: Boise, Idaho

1. They had recently traded in for a new car the 1936 Plymouth that Tom had purchased from his father after he returned home from Japan.
2. The program that is now called home teaching.
3. Ward boundaries had changed, and the Perrys now resided in the Logan 15th Ward but met in the same building.
4. Doctrine & Covenants 81:5.
5. Leslie Thomas Perry, *Life Story of Leslie Thomas Perry* (privately published, 1964), 53.
6. When a woman with the potential to develop Rh incompatibility is

pregnant, doctors administer a series of two Rh immune-globulin shots during her first pregnancy that act like a vaccination to prevent the production of potentially dangerous Rh antibodies.

7. Two thoughts come to mind from my father's description of his typical day that pertain to him as much now as they did back in 1951. First, he likes a routine, and second, he is very fond of desserts.
8. I have never felt I measured up to my father. The most obvious reason is he is six foot four and I am only six foot two, but there are many other ways I don't quite measure up. I consider it an honor just to be close, always looking up to him.
9. Because this is when I enter my father's life, I intend to write only in third person going forward. While it feels a little awkward to refer to myself in the third person, I believe this a wise and necessary choice. The only exception to this self-imposed rule will be in the notes, where I will continue to insert first-person commentary.
10. I was given the nickname Two-ton Tommy.

Chapter 16: Lewiston, Idaho, and Clarkston, Washington

1. This was long before the consolidated meeting schedule, when priesthood and Sunday School classes were held in the morning and sacrament meeting was held in the early evening.
2. They never were able to purchase a home in Lewiston.
3. During this time, the stake center was in Spokane, Washington.
4. Exodus 18:14.
5. Exodus 18:17–18.
6. See Exodus 18:21.
7. Lewis Carroll, *Through the Looking-Glass, and What Alice Found There,* ed. Florence Milner (Chicago: Rand McNally & Company, 1917), 39.
8. Just as in Tom and Virginia's dating days, dancers had dance cards that they would fill when they arrived at dances. Virginia was a much better dancer than Tom, and her dance card always filled up quickly. Tom would occasionally end up sitting in the corner watching his wife dance with someone else.
9. The cottage on Lake Chatcolet is the scene of one of my earliest memories as a child. I had found a clump of bushes with red berries just outside the cabin. I was told not to eat them, but I loved to pick them. As I worked my way around to the back side of the bushes, I saw a large object hanging in front of me that interested me more than the berries. As I discovered after I disturbed it, the object was a beehive. Soon the bees swarmed around me, and I ran into the

cottage screaming my lungs out. My father bravely leaped to my rescue, pushed me into the bathroom, closed the door, and began killing bees. Later my mother packed mud on me from head to toe.

10. Tom's sister Gay and her husband, Albert Kowallis, purchased the home at 472 North 100 West the year following Nora Perry's death.
11. L. Tom Perry, "For a Bishop Must Be Blameless," *Ensign,* November 1982, 29.

Chapter 17: Sacramento, California

1. This letter to Gay and her family was dated April 8, 1955.
2. I recall playing a midday Little League game in 113 degrees.
3. The Church participated in financing meetinghouses and temples using general tithing funds.
4. L. Tom Perry, "Nauvoo—A Demonstration of Faith," *Ensign,* May 1980, 75–76.
5. I'm sure I needed more parental influence than my two well-behaved sisters.
6. Although no longer the case, in the 1950s and 1960s, such clubs were open only to men.
7. L. Tom Perry, "In the World," *Ensign,* May 1988, 14.
8. L. Tom Perry, "In the World," *Ensign,* May 1988, 14.
9. See Daniel 1:5–21.
10. Based on profit per square foot of floor space.
11. The pretext for the letter to Mignon Perry was that she had invited her brother and his family to visit her in Pullman, Washington, during the summer of 1962. My father likely thought to write to his older sister during the flight because she had lived in the state of New York while studying for her PhD from Cornell University in the upstate city of Ithaca.

Chapter 18: Scarsdale, New York

1. The Bluebird was Aunt Emma's favorite place to dine.
2. Lee Perry, "Elder L. Tom Perry," See chapter 10 fn 11, pages 15–16. My father told a version of the same story at the October 1977 general conference (see L. Tom Perry, "Father—Your Role, Your Responsibility," *Ensign,* November 1977, 63).
3. A version of this story was shared in L. Tom Perry, *Living with Enthusiasm* (Salt Lake City: Deseret Book, 1996), 79–82.
4. L. Tom Perry, "Teach Them the Word of God with All Diligence," *Ensign,* May 1999, 8.

5. Elder Perry has the latest iPad and iPhone as well as a notebook computer, and he is quite adept with all of them.
6. This is a story for the second volume of my father's biography, but for many years he was chairman of the board of the Management Services Corporation (MSC), which provided computer and information services for both the LDS Church and LDS Hospitals. When the Church divested itself of its hospital system, the Information Systems Department (ISD) was created to support the Church. My father's combined service with MSC and ISD totals more than twenty years.
7. Perry, "Elder L. Tom Perry," 14.
8. Brent L. Top, "Legacy of the Mormon Pavilion," *Ensign,* October 1989, 28.
9. Perry, "Elder L. Tom Perry," 17.
10. Perry, "Father—Your Role, Your Responsibility," 62.
11. I firmly believe, and my father agrees, that one of the great benefits of teaching others is that we also teach ourselves.
12. Virginia added another reason. She wrote in the Perry 1966 Christmas letter the following explanation for their move to the Boston area: "When the New York Central Railroad tore up the station platform board where Tom always stood to catch the commuter train, he became frustrated. So when an offer came from a new, rapidly growing firm, he couldn't resist the challenge of getting in on the ground floor and made the change to join Lechmere Sales Corporation." I suspect my mother's comments weren't entirely serious.

Chapter 19: Weston, Massachusetts

1. Barbara spent the summer in Utah with Tom's sister Gay, and her husband, Albert, who had invited her to go on several trips with them, mostly to the Pacific Northwest and Yellowstone National Park.
2. The letter was undated, but it was written prior to Christmas 1966.
3. Linda Gay is still by far the most avid Red Sox fan.
4. In 2012 the book by Kristen Smith Dayley was published as *For All the Saints: Lessons Learned in Building the Kingdom* (Springville, Utah: Cedar Fort).
5. Elder L. Tom Perry, Lee Perry, and Linda Perry Nelson, interview by Clayton Christensen, May 9, 2004, Weston, Massachusetts, in Clayton M. Christensen collection of Boston Latter-day Saint Oral Histories, MSS 7770, L. Tom Perry Special Collections, Harold B. Lee Library, Brigham Young University, Provo, Utah; hereafter cited as L. Tom Perry Special Collections.

6. When I worked for Lechmere for two summers, my father would sometimes take me to lunch, and we would go up to the room and take a short nap afterwards.
7. Perry, Perry, and Nelson interview by Christensen.
8. William A. Fresh, interview by Clayton Christensen, April 26, 1999, St. George, Utah, in Clayton M. Christensen collection of Boston Latter-day Saint Oral Histories, MSS 7770, L. Tom Perry Special Collections.
9. Fresh, interview by Christensen.
10. The trip was sponsored by General Electric, one of Lechmere's largest vendors.
11. They were able to arrange with the tour sponsors for a one-day stopover in Salt Lake City on the way home, which allowed them to make a surprise visit to Barbara at BYU. They also visited Virginia's sister Maud and her husband, Lew, who lived in Orem, Utah.
12. The letter was dated July 12, 1970.

Chapter 20: President of the Boston Stake

1. Only six weeks later, Bill was called to serve as the first stake president of the Manchester New Hampshire Stake.
2. Elder L. Tom Perry, Lee Perry, and Linda Perry Nelson, interview by Clayton Christensen, May 9, 2004.
3. Elder Perry continues to use the Creation account as recorded in the scriptures to train new stake presidencies.
4. See Moses 1:39.
5. Quoted from training session for the presidency of the BYU 15th Stake, April 9, 1978.
6. See Moses 2:3–5.
7. See Harold B. Lee, *Stand Ye in Holy Places* (Salt Lake City: Deseret Book, 1974), 309.
8. Both of these statements by Helen Claire Sievers were taken from an article by Peggy Fletcher Stack, "Meet the Unassuming, Optimistic LDS Apostle," *Salt Lake Tribune*, April 4, 2011.
9. See Moses 2:9–13.
10. BYU 15th Stake training.
11. Moses 2:14.
12. Also while training the presidency of the BYU 15th Stake, Elder Perry taught: "I do not believe in long meetings where you have large numbers attending. . . . Now, it is easy to forget that time is valuable to these men. They would be much better off not holding a long meeting where you have twelve high councilors, and all of them want to say about the same thing, and every one of them have to make a

contribution to everything that you bring up. You see, I don't think that is the meeting to solve your problems. I think it is a way of communicating, giving of some spirituality, clearing the calendar and doing that sort of thing. But really, the problem solving should be done in smaller groups. We used to hold between 45 minutes to an hour where we'd have a high council meeting. Then Gene [Dalton] would take his high councilors and my other counselor would take his, and they would go into review sections where they were working on adult functions and youth functions. They would clear all of those on that night."

13. BYU 15th Stake training.
14. For example, see Moses 2:4, 10, 12, 18.
15. He also maintained a direct reporting relationship with the stake Relief Society president, according to the guidelines in the Church's *General Handbook of Instructions.*
16. Loren C. Dunn, "Elder L. Tom Perry: Serving with Enthusiasm," *Ensign,* August 1986, 19.
17. Soon after Tom was called as an Assistant to the Twelve, Dayton Hudson settled with him for its violation of his multiyear contract.
18. I have wondered for many years why my mother never fully disclosed the severity of her illness to Linda. Part of her reason was obvious—Linda was very young at the time, and my mother wanted to protect her from worry. I also think my mother genuinely believed she was going to beat cancer. Because she never gave up hope, she felt it was unnecessary to disclose fully the seriousness of her condition to her youngest child.
19. Two other medical professionals were deeply involved in coordinating Virginia's treatments and are deserving of mentioning—Dr. Leroy Wirthlin, also a devoted member of the LDS Church, and Dr. Rita Kelley, an oncologist at Massachusetts General Hospital, who died after a three-year battle with cancer in 1981. In a letter to Elder Perry dated December 18, 1974, just after Virginia's death, Dr. Kelley wrote: "Dr. Wirthlin told me of your wife, Virginia's, sudden death on the weekend. I did not know of the details of her death, but it was obvious when she was here a couple of weeks ago that things were going poorly for her and that from here on her course was going to be a rough one. In a way, such a sudden episode for her was the kindest thing that could have happened. She would have adjusted very poorly to a period of chronic invalidism which could easily have accompanied her disease as she declined. She was a lovely person and a very cooperative patient. Please accept my sincere sympathy."
20. L. Tom Perry, "A Tribute," *Ensign,* May 1975, 33.

21. Perry, "Tribute," 33.
22. L. Tom Perry, "Let Him Do It with Simplicity," *Ensign*, November 2008, 7.
23. Perry, "Elder L. Tom Perry," 17.
24. Elaine Cannon later served as the general president of the Young Women of the Church.
25. Perry, Perry, and Nelson, interview by Christensen.

Chapter 21: The October 1972 General Conference

1. For readers under thirty, this was long before cell phones.
2. The Perrys did not realize that if they had driven another 50 miles on I-15, they could have taken a route to Delta that was both faster and fifteen miles shorter.
3. Orlin Hunsaker, who had diabetes, died less than a year later, on April 17, 1973.
4. "Conference Visit Wasn't Routine," *Church News*, November 11, 1972, 5.
5. This might not be the stupidest thing I've ever said, but it's certainly high on the list.
6. The Perrys had even contemplated watching several sessions of general conference on television in their motel room so they could stay together as a family.
7. This was the second Salt Palace, completed in 1969 and later torn down for the construction of the present Salt Palace Convention Center, which is named for former Utah governor Calvin Rampton.
8. By Heinrich Schutz.
9. Jay M. Todd, "The Sustaining of President Harold B. Lee," *Ensign*, January 1973, 1–4.
10. Paul James Toscano, "Elder L. Tom Perry: Assistant to the Council of the Twelve," *Ensign*, January 1973, 16.
11. The predecessor of the *Ensign* magazine.
12. Lee Perry, "Elder L. Tom Perry of the Council of the Twelve," *Ensign*, February 1975, 14.
13. They drove the Vega to Utah and then gave it to me.

Chapter 22: Bountiful, Utah

1. My father always wanted his friends in Boston to call him Tom (or President Perry until he was released as stake president). For example, Paul Thompson, former Weber State University president, said, "He never wanted me to call him 'Elder Perry.' We were just Tom and Paul." However, because of my father's call as a General

Authority, this seems like the appropriate time to begin referring to him as Elder Perry.

2. Weston and Pauline Roe eventually moved to Orem, Utah, and became members of the Orem Canyon View Eighth Ward. I was their home teacher, served as their bishop, and spoke at Wes's funeral in March 2005. He was a great man and a pioneer for the Church in northern California.
3. Adapted from L. Tom Perry, "Christmas Giving and Receiving," in *Christmas Treasures: Stories and Reminiscences from General Authorities* (Salt Lake City: Deseret Book, 1994), 6–8.
4. In James P. Bell, *In the Strength of the Lord: The Life and Teachings of James E. Faust* (Salt Lake City: Deseret Book, 1999), 102.
5. The Bountiful 29th Ward.
6. L. Tom Perry, "Consider Your Ways," *Ensign,* July 1973, 21.
7. Later the groups were called Young Single Adults and Single Adults, and the ages of the groups were adjusted.
8. See "First Presidency Announces Priesthood MIA Programs," *Ensign,* January 1973, 135–36.
9. In Bell, *In the Strength of the Lord,* 100.
10. Lee Perry, "Elder L. Tom Perry of the Council of the Twelve," *Ensign,* February 1975, 15.
11. See chapter 20, "President of the Boston Stake."
12. It almost certainly had something to do with her cancer and chemotherapy treatments.
13. She served as the general president of the Relief Society from April 6, 1945, until October 3, 1974.
14. "Constitutional Responsibility Encouraged by First Presidency As Elder L. Tom Perry Appointed Chairman of Bicentennial Committee," *Ensign,* November 1973, 90.
15. L. Tom Perry, "I Will Go and Do the Things Which the Lord Hath Commanded," *Ensign,* January 1974, 53.

Chapter 23: Christmas to Christmas 1973–74

1. "The Solemn Assembly," presented by President N. Eldon Tanner, *Ensign,* May 1974, 41; emphasis added.
2. Ephesians 6:10.
3. L. Tom Perry, "Build Your Shield of Faith," *Ensign,* May 1974, 98–99.
4. I do not want to make this sound as if my contributions were heroic. I loved my mother deeply, but I was too self-centered to truly appreciate all she had done and was doing for me. I remember on a few occasions thinking that my life would be so much simpler if, instead

of going to Ogden, my mother would receive her treatments in Salt Lake. Fortunately, I never complained openly to her, but I thought it from time to time; even thinking it shows an unconscionable underappreciation for my dear mother, who would have done anything humanly possible for me. I still carry the guilt of my all-too-frequent lapses in gratitude for my mother and for God for allowing me to be born of such a noble woman.

5. L. Tom Perry, "A Tribute," *Ensign,* May 1975, 33.
6. L. Tom Perry, "A Tribute," *Ensign,* May 1975, 33.

Chapter 24: A Tribute to a Noble Soul

1. Mr. Warner later served as a U.S. senator from Virginia for thirty years (1979–2009) and is well known as Elizabeth Taylor's sixth husband.
2. "Elder Perry to Serve on Bicentennial Council," *Ensign,* March 1975, 77.
3. "Elder Perry Enjoys Mingling," *Church News,* February 1, 1976, 7.
4. L. Tom Perry, "A Tribute," *Ensign,* May 1975, 31.
5. L. Tom Perry, "A Tribute," *Ensign,* May 1975, 31.
6. L. Tom Perry, "A Tribute," *Ensign,* May 1975, 33.
7. I had an experience only a few years ago that helped me recall and marvel at my mother's missionary spirit. At a gathering I attended, a man approached me and introduced himself as a current member of the Westchester Ward in New York. He told me how he had gone to a yard sale a few years before, and he noticed that one of the items for sale was a used copy of the Book of Mormon. He picked up the book to examine it. Inside the front cover of the book was a testimony written and signed by Virginia Perry.
8. Perry, "Tribute," 33.
9. Perry, "Tribute," 33.
10. Elder Jeffrey R. Holland, interview by the author June 28, 2012, in the Church Administration Building, Salt Lake City, Utah.
11. L. Tom Perry, "For the Time Will Come When They Will Not Endure Sound Doctrine," *Ensign,* November 1975, 85.
12. Elder Perry's "bright young colleague" was Richard Eyre.
13. Perry, "For the Time Will Come," 86.
14. Perry, "For the Time Will Come," 86–87.
15. Ephesians 6:10.

Index

INDEX